THE OTHER SIDE OF THE RISING SUN

Tatsui Sato

and the growth of the
Church of Jesus Christ of
Latter-day Saints
in Japan

KOMAE MORI
with David W. Harris

The Other Side of the Rising Sun: Tatsui Sato

Published by:
Lutes Publishing

Distributed by:

Granite Publishing and Distribution, LLC
868 North 1430 West
Orem, Utah 84057
(801) 229-9023 • Toll Free (800) 574-5779
Fax (801) 229-1924

ISBN: 1-59936-004-7

Library of Congress Control Number: 2005934617

First Printing October 2005

10 9 8 7 6 5 4 3 2 1

Printed in the United States of America

Cover photo

Back from left: Boyd Packer, Norton Nixon, Tatsui Sato, Elliott Richards.
Front from left: Yasuo Sato, Chiyo Sato

This book is dedicated
with love and gratitude to
Tatsui Sato
and the Latter-day Saint servicemen
who brought him the greatest of gifts—
the gospel of Jesus Christ.

Contents

Preface

Few who met Tatsui Sato (1889–1996) can forget his faith and intellect. Despite his always modest, unassuming appearance, he was a man of remarkable depth and insight. During his long life, Brother Sato (or Sato Kyodai as he was affectionately known among Japanese speakers and close friends) made a lasting impression and forged friendships with countless Church members, missionaries and others who had the privilege of his acquaintance.

Tatsui was a voracious reader and a man of deep thought. He also had an exceptional command of the classical Japanese language and literature, as well as a keen understanding of English and its many nuances. Brother Sato was a man of great compassion who had a great sensitivity to the Spirit. He is most remembered for being a pioneer member of The Church of Jesus Christ of Latter-day Saints (the Church) during the postwar era and for his translations of the scriptures into Japanese, including the Book of Mormon. But his life was much more than that, as he made contributions in many diverse areas. Really, he had several careers. We know Tatsui primarily for what he did in his later years. He is an inspiration to all of us as he truly endured and contributed to the end. His mind was lucid and his insights penetrating even in his nineties. He was always a joy to visit, and one always felt at home in the modest dwelling Tatsui and his second wife, Tomiko, shared in southeast Salt Lake City.

Elder Boyd K. Packer—who played an important role in the baptism of the Sato family and was a lifelong friend—called Tatsui "one of the most interesting men I have ever met. I treasure my memories of him."[1] Harrison "Ted" Price, who first met him in Narumi as a missionary, called him one of the most "unique" men he had ever met, and emphasized the great debt the Church in Japan owed to him.[2] Kazuo Imai, who worked with Tatsui in Church Translation Services, was amazed at Tatsui's vast understanding of the gospel and his ability to communicate it with "easy explanations." Brother Sato, he remembered, quietly strengthened the testimony and faith of many members and their families.[3] Masao Watabe, who joined Translation Services a decade later, paid his dear friend many great compliments; he felt Tatsui "walked with God" and was full of love and charity toward all people.[4] Kenji Suzuki, who worked closely with Tatsui in his later years at the Genealogical Society, put it succinctly, "There will never be another person like Brother Sato."[5] To so many people, the warm, ever-faithful Tatsui was an example of a true Christian gentleman and will remain an unforgettable character. As for me, he was both a spiritual father and a man of remarkable talents and insights.

This book is not intended to be a biography of Brother Sato. The author has tried to weave letters, interviews and materials about him through his many decades of Church activity and devotion to the Savior and his fellowmen into a story that he, himself, and his friends tell. The record portrays the struggle he and his family went through, the greatness of his character and the wonderful relationships he made. There is not much material available on the story of his life up to the end of World War II. However, the touching story of his conversion and lifelong friendship with the Latter-day Saint servicemen who brought him and his family into the faith is well documented in the many letters written back and forth over the years.

These letters and conversations with people central to his later life form the basis of this book about the life of Tatsui Sato. Tatsui speaks for himself many times, and his generous, caring personality comes out as he and his family endured the struggles of trying to survive in the difficult period after the war. His excitement during his conversion to the gospel of Jesus Christ and his many achievements in succeeding years are also included. Examples of the letters and a few important photos are included to illustrate this trail of evidence of his remarkable life.

The humble beginnings of the Lord's work among the Japanese people is similar to that of another great people portrayed in Elder John H. Groberg's well-known book and movie, *The Other Side of Heaven*. When asked about using a similar title for this book *(The Other Side of the Rising Sun)* Elder Groberg said, "It would be an honor." Moreover, the title implies that Brother Sato was very unique and remarkable for his generation, and that he represents another side of the character of the Japanese people. Tatsui Sato, indeed, captured the true vision of the gospel, made a great contribution as a pioneer member of the Church, and served and remained faithful to the very end. In the minds of many, he will always be seen as a great example of quiet faith, true humility and Christian love.

Acknowledgments

Collecting AND ORGANIZING the many boxes of source materials was a monumental task and could not have been done without the encouragement and contributions of friends and people willing to help with a book on Brother Sato. I acknowledge the contributions of many that have helped bring this project to fruition.

First, thanks go to Brother Sato, himself, who methodically recorded many of the events of his life and saved many boxes of letters and materials dear to his life (almost every scrap of paper, it seems) since his coming into contact with the gospel immediately after World War II.

I thank Sister Tomiko Sato for making his writings, letters and other material available to me. Without these, this book would not have been possible.

I am particularly indebted to Tatsui's many lifelong friends, particularly the Latter-day Saint servicemen: Ray Hanks, Reed Davis, Mel Arnold, Chaplain Warren Richard Nelson, Norton Nixon, George Swett, Elliott Richards, Boyd Packer, Thomas Bauman and Bob Swenson, who brought him the gospel and maintained contact with him over the years. They have allowed me to use their photographs and letters, though many are personal in nature, and want their posterity to know of their involvement with Tatsui and the great friendships that spanned the years.

Special appreciation should also be given to Glenn N. Rowe of the Family and Church History Department for being so helpful. He served in the Japan West Mission with me and later as the president of the Tokyo South Mission (1993–96). Without his willingness to help with contacts, offer suggestions and thoroughly review the manuscript, I would never have completed this task. His assistance, even at inconvenient times, greatly impressed me.

I am indebted to Professor Greg Gubler of BYU—Hawaii (Brigham Young University), who was tutored by Brother Sato as his replacement in the Genealogical Department, and who assisted with additional source materials and with editorial suggestions. He also helped with historical context, interviews and particularly with Chapter 9, on "Pioneering Efforts in Genealogy."

Rose Pfaffle, who was my missionary companion in the Japan West Mission for nearly two years, deserves my special thanks. She supported my project and encouraged me these past years. She copied by hand from microfilm a letter, which was written to President Lee containing a brief history of Tatsui Sato by Thomas Bauman. Rose is my lifelong friend.

I appreciate my missionary friend, Douglas Macdonald, Chief Economist, Utah Sate Tax Commission. He was very helpful in introducing me to a publisher in Japan for the Japanese version of this book.

When I went to Japan to visit Tatsui Sato's birthplace, several nonmembers assisted me. I have been very indebted to Junko Kataoka, who lives in Kyoto, Japan for many years. Not only has she assisted my school—which is the first public Japanese Immersion School in the United States—but in order to do my research on the hometown of Tatsui Sato, Junko welcomed me as a guest in her home and helped me to accomplish my task. Dr. Rihe Goshima, who is a friend and a college professor in Nagoya, served as my guide in Narumi, where Tatsui Sato was born. And thanks also to Professor Takashi Shiba, who is also known as a historian of Narumi. He was willing to help me by sharing his research and has supported my project all of these years.

I wish to express my appreciation to Takashi Fukunaga, who is a publisher of the Japanese version of this book. He was born in Kagoshima, Japan, and is a member of the Shibuya Ward of Tokyo, Japan. He was very patient and donated his time and talents to make it possible for members in Japan to read the wonderful and spiritual life story of Tatsui Sato.

To Maya Nakahara, I express my gratitude. She served as a temple missionary in the Tokyo and Taiwan temples. She also served as a missionary for the Family and Church History Department for almost eight years. Maya was Tatsui's lifelong friend, really knew him well and highly respected him. She helped find important material and information about Brother Sato for me and was always willing to help throughout the years. She was my editor for the Japanese version of this book, and has been most generous and patient with her time and talents.

A special thanks to Masao Watabe, who is a patriarch in a BYU stake. He also contributed from his memories of Tatsui Sato. Brother Watabe gave me a special blessing, which stated that I would be able to accomplish my book about Brother Sato.

Many thanks also to Ralph Shino for the information he provided about Tatsui Sato. Ralph was a great help to Tatsui while he was a member of the Japanese Dai Ichi Ward.

I wish to express my appreciation to Chiyo Nelson Christensen, a daughter of Richard Nelson. She provided a few pictures of her father and shared information about him.

My appreciation also goes to Eva Swett, wife of George Swett. She was kind enough to go through her husband's pictures for use in the book. She was very helpful in giving me some information about her husband's experiences with the Sato family.

I wish to thank Gary and Cathy Keller, who are George Swett's son-in-law and daughter. They contacted their mother and provided information to me about Brother Swett.

Special thanks must be made to Carly Potter, who is a returned missionary from Hokkaido, Japan. He contacted me on behalf of the Swett family and relayed messages between the Swetts and myself. Because of his help, I was able to obtain valuable information about George Swett.

I also thank my son David for his assistance in typing all of those old and faded letters, newspaper and magazine articles, as well as Brother Sato's documents. He helped edit my translation and gave me many suggestions to improve the final product. Translating English to Japanese was not much of a problem; I struggled, however, when it came to translating old Japanese into English. David patiently listened to my explanations and translated what I really wanted to say. David surely knows my thoughts and helped successfully transfer them into English. Without his help, this English version of Brother Sato's story would not have been possible.

I wish to thank Keith Harker, who is a patriarch in the Eugene Oregon Santa Clara Stake, and who is also my home teacher. (Interestingly enough, Brother Harker is Ray Hanks' second cousin.) Brother Harker is a very kind and spiritual man. He prayed for me, gave me blessings when I was sick, and has constantly encouraged and assisted me during all of these years. Like our Savior, Jesus Christ, Brother Harker has great love toward everyone.

Thanks also to Sharon Downing Jarvis who has authored several books, including, the *Fairhaven Chronicles* series, *The Kaleidoscope Season, The Healing Place* and *Priceless Discoveries*. She thoughtfully reviewed my manuscript and recommended numerous improvements.

I wish to express my thanks to Kenneth and Lyndell Lutes, who dedicated themselves to preparing this manuscript for publication as my editors, designers, typographers, and publishers. They are the authors and publishers of *The Bible Corrected by Joseph Smith*, *Words of Christ Restored for the Last Days,* and other books. I feel like this humble, spiritual, kind, and talented couple was chosen by the Lord to prepare this book for publication. As soon as I met them, I couldn't stop smiling because I was confident that the Lord had sent them to do this work.

In conclusion, I thank my dear friend, Wesley Jarvis, who has been invaluable to me in coordinating the publishing of this book. He has also co-authored several books, including, *The Remnant, The Greater Things,* and *Priceless Discoveries*. When I attended BYU, Brother Jarvis and his wife welcomed me to stay at their home. They shared their love and treated me as their own daughter.

Brief Chronology (1899–1996)*

1899 Born 16 October in Narumi, Aiichi Prefecture (presently Midori Ward, Nagoya).

1903 Birth of wife, Chiyo, on 26 April in Watagashima, Shimo-Atago, Shizuoka Prefecture.

1905 Entered Narumi Elementary School.

1912 Entered Aiichi Prefectural Middle School (Nagoya).

1917 Entered (National) Second High School in Sendai (Miyagi Prefecture).

1920 Graduated from National Number High School; entered Tohoku Imperial University in Sendai (majoring in chemistry).

1923 Married Chiyo Akizuki (daughter of the Principal of Miyagi High School) on 28 December.

1924 Graduated in chemistry from the Tohoku Imperial University in Sendai; employed as teacher by Mie Prefectural Girl's Normal School.

1926 Returned to Sendai to teach at Miyagi Prefectural Higher Normal School.

1931 Resigned from teaching and became a research assistant at the Metallurgy Research Center at Tohoku University in Sendai—conducted scientific research on metal alloys.

1937 Employed as supervising engineer at Nippon Metal Industry Company in Kawasaki (Yamanashi Prefecture)—involved in developing stainless steel and metal alloys.

1939 Son, Yasuo, was born on 9 April in Yokohama.

1941 Daughter, Atsuko, was born in Naka-ku, Yokohama on 22 May.

1944 Returned to Narumi (near Nagoya) because of illness; passing of daughter, Atsuko, on 2 September from malnutrition and disease.

1945 Emperor Hirohito announces surrender on 15 August; surrender treaty signed on 2 September; worked as interpreter and salesman for local shops in Narumi; 27–28 November, met members of the Church stationed at nearby Camp Okazaki.

1946 Employed at Civil Censorship Detachment in Nagoya; passed exam and obtained credentials as an interpreter; baptized along with wife, Chiyo, in pool at Kansai University (Nishinomiya).

1948 Japanese Mission reopened by Edward L. Clissold; first missionaries came to Nagoya—Elder Harrison T. Price and Kojin Goya—where Brother Sato had a thriving Jr. Sunday School.

1949 Ordained an elder by Elder Matthew Cowley on 12 June; set apart in August as official translator and interpreter for the Church in Japan—initially translated sacrament prayers, and then over a 9-year period, the Book of Mormon, Doctrine and Covenants, Pearl of Great Price, the *Articles of Faith*, and *Jesus the Christ.*

1958 Triple combination published in Japan; wife, Chiyo, passed away on 8 October and was buried on 9 October in Ota Ward, Tokyo.

1965 Chosen to translate the temple ceremony into Japanese (Laie, Hawaii); attended general conference in Salt Lake City as special guest in April; officially retired as translator.

1966 Attended Brigham Young University in Provo as graduate student; employed as special instructor for Japanese and comparative world religion classes (winter and spring); hired in July to do pioneer research on Japanese genealogy (Research Department, Genealogical Society); compiled a dictionary of Japanese surnames and conducted research (including trips to the field) on Japanese genealogical sources; married and sealed on 29 July to Sister Tomiko Hiranishi in Salt Lake Temple.

1967 Called as a sealer in the Salt Lake Temple.

c.1970 Called as a member of the Dai Ichi Branch presidency in Liberty Stake.

1976 Retired from the Genealogical Society; continued to serve as consultant/trainee until 1979.

1980 Called, along with his wife, Tomiko, to serve temple mission at Tokyo Temple where he served as a sealer.

1984 Served as editor and writer for Dai Ichi Branch newsletter [*Tayori*].

1986 Wrote a series of articles for the *Utah Nippo Japanese* newspaper.

1996 Passed away in Salt Lake City on 15 June.

* Based on "Sato Tatsui Kyodai no ryakureki" [Brother Tatsui Sato's brief history], dated 12 March 1987.

Endnotes

1. Watabe Masao, Imai Kazui, and Ishizaka Kouichi, eds., *Ametsuchi wo miyou: Sato Tatsui Ou no omoide* [Looking at heaven and earth (nature): memories of our venerable Tatsui Sato] (Tokyo: Yunikkusu, 2004, introduction).
2. Interview, Greg Gubler with Harrison "Ted" Price, Murray, Utah, 12 August 2004.
3. "Sato Kyodai no omoide [memories of Brother Sato]," *Ametsuchi o miyou*, preface.
4. Ibid., preface.
5. Interview, Kenji Suzuki, Salt Lake City, Utah, 19 June 1996.

Editor's Note

Lyndell and I are sincerely humbled to have had the privilege to work with Sister Komae Mori to prepare this book for publication. The Spirit indeed brought us together to bring forth the story of this great servant of our Heavenly Father. Tatsui Sato is a tremendous example to all of us who would follow Jesus Christ. His story brings hope to not only Japanese people, but to all of God's children. Brother Sato performed a great service in building up the kingdom of God on the earth and endured all things to the very end.

May this book be an instrument in the hands of the Almighty to bring many souls unto Him. We pray that more and more people will find the true gospel and be able to work out their salvation. The beautiful testimonies and examples of Christ-like love found in this book can provide a spiritual experience to all who are seeking the truth.

I know for a certainty that Joseph Smith is a prophet of God and that the Church that he restored to the earth as a servant of God is the only true church on the face of the earth. As one who was blessed by God to have my employer bring the missionaries of The Church of Jesus Christ of Latter-day Saints to my door, I am eternally grateful. Upon hearing the "First Discussion," I was inspired to accept the challenge to read the Book of Mormon, and I felt the Spirit through that God-sent book and knew that what it contained was undeniably true.

That same Spirit, who has guided so many aspects of my life since receiving the true gospel, led us to Sister Komae Mori. Preparing this book for publication has truly been a joyful, rewarding and spiritual experience. We have learned so much and have grown to love the Japanese people through the association with our new friends and through the example of Brother Tatsui Sato.

Please do not let any errors in this book detract from the message that it sends to the world—that Joseph Smith is a prophet and Jesus is the Christ!

Kenneth O. Lutes

Chapter 1

Beginnings in Narumi

TATSUI SATO WAS BORN 16 OCTOBER 1899 in the village of Narumi (now Midori-ku Nagoya-shi), Japan. He was the first child of his father Magoichi (16 October 1876–17 August 1948) and mother Tai Mizuta (17 March 1878 to about 1966).

In March of 2001, I made a trip to visit Tatsui Sato's birthplace. My good friend, Dr. Rihe Goshima (a professor of architecture at the Department of Architecture at Daido Institute of Technology in Nagoya) and his family came to meet me at 10:03 a.m. at the Nagoya train station. The day before I arrived in Narumi, Dr. Goshima had generously offered his time and made finding Tatsui Sato's place of birth part of his itinerary. As Dr. Goshima drove us through Nagoya, he expounded on Narumi's rich historical background.

In 1603, after Tokugawa Ieyasu became Shogun, he improved the existing trail from his castle at Edo (now Tokyo) to the Imperial Palace at Kyoto. The new road was approximately 320 miles long. Every four to seven miles along this route, the powerful Shogun established way stations where travelers could obtain food, shelter, porters, horses, and other necessities. These stations attracted merchants, innkeepers, and others who settled nearby; and thus the stations soon evolved into towns. Visiting Narumi was like traveling back in time to a more ancient Japan. To feel as if I lived during the Edo period (1839–1854) while walking down the street was an interesting, exciting sensation.

Narumi and its neighboring towns used to be small. At the Arimatsu Shibori Kaikan (tie-dying museum), I received a pamphlet that briefly covers Narumi's history. I learned that a man called Takeda Hokuro had moved to the area with nine other people, and since there was no local industry, they had a very hard time making a living. One day, they got the idea to make what is called *Shibori*—a unique tie-dying technique that a visitor from Northern Kyushu (a southern island) introduced. This fledgling industry became a boon to Narumi's local economy, and various new *Shibori* methods were refined there.

The two Hiroshige Ukiyoe (wood block prints) were on display at the historical site where his prints were produced. In 1834, Ando Hiroshige published his first set of *Fifty-three Stations of the Tokaido*, one of the greatest art treasures of Japan.

Hiroshige's Ukiyoe print of Narumi

Narumi is located in the southeast section of Nagoya city, and has a population just over 20,000. When I was there, the citizens of

Narumi were preparing for the commemoration of their 400-year anniversary in 2002. Mr. Kojima, the president of the local chamber of commerce, mentions in the pamphlet's greeting that the people of Narumi should strive to reconfirm their culture, tradition, history, and industry. He expresses his hope that the people will feel a strong attachment to their town.

Tatsui Sato's grandfather, Tanuemon Sato, and his grandmother, Yone Kojima, operated a *hatagoya* (traveler's inn) located right on the Tokaido Road. The family lived on the second floor, and the guests stayed on the first floor in traditional *tatami* (straw mat) rooms with *shoji* (rice paper) wall partitions.

Just before noon, Dr. Goshima took me to the place where Tatsui Sato was born. When he stopped his car and said, "That's the house," I immediately looked in the direction he was pointing. I read the signboards on the building: "Takejin shoten kanamono bu" (The Takejin Hardware Store).

I went inside the store and called for help. The owner was inside eating; so when he heard me, he came out and greeted us. I asked if it would be possible to see the inside of the house, but the proprietor declined, as it was lunchtime and the house was unkempt. I had many queries, such as when his family began to live at this location, but he was unable to answer any of them.

There was only one floor, but I assumed the frame of this house was the old original. On the ground, many long water pipes lay in an untidy manner. The right side consisted of a little old room measuring about 12′ x 12′. I had to use my imagination to envision this room as it looked in days long past, occupied by weary travelers who were resting from the long journey along the famous Tokaido Road.

After leaving the old house, we went to a sake liquor store owned by a friend of Dr. Goshima. He told us we should visit a well-known Narumi historian, who happened to live across from his store—Shiba Takashi, Dean of the Management Department at the Aichi Gakuin University. His 88-year-old mother, Nobuko, and his aunt welcomed us into their home. The entrance of their house has remained the same as it was 400 years ago—a reminder of Japan's enduring history.

After passing through the ancient gate and courtyard, we arrived at the two modern buildings, which make up their home. Professor Shiba, as well as his mother and aunt, shared very precious information with us about Narumi. The ladies told me that when they were little, Tatsui had already gone to Sendai University; and among the local villagers, it was well-known that he was a genius. They used to play with Tatsui's younger sisters and younger brother. It was very special to meet people like the Shibas—who knew the Satos directly and whose ancestors had also managed the old traveler inns. My visit was incredibly successful due to these kind, special folks who were so willing to help me in Narumi and made the history come alive for me.

Shortly after I came back to the United States, I received a copy of Professor Shiba's publication, *A History of Narumi,* and his collection of ancient manuscripts. A diagram from his collection shows the record book from Tanuemon Sato's inn. Thanks to this material, I learned the name of Tatsui's grandfather and also the name of his inn: Echigoya.[1]

The diagram further shows the allotment of lodgings in the possession of Senga Yohachiro in 1853, near the end of the Edo period. From 1639–1853, the population of Narumi remained about 3,500. More than twenty shrines and temples were built during this time. Once, more than sixty inns were operating in Narumi. Among those inns was the Honjin, an officially appointed inn at which Daimyos, nobles, and high officials were lodged. The plot of ground for an officially appointed inn was 667.5 tsubo (one tsubo is equal to two tatami mats in size, which is 6′ x 6′, or 36 square feet), and the floor space of the building was 235 tsubo. All other inn plots, including Tatsui's grandfather's, were limited to 185 tsubo.[2]

During the Edo Period, Japan had a policy called *Sakoku* (National Seclusion, 1639–1854), adopted by the Tokugawa Shogunate (1603–1867) in an effort to legitimize and strengthen its authority, both, domestically and in East Asia. The main element of this policy was the exclusion of Roman Catholic Christianity in Japan, and also the prohibition of foreign travel by Japanese citizens. Designated officials and traders from the Domains of Satsuma (now Kagoshima) and Tsushima (now part of Nagasaki) were allowed to go to the Ryukyu (now Okinawa) and to Korea, respectively. However, the Korean trade in Japan was confined to Tsushima, and the only Japanese port open to the Dutch and Chinese was at Nagasaki.

In 1853, Matthew Perry, a U.S. Navy commander, arrived in Japan and forced the Shogunate to abandon its seclusion policy. The Kanagawa Treaty of 1854 and the Ansei Commercial Treaties of 1858 formally brought national seclusion to an end.

To my inquiry about the downfall of more than 60 Tokaido Road inns, Professor Shiba responded, "In Meiji Ishin (Imperial Restoration, 1868), the inns on the Tokaido (Imperial) Road did not meet their role anymore, because of the decreasing traffic. Therefore, most inn owners had to let their business go, and reduce their large lots, and were forced to move to smaller plots of land."[3]

The Echigoya, run by Tatsui's grandfather, was one of the inns forced to downsize. Professor Shiba, recounting his grandfather's story, told how he managed to keep his land. He began to operate a new trade—the rickshaw business. Because of those efforts, the family was able to remain on the spacious lot right up to the present day. (An average Japanese home lot is about 30–40 tsubo, and some have less than 20 tsubo.)

Narumi, the 40th stop along the Tokaido Road, has an affluent history, tradition, and culture. Brother Sato often spoke with pride of his birth town. The people of Narumi show great affection and kindness, and welcome strangers to their town warmly. Narumi has magically adapted to the new and modern while still preserving and proudly exhibiting its 400 years of history. Narumi was surely the type of town that could produce a great scholar, scientist, professor, father, researcher, interpreter, translator, church leader, temple sealer, genealogist, temple missionary, and saint whose works and name will remain with us imperishably.

Tatsui Sato's Childhood

Because Tatsui was the eldest son of the Sato's, his grandmother, Yone, pampered him. As firstborn, he was heir to the family's home. Tatsui often talked about memories of his grandmother, and how she took care of him so lovingly. In 1905, when Tatsui was six years old, Japan was fighting with Russia. At that time, a rumor spread among the villagers that a Russian battle ship might come and take them away. Talk like that caused great fright, and Tatsui's grandmother slept with him every night for his safety. Eventually that year, Japan scored a monumental victory in the Straits of Tsushima by sinking most of Russia's Baltic Fleet and achieving victory in the Russo-Japanese War (1904–5).

When Tatsui was seven years old, he was ill quite often. The doctor claimed that the cause was a weak liver. Although this reduced Tatsui's stamina for physical activity, his mind was fierce to embrace knowledge, and he exercised it vigorously. First, Tatsui was placed in a private preschool to learn Chinese characters *(kanji)* and the classics. His *sensei* (teacher) was an old scholar of Confucianism named Seran Takashima. The textbook, *The Classical Teachings of Confucius, Vol. 4*, instilled traits of filial piety and ancestor worship in Tatsui. These studies went on for a year, until he entered Narumi Elementary School.

Tatsui's grandparents wanted him to become physically strong, so they sent him to take *naginata* lessons (similar to kendo—a martial art employing a very long handled sword). He also played with the other children in the neighborhood at the Buddhist Temple. But when the kids built sand castles out of the carefully raked and contoured sand gardens surrounding the temples, the monks would scold them vehemently and smack them on their backs. Because of that, Tatsui never did like Buddhism.

When he was about nine years old, Tatsui became fascinated with trains and railroads. Every evening, he would wait patiently at the Narumi train station for his father's return from his bank clerk work in nearby Nagoya, eight miles away.

The boy entered the Narumi Elementary School, where he was made president of his first grade class. Upon graduating in 1912, he entered the Aichi Prefecture Middle School that was located five miles from his home. His mother arose at 4:00 a.m. to prepare breakfast and lunch for him. Tatsui got up at 5:00 a.m. every morning and left for school on foot. Tatsui had five school friends. Sometimes they would buy yams for one or two yen, salt them, and put them in their pockets to eat. Tatsui usually used a bicycle as his form of transportation. He spent five years at the school, graduating in March of 1917.[4]

Tatsui touched on his interest in Christianity in a letter he wrote (with the help of Thomas Bauman) to Elder Harold B. Lee in 1946. After acknowledging the warm feelings Elder Lee had for the Sato family, Tatsui expressed gratitude for Brother Lee's Church Welfare activities. He then relates his early experiences with Christianity:

> The first time I came in touch with Christianity was as early as 1910 when I was a primary school boy. An American missionary and a Japanese pastor came to my town and they held Sunday school every Sunday. I attended Sunday school, sang hymns, listened [to] stories that were never heard of before at the primary school. The Sunday school continued for several years with a Japanese pastor that settled in my town and opened a "preaching station." We called it so when several American missionaries came to preach and hold meetings (1915–1920). They were the Reverends VanDyke, Reverend J. Obee, Miss Cronise, and others who belonged to the Methodist and Protestant Mission and were competing for their missionary territory on the Tokaido District.[5]

It was during his middle school days that Tatsui came in contact with an American reverend from Ohio, of the Methodist Protestant church, who called himself "O.B." He would not disclose his real identity due to the persecution of Christian faiths at that time. But Tatsui liked the association and, at age 18, served as a clerk for the church for about a year.

While Tatsui attended this church and middle school, he developed an interest in English and began to study it in school. Middle school was the equivalent of American junior high; and when graduation came, it was time to take an examination for higher education. There were eight school levels that were the highest and most difficult to enter. Then the system of testing changed. A standard test for all high schools was introduced. Tatsui, with hearty support from his mother, took the new examination. A letter came saying Tatsui had been accepted for higher education at the Second High School in Sendai.[6]

Tatsui worked as a helper for Reverend Obee for several months, until he left home for Sendai to enter the Second High School. Reverend Obee was kind enough to write a letter of introduction to William G. Seiple, who was a professor of theology at Tohoku Gakuin (a Christian university) in Sendai. Sendai was like a foreign country to Tatsui. He didn't even know where it was. Located 260 miles north of Nagoya, it took a roundabout trip on the existing railways through Tokyo to get there. Despite the difficulty, Tatsui arrived in September 1917 with his *kori* (suitcase). He graduated in March of 1920. Since Tatsui spoke Nagoya-ben (the dialect of Nagoya), it was quite an experience for him, clashing with Sendai-ben (the local dialect).

Dr. Seiple belonged to the Dutch Reformed Mission. Tatsui became Dr. Seiple's assistant for the next four years. He considered him to be "a true gentlemen and scholar." The boy was extremely grateful for his mentor, especially for Dr. Seiple's "warm heart and understanding nature."[7]

Tohoku Imperial University

Tatsui applied and was admitted to the prestigious Tohoku Imperial University, also located in Sendai, where he immediately started studies in April of 1920. There he studied theoretical chemistry and met and took English classes from Professor Tsuchii Bansui—author of the lyrics to the famous hymn "Kojo no Tsuki" (The Moon Above the Ruined Castle). Professor Bansui's text happened to be the works of Shakespeare. Tatsui soon acquired a competent ability to read and speak English.[8]

While in Sendai, Tatsui visited and attended many Christian churches and helped some with interpreting or translation, although he never really affiliated with any of them.[9] As Tatsui studied and lived in Sendai, unbeknownst to him, a small branch of worshipers who called themselves "Latter-day Saints" were holding religious services just 200 meters away from where he resided. This branch existed until the Japan Mission of the Church was closed in August 1924, due to rising Japanese militarism and the deterioration of relations with the United States.

Shortly before Tatsui graduated with a B.C. (Bachelor in Chemistry) degree from Tohoku Imperial University, Professor Bansui introduced him to Chiyo Akizuki, a graduate student of the Miyagi Girl's School in Sendai. Her father was principal of a technical college in Sendai. She was three-and-a-half years younger than Tatsui and a perfect match. She was born on 26 April 1903 to Gentaro Akizuki. They were married on 28 December 1923; and Tatsui graduated from Tohoku Imperial University 31 March 1924.[10]

According to research by Shinji Takagi, Tatsui's graduation from both—a higher school and a degree from a prestigious national university—were equivalent to a master's degree in prewar Japan.[11] Upon graduation, Tatsui was employed as an assistant researcher for two years at the university until he found a teaching position.

In 1926, Tatsui left Sendai to become a teacher at a girl's school in Mie Prefecture, where he taught for one year. Again he returned to his old Sendai, and this time he taught chemistry for nine years in the normal school in Sendai. However, because of the Manchurian Incident and the commencement of war with China in 1937, Tatsui was forced to leave school—the militarists did not want to have a teacher who cherished the idea of liberty and believed in a religion other than Shintoism. Tatsui resigned from his teaching assignment and found employment with the Iron and Steel Institute of Tohoku, where he conducted studies on stainless steel and wrote several scientific papers.[12]

On the following page is a sample from a paper published by Tatsui Sato and a colleague, Takejiro Murakami, in 1938. It was entitled, "The Acid-resistivity of Iron Alloys." The introduction is written in English as follows:

> In an attempt to investigate the acid-resistivity of iron alloys containing a trace of carbon, a series of corrosion tests were conducted by the dip method with specimens of binary iron alloys. As an alloying element Ni, Co, Cu, Mn, V, Cr, Mo, W, Si, and Ai were selected, and the specimens were prepared by rolling and annealing from the ingot. The corrosion was examined . . . [as follows].[13]

Engineer at Nippon Metal

Again, Tatsui had to leave Sendai, this time to become an engineer. He moved to Yokohama and lived there until 1944. Tatsui was a supervisor of a lab at the Nippon Metal Industry Company (special steel manufacturing) in Kawasaki City, near Tokyo. Tatsui took daily train rides of about two hours each way to and from work. The company produced stainless steel exhaust pipe for Japanese aircraft.

It is interesting that Tatsui and his family lived several years in Yokohama, the same city where future Latter-day Saint prophet Heber J. Grant had dedicated Japan for the preaching of the gospel as a young Latter-day Saint Apostle on 1 September 1901.

NIPPON KINZOKU GAKKAI-SI

Vol. 2, No. 3, March 1938

日本金屬學會誌

第2卷 第3號 昭和13年3月

研　究

鐵合金の耐酸性（第1報）*

二元鐵合金の耐酸性（其一）

Fe-Ni系, Fe-Co系, Fe-Cu系, Fe-Mn系及Fe-V系合金

村上武次郎**　佐藤龍猪**

Takejirō Murakami and Tatui Satō: The Acid-resistivity of Iron Alloys. (lst. and 2nd. Reports). The Acid-resistivity of Binary Iron Alloys. In an attempt to investigate the acid-resistivity of iron alloys containing a trace of carbon, a series of corrosion tests were conducted by the dip method with specimens of binary iron alloys. As an alloying element Ni, Co, Cu, Mn, V, Cr, Mo, W, Si, and Al were selected, and the specimens were prepared by rolling and annealing from the ingot. The corrosion was examined in 10% HNO_3, 10% HCl and 10% H_2SO_4 aqueous solutions at 25° by measuring the loss in weight, and the extent of the corrosion was expressed as mg/cm²/hour. The results were discussed by referring equilibrium diagrams. The effect of heat treatments for some alloys on the corrosion was also studied.

(Received November 9, 1937)

緒　言

鐵鋼の耐酸性に就ては古來多くの研究結果が發表せられて居るが多くは炭素を含有せるものに就て實驗せられて居る．炭素を含有する時は一般に耐酸性を減ずるに因つて炭素を含有せない又は微量を含むに過ぎない所の鐵合金を造り其の組成及び熱處理並に酸の種類，濃度，溫度等を變化し系統的に耐酸性を研究することゝした．先づ二元合金より始め鐵に相當量迄固溶する金屬元素をアームコ鐵と配合して各種の二元鐵合金を調製し之をHNO_3, HCl, H_2SO_4等の酸に浸漬して一定時間後の腐蝕減量を求め之を以て各合金の耐酸性を比較し又熱處理其他が耐酸性に及ぼす影響を調べた．

試片の調製並に實驗方法

アームコ鐵の角材（約6cm角）を鍛錬して直徑約3cmの丸棒となし黑皮を旋削除去した後之を適當に切斷し，之に所要の各種元素を配合し高周波誘導電氣爐で熔融し金屬マンガン（0·3%）及び金屬硅素（0·1%）を添加して脫酸を行ひ之を鐵製鑄型に注入して約3cm角の角棒を造つた．次に之を鍛錬，壓延して直徑7mmの丸棒となし，電氣爐中で後に述べる如く夫々適當なる溫度に於て3時間保持した後電流を切り爐中で自然に冷却せしめて燒鈍したものを旋削研磨して直徑5mm長さ30mmの

** 東北帝國大學金屬材料研究所

* 本報告は著者の一人（村上）が日本學術振興會第5小委員會に提出したものゝ一部である．

Scientific paper of Takejiro Murakami and Tatsui Sato, 1938

On 9 April 1939, Tatsui and his wife, Chiyo, were blessed with their first and only son, Yasuo. (He took a liking to trains as much as Tatsui had, and later entered a lifetime profession working for the Japan National Railroad.) Two years later, the couple was blessed with a daughter named Atsuko, born on 22 May 1941 in Naka-ku, Yokohama.

When America entered World War II in April 1942, Tatsui vividly remembers the day when the first air strike on the Tokyo area by American bombers took place. He recalls looking out the window of his factory office towards the adjacent ocean, when suddenly a bomb exploded in midair over the water. Another exploded in the middle of a road, and Tatsui later examined the gaping crater it left.[14]

Return to Narumi

Tatsui gave up his job at this time, because from the standpoint of an expert on special alloy steels, he intuited that Japan could never achieve victory in this war. Tatsui took a release from his company, claiming illness, and returned to his hometown, Narumi. During the last year of the war, Tatsui remained a civilian and did nothing for the militarists except construct air raid shelters for people and serve as a volunteer to watch for the air raids. The war ended on August 15th, 1945.

Eleven days later, Tatsui's son and daughter were attacked by a terrible epidemic, perhaps as a result of malnutrition and lack of hygienic care during the war. After six days, on the anniversary of the surrender of Japan on the Battleship Missouri (2 September 1945), Tatsui's daughter, Atsuko, passed away—despite her parents' desperate efforts to retain her soul in this world. Tatsui's son, Yasuo, survived, very narrowly escaping death. He had to lie in his sick bed for five months before he was strong enough to walk about as before.

Tatsui's health and spirit also failed, and he too had to lie in bed, but only for about two weeks.[15] To lose his beloved daughter in this way was personally the most difficult and traumatic event in Tatsui's life. He related later how he had put a small photo of his departed Atsuko in his shirt pocket and carried it with him. As soon as he had strength enough to make the trip, he went up into the hills near Narumi, where he wept and said private prayers on her behalf. It was only a month or so later that he was to come into contact with members of the Church.[16]

While he was thus stricken, the American occupation army landed nearby, on the shore at Wakayama near Osaka. Soon, countless numbers of jeeps, tanks and amphibious vehicles came along the main road, Tokaido, on their way to the Uto—an ex-Japanese airdrome that was converted to a replacement depot by the U.S. Army. Uto was about 18 miles southeast of Narumi.

At first, rumors spread that American soldiers sought revenge against the Japanese and would commit every sort of atrocity. However, when the GI's generously distributed chocolate bars, chewing gum, and yen notes instead of bullets and TNT, the populace began to witness the true spirit of Americans and the gentility on display by the young soldiers.

Tatsui was lying in bed when he heard the astounding news that Japanese were carrying on trade with Americans—that the soldiers were willing to buy Japanese kimonos and ready to trade American food for silk or other goods. There were very few people who could speak English in the little town of Narumi, so merchants were looking for interpreters. Tatsui definitely needed work, as the calamities of war and unemployment had emptied his purse. He made up his mind to obtain a job and very soon found himself working as an English-speaking clerk at a silk shop near his home.

Business was prosperous on the part of his master, but not for Tatsui, as he was paid such a small sum of money. So Tatsui became a freelancer, and he was soon strolling about the street acting as an unlicensed interpreter.[17] While Tatsui was thus working aimlessly one night, a truly epochal meeting occurred. Like small pebbles that cascade into a roaring landslide, this innocuous event would lift humble Tatsui to the most majestic spiritual heights.

Endnotes

1. Takeshi Ishida, The Culture and Folklore of Narumi and Its Environs.
2. Ibid.
3. Interview with Takeshi Shiba, Narumi, 21 March 2002.
4. From Tatsui Sato, biographical account.
5. Correspondence, Tatsui Sato to Harold B. Lee, December 1946.
6. From Tatsui Sato, biographical account.

7. Correspondence, Tatsui Sato to Harold B. Lee, December 1946.
8. From Tatsui Sato, biographical account.
9. Correspondence, Tatsui Sato to Harold B. Lee, December 1946.
10. From Tatsui Sato, biographical account.
11. Shinji Takagi, "The Eagle and the Scattered Flock: Church Beginnings in Occupied Japan," unpublished manuscript, August 2001, pp. 17–18.
12. Ibid.
13. "The Acid-resistivity of Iron Alloys," paper by Takejiro Murakami and Tatsui Sato, Iron and Steel Institute, Tohoku University, Sendai, 1938.
14. From Tatsui Sato, biographical account.
15. Ibid.
16. Interview by Greg Gubler with Harrison "Ted" Price, Murray, Utah, 15 August 2004.
17. From Tatsui Sato, biographical account.

Chapter 2

Meeting Latter-day Saint Soldiers

ON JULY 25TH, 2002, I visited 86-year-old Reed Davis in Saint George, Utah. I was there to ask Brother Davis about his time as a soldier and an early missionary in Japan, where he first met Tatsui Sato. Brother Davis told me that just by thinking about those days with Tatsui, he was filled with the Spirit and tears came to his eyes.[1]

Reed Davis was with a group of Latter-day Saint soldiers during World War II in Manila, Philippines. In the beginning of November 1945, they were sent to Japan to be part of the occupying forces stationed there in the aftermath of the war. Upon their arrival, Reed's friend from Utah, Raymond Hanks, went to Narumi to buy souvenirs. There he met a Japanese gentleman who spoke English, in a silk shop. Later, on Saturday afternoon, November 22nd, Ray, Mel Arnold and Reed Davis were standing by a bridge. Tatsui Sato noticed the trio and invited them into a nearby teahouse. When Tatsui offered them tea or coffee, the three soldiers simultaneously declined, saying, "No, thank you!" Tatsui declared, "You must be Mormons!" Brother Davis and his friends wondered where Mr. Sato could have learned about their Church.

Brother Sato told them he remembered a drunk who lived in Narumi a long time ago. Narumi citizens for the most part ignored him, but he often told interesting stories. Tatsui was curious, and did pay attention to the man sometimes. One thing he told Tatsui was about meeting Heber J. Grant, and how he had learned that Mormons don't drink alcohol, tea, or coffee.

Brother Davis and his friends began to visit the Sato family every Tuesday and Thursday, because they finished their job at the military base early on those days. They left around 11 a.m. or noon from Okazaki airport, and walked about 15 miles to the Sato's home, arriving at four or five in the afternoon. Mel Arnold was 27, and Ray Hanks and Reed Davis were 28 at the time.

Back from left: Ray Hanks, Lee Blanchard, Reed Davis, Lewis Nypower
Front from left: Grover Dye, Kenneth Goodrich, Keith Armitsted

One day Ray, Mel, Reed, and their friends, Brothers Richards, Swett, and Kocherhans, were summoned to a military court-martial. Brother Davis was the first one called to present himself for questioning. Seven stern military personnel were waiting with hard questions.

They wanted to know why food was missing from the storage house, and suspected it had been trucked away somewhere. Brother Swett, as quartermaster, was in charge of the food storage key. Brother Davis had to reply honestly. He explained that after seeing kids go hungry in a local orphanage, the soldiers felt they had no choice but to help.

Brother Davis told them that every day they were witnesses to men and women, young and old, starving before their eyes, and they simply couldn't do nothing. "If you guys were in our position, you would do the same thing," Reed Davis admonished, and asked to receive his punishment. Evidently Brother Davis was right, because instead of punishing the soldiers, the military agreed with Reed and allowed for even more donations of food.

When they were with the Sato family one afternoon, Brother Hanks asked Brother Davis to do a lesson on Joseph Smith. Tatsui had invited several of his Japanese friends that day, and he was acting as a translator. After speaking for a few minutes, Reed realized that the Sato couple was crying and Tatsui had stopped translating. Reed asked them what had happened, and was astonished when Tatsui told Reed that he was speaking Japanese very well, and there was no need for translation. Evidently, the Spirit was aiding Brother Davis' communication and "the gift of tongues" became a very real phenomenon to him.

Reed Davis recounted an unforgettable story about Tatsui's mother, Tae. One day they taught a lesson about tithing, and when they returned again Tae brought the missionaries one egg. It was all she had to tithe, but she told them she would like to give it to God. The missionaries hesitated to accept Tae's egg, as it represented all of her possessions at the moment, but Tatsui politely told them to please accept Tae's offering.[2]

It was the middle of November 1945 when Tatsui Sato first became acquainted with these pioneering Latter-day Saint soldiers—Ray Hanks, Mel Arnold and Reed Davis. Tatsui recorded several of these experiences with the soldiers written in English in his diary:

November 15, 1945

On the night of Nov. 15th, 1945 at about 7 o'clock, I met two American soldiers going westward on the main street at Narumi. Saying "Good evening" to them, I remembered that I had met one of them before when I had been working at a silk shop as an interpreter. He remembered me and introduced me to his friend Mr. Mel, saying that I might call him Ray. When I confessed that I am a Christian and belonged to the Methodist church they were very pleased. Shaking my hand warmly, they said that they were Mormons.

They said that on that night they were going to pay a visit to Mr. Miyata—one of their friends who is now living in Narumi but who had been in the States for several years.

This was the night when I first met Mr. Raymond Hanks and his friend Mr. Mel Arnold.[3]

Tatsui had worked at a silk store called Ichi Roku. Many soldiers went there to buy souvenirs, old silk kimonos, and Japanese antiques. Raymond Hanks had met Tatsui Sato there.

From left: Mel Arnold, Ray Hanks, Reed Davis, Grant Flygare

November 22nd, 1945

It was a cold but silent night and I was chatting with several friends of mine at the little shop near the bridge, when someone noticed that there were three American soldiers waiting for a jeep or Japanese truck which might pass from west to east.

Hearing what they said, I went out and found there at the foot of the bridge Mr. Ray, Mr. Mel, and another new friend (Mr. Reed Davis).

I invited them to come into the shop and asked them to come nearer to the fire pot in order to warm their cold hands. Japanese folks who were there seemed to be astonished at the coming of strangers into the room, but after a minute they became good friends and had pleasant talks with them.

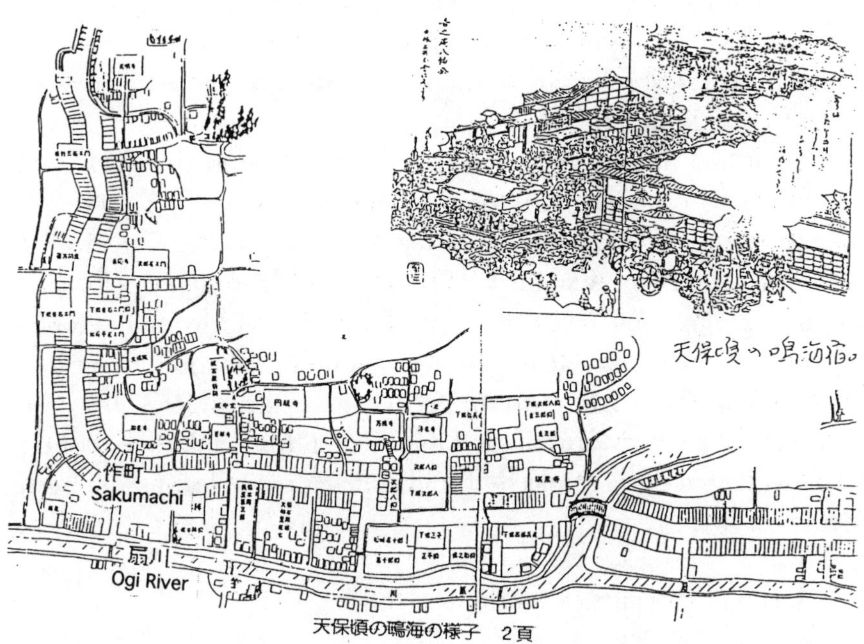

Map showing the Ogi River, which runs through Narumi (Sato was born in Sakumachi near the bridge over the river. According to Mr. Arnold, Sato crossed the bridge to meet Hanks, Davis and himself and took them to the teahouse on the east bank of the river.)

> *I presented them six boiled eggs, which were hot in order to warm their hands on their way to camp and advised them to eat if they would find it good to eat. They said thanks for our invitation to hot Japanese tea but making apologies that according to their religious faith they do not drink tea and coffee. They caught a Japanese truck and said good-bye, and then they would come to my home next time.*[4]

In the *Seito no Michi*, which is now the *Liahona*, Tatsui describes how he first met the soldiers. The beginning of the article is the same as his diary, but he also mentions two early sources of information about the Church. Brother Sato read something written by Sir Arthur Conan Doyle, and felt Doyle didn't describe Church elders in a flattering manner. Tatsui thought Mormonism was a strange type of Christianity existing in America. The other thing Brother Sato read about Mormonism was an article in the *Asahi Shimbun* newspaper when he was in middle school.

Sugimura Sojin Kan, who was traveling around the world and recording his experiences, wrote it. Sugimura wrote of a midnight train stop in Salt Lake City, and his article captivated Tatsui. The scene that Sugimura described, of having come through the Rockies and then seeing snow falling in front of the ethereal Mormon temple, was very moving; and Tatsui Sato never forgot and would never lose his curiosity about Mormonism. When he heard Elder Hanks tell him that they were Mormons and therefore didn't drink tea or coffee, he remembered those things he'd read and wanted to learn more from them.[5]

Tatsui's diary entries continue as follows:

November 28th, 1945

> *In the morning Mr. Ray, Mr. Mel and Mr. Davis came to my home as they had promised me the other night. When I showed them my New Testament, which is a private translation of Dr. Mophet and*

said that I had lost another New Testament—the authorized edition—and have no Old Testament, they loaned me [a] book which bears a title [which] says The Book of Mormon and advised me to read it. They also promised to get an Old and New Testament for me: I have a memory that I had heard about Mormon long before as one of the sects of Christianity, but I had such little knowledge about it at first sight of the book that I could not understand what was written in that book—but I promised I would read it and ask them questions next time when they would be here. They were the first Americans who trod the country road and came to my community—above all they were the very pioneers who introduced Mormon to this district of our country.[6]

Brother Hanks presenting the Book of Mormon to the Satos

December 3rd, 1945

Mr. Ray, Mr. Mel, Mr. Davis and Mr. Morley came to my home in the night for the first time, and they gave me a New Testament. This night we had good talks about the Book of Mormon and Mr. Ray exerted himself to explain about the faith of the Mormon people and the characteristic point of the Mormons. This night they fortunately caught a Japanese taxi at the foot of the bridge.[7]

Ray Hanks wrote a letter to his parents, regarding his experience meeting the Satos:

December 5th, 1945

The following is a page or two of a letter I wrote to Mother and Dad, while in the service in Japan. It is getting time to say (Siyonara) (good-bye), though I would like to mention about a little trip we took the other evening to one of the small Japanese towns. We, Reed Davis, Mel Arnold, Ralph Morley and Archie Gailey and I met in Narumi a very kind and honest Christian Japanese gentleman, Mr. Sato. He invited us to his home. In the course of our conversation, he said he wanted us to teach him Mormonism. He said he felt the Lord sent us to him, to come clear from America and find him and bring him a Book of Mormon, which we had given him prior to this date. We have an appointment to visit him Saturday evening. He wants us to come every chance we can. He speaks and understands English very good. He has one little boy, 6 years old, named Yasuo, which means, he says, "to live in peace."

Such men like Mr. Sato has shown me that the average Japanese is a peace-loving individual who loves life as we do, and wants to live it the best he knows how. As for me I have no enmity toward them. Their warlords are the guilty ones and not the masses. If they had had the freedom of democracy as we have had it they would be equally as great as we. America must destroy her own mental individual hatred and prejudices, while she is destroying warlords, if she is to have the permanent peace—hoped for by all.

Well, so much for the problems of the world—we'll not try to solve them all tonight.

Always,
Love "Ray" [8]

Embracing the Message and Messengers

Tatsui continues his English diary:

December 10th, 1945

Mr. Ray and Mr. Davis came to my home in the morning and they gave me a new the Book of Mormon and Principle of the Gospel. They also presented me an Old Testament. Mr. Ray explained about the general history of Christianity in relation to the history of Mormonism. Between Dec. 3rd and Dec. 10th, I introduced Mr. Ray, Mr. Mel and Mr. Davis to my neighbor Mr. Ito's and they have enjoyed some time at his house.[9]

Tatsui prepared a notebook for the soldiers to write notes for him. The following are those soldiers' notes:

December 10th, 1945

Dear Mr. and Mrs. Sato and Yasuo,

We shall always remember you as good people, who are interested in always living a good Christian life.

May you always enjoy the good things of this life!

With the sincere wish of your friend and brother,

Ray E. Hanks, Orem, Utah

December 10th, 1945

Dear Mr. and Mrs. Sato and Yasuo,

We all feel it a great honor to have you as our friends. We hope to have you visit us in America someday.

May the Lord bless you for your work.

Sincerely your friend,

Reed Davis, Susanville, California

Tatsui's diary continues:

December 15th, 1945

Mr. Ray, Mr. Davis, Mr. Mel and Mr. Gailey came to my home in the morning. Mr. Ray gave me a large the Book of Mormon which was sent from his mother. I presented my Japanese New Testament to Mr. Ray as a memorial. They took several photographs of my family.[12]

Mel Arnold and Archie Bruce Gailey wrote a short note of thanks that same day to the Satos:

December 15th, 1945

Mr. Sato—Wife and son, Yasuo,

It has been one of the highlights of my stay in your country, to be able to call you my friend. May I have the opportunity in the very near future to repay your hospitality. May our relationship continue to grow!

Your friend,

Mel Arnold, Provo, Utah

December 15th, 1945

Mr. Sato and Wife,

I have enjoyed being your friend and the things you have told and what you have showed us while we visit your home country.

Your friend,

Archie Bruce, Ridgeland, Utah

Tatsui's diary continues:

December 19th, 1945

Mr. Ray, Mr. Morley and Mr. Richards came to my home in the night. We had a very good talk about the characteristic faith and organization of the Mormon Church. The day before, we had the heaviest snowfall that we experienced for about 40 years, and this night we had a very beautiful moonlight.

Richards wrote the following note to the Satos:

December 19th, 1945

Dear Mr. and Mrs. Sato,

This has really been the most enjoyable evening that I have spent here in Japan. Your hospitality, sincerity, and open hearts will always be remembered. I hope that I can be with you folks often while I am stationed here. May the Lord help us to answer your questions and satisfy your desires.

Sincerely your friend,
C. Elliott Richards,
Salt Lake City

C. Elliott Richards

Tatsui's diary continues:

December 22nd, 1945

Mr. Ray, Mr. Richards, Mr. Morley and Mr. Kocherhans came to my home in the night. We had a vivid question and answer session about the history, faith and organization of The Church of Jesus Christ of Latter-day Saints. I heard from Mr. Ray that as they could not catch any truck, they had to walk all the way to their camp, which was about 15 miles, but they did enjoy the beautiful moonlight and snowy road.

Lavor P. Kocherhans also wrote a note of encouragement to the Satos:

> December 22nd, 1945
>
> Mr. and Mrs. Sato,
>
> I am very much delighted with the fine spirit of Christian brotherhood that you have and with the fervent desire you have for all good and noble things. It is my promise to you that if you continue to search for the things of lasting value and study diligently the principles of the gospel you will be very happy. Be prayerful and studious and you will be blessed.[10]

Ralph Morley also expressed his gratitude for this special experience:

> December 22nd, 1945
>
> Dear Mr. and Mrs. Sato,
>
> I have enjoyed knowing you very much. I think you are a nice family, and also your son. I will always remember you; this will be a great experience while I am in Japan. I have enjoyed coming here, and to know you are interested in our Mormon religion. I wish you all the pleasures and happiness in your future and trying days. Pray often and your prayers will be answered.[11]

On Christmas day, 1945, Brother Sato recorded the following in his journal:

> *December 25th, 1945*
>
> *Chaplain Nelson came to my home to take us to Okazaki camp to attend the Christmas evening service. To my regret I could not do so. He left a note for us as a memorial.*[12]

Chaplain W. Richard Nelson

The following is a memo from Chaplain Nelson:

On Christmas Day, 1945

I have learned about you from many of your American friends who are members of the Church of Jesus Christ of Latter-day Saints. They speak very highly of you, and I know that you have brought them a lot of happiness during their stay in Japan. I have been pleased to learn that you are interested in the truths believed, taught, and lived by the Saints of the Church of Jesus Christ. I hope that you may come to a full knowledge of the truth and enjoy the blessings of the kingdom of God. In the future, I hope to get better acquainted with you. I will come to visit you whenever I can.[13]

Tatsui's diary continues:

December 30th, 1945

Mr. Richards, Mr. Kocherhans and Mr. Davis came in the night. We had three Santa Clauses at my home on this night, and they gave us a lot of Christmas presents—especially for my son Yasuo. They sent me a lot of presents and a sincere prayer from Mr. Raymond Hanks who had started for the United States after several months stay in this country, leaving an imperishable impression upon our family.

I believe it's a wonderful thing that I could meet Mr. Ray and his friends and have my eyes opened towards being a new evangel of the Book of Mormon.[14]

Sharing the Gospel

Tatsui's diary continues:

January 6th, 1946

Attendants: Mr. Richards, Mr. Kocherhans, Mr. Miller, Mr. Tidwell, my neighbor Mr. Kimura's family (5), Sato's family

We had a first meeting of this year with 12 attendants. I invited my neighbor Mr. Kimura's family to attend this meeting. They attended with great joy and had fun freely. We sang a hymn and the closing prayer was by Mr. Tidwell.

January 9th, 1946

Attendants: Mr. Richards, Mr. Davis, Mr. Gailey, Mr. Valleau, Mr. Flygare, the Satos (3)

After we had a Christian meeting, we went to the orphanage of Narumi and they gave a donation to that orphanage.

Brother Flygare from Heber City, Utah, expressed his appreciation to the Satos in a note the same day:

> I'm very happy to have met you and be a friend of yours. I pray that everything will turn out for the best and that all will be well with you folks. May God bless us all.[15]

Brother Reed Davis wrote a detailed letter to Brother Ray Hanks, who had returned home on 12 January 1946 to report on how things were going in Japan; portions of the letter follow:

> I have made four trips to Narumi since you left, and each time I come back with a stronger testimony of the gospel. Mr. Sato is working in a new place now. It's about two miles northwest of Narumi. He said he gets more money, and the man lets him have plenty of time off. We are holding regular meetings at Sato's house each Sunday night, and he invites some of his friends to attend. Mrs. Sato is organizing a ladies club to come to her home once a week to do fancy work, and at this little group meeting of women, Mr. Sato is teaching them Mormonism. How's he doing? To me, he is a remarkable man. Our last trip there was Wednesday the 10th, and they expected that would be my last visit. So they had a special dinner prepared for us and Flygare, Richards, Valleau (a new boy from Alpine) and Davis. We all ate a hearty meal. No kidding, the food was OK. To finish the evening at Satos we sang songs, and then Lt. Richards gave the closing prayer. It was very enjoyable, but we missed you, Ray. You were the hub.
>
> We all thank you for the help you gave us. The Satos also thank you. They were very happy with the Christmas presents you gave them.
>
> Hank, we went up to visit the orphanage in Narumi. Sato took us. It was very impressive, and as we signed a book of remembrance at the Orphanage, Mr. Sato asked if we would please put Mr. Ray's name first.
>
> We were so impressed that we gave them a donation then and promised to do more.
>
> So, yesterday I went to see the American Red Cross to see if they could contact the Japanese Red Cross and get them to help,

> but no was the answer. Then I went to see the chaplain here at headquarters and he said that he would match anything that I could bring in. That was a challenge, so yesterday afternoon, Hap and I were visiting elders to all the brothers. We did a good job I think. I will tell you the total after we meet tomorrow and get in the rest. Anyway the chaplain is going to shell out a bit of dough to match ours. It was your idea, Ray, so you won't be cheated out of the blessings. The nuns at the orphanage say we must have a wonderful religion, because we are so kind (she doesn't know me). She said that even the people of Narumi do not offer them help.[16]

Tatsui's diary continues:

> *January 13th, 1946*
>
> *Attendants: Mr. Richards, Mr. Kocherhans, Mr. Davis, Mr. Miller, Mr. Nixon, Mr. Swett, Sato family (3)*
>
> *We discussed the principles [of] the Church, and learned more about its organization. Opening prayer was by Mr. Richards. Closing prayer was by Mr. Swett.*
>
> *January 20th, 1946*
>
> *Attendants: Mr. Richards, Mr. Kocherhans, Mr. Swett, Mr. Nixon, Mr. Mellor, Mr. Berrett, Mr. Otten, Kimura (3), Kato (1), Shikano (1), Sato (3)*
>
> *Hymn and prayer was (in Japanese) by Sato. Free talking about the nationalities of the United States of America, and the organization of the congress. Hymn and prayer was by Mr. Nixon.*

Becoming Friends for Life

George Swett, a serviceman from Vernal, Utah, wrote a note to his "Dearest friends" dated 20 January 1946:

> I hope you don't mind me calling you friends 'cause it is a great privilege to be called a friend of folks like you. I'm very

> thankful for knowing you, and may God bless you in your efforts to do your best. I only wish that more people could know people like you. I know that God will bless you, and I know that God lives, as you and I will if we live to deserve it. [17]

George Swett was the quartermaster at the base, and he made many trips back and forth to Nagoya, usually dropping off a fresh loaf of bread to the Satos on the return trip. In those difficult and lean times, extra food, beyond the limited rations was a tremendous blessing. Although done anonymously, Sato found out later who his benefactor was.[18]

George Swett

Another note of gratitude was delivered by Norton D. Nixon of Salt Lake City, from the same servicemen's group that same day:

> Many sincere wishes and prayers are yours. I pray that God will always bless you and help you in your search for truth. May he always bless you and your wife and family with health and

> happiness! It has been wonderful to know you and visit with you. Thank you very much.[19]

Max Mellor, in a letter dated 27 January 1946, spoke specifically to Brother Sato and his son:

> May you be able to teach your son the right and worthwhile things. Maybe you will be able to send him to America to be educated, so that he will be able to return to Japan and better the conditions in Japan.[20]

Ross Berrett, a serviceman from Draper, Utah, in a letter undated but written about this same time, also expressed his feelings with the Satos about the meaning of Christian fellowship:

> It gives me a great deal of pleasure to meet people such as you. There is much to be gained by Christians meeting together. While we are of different nationalities, we should still have much in common, because we are striving to be happy and to live useful lives. As Christians, we worship the same God and are trying to earn the same life hereafter. Because of our hope of sanctity beyond this life, we should live closely in our relations here on Earth. This means brotherhood must exist among us.
>
> It is my prayer that as Christians we may live friendly lives, thus bringing our countries to understand each other and to further the cause of Christianity—that the light of Christ might guide us in the desired paths. May God bless you always! [21]

Tatsui's diary continues:

January 27th, 1946

Attendants: Mr. Richards, Mr. Nixon, Mr. Swett, Mr. Davis, Mr. Berrett, Sato (3)

Hymn and prayer was by Mr. Davis. About "the articles of faith (1)" of the "Principles of the Gospels"—Mr. Nixon and Mr. Richards explained for us. Closing prayer was by Mr. Berrett.

February 3rd, 1946

Attendants: Mr. Richards, Mr. Swett, Mr. Davis, Mr. Berrett, Tamon, Kimura, Satos

Hymn and prayer was by Sato (in Japanese). We had a free talk about the principal of Christianity. Hymn and prayer was by Mr. Richards.

Norton Nixon

February 10th, 1946

Attendants: Mr. Richards, Mr. Swett, Mr. Nakamura's family, Mr. Horike, Satos

About 5 o'clock in the afternoon Mr. Richards and Mr. Swett came and we went to the orphanage of Narumi and they made a donation of Mormon brothers to that orphanage. We had Mr. Nakamura, an English teacher at Kinjo girls' school (mission school) in Nagoya. Mr. Horike a graduate from Tokyo University as attendants and Mr. Richards explained about the characteristic faith and organization of "The Church of Jesus Christ" to them.

Hymn and prayer was by Mr. Richards, closing prayer was by Sato.

February 17th, 1946

Attendants: Mr. Richards, Mr. Swett, Mr. Berrett, Mr. Nixon, Nakamuras (3), Horike

About 6 o'clock in the afternoon Mr. Richards, Mr. Swett, Mr. Berrett and Mr. Nixon came, and we had Mr. Nakamura's family and Mr. Horike at the meeting as before. Mr. Nakmura questioned about "the original sin of human being" and "the Lord's plan and free will." Mr. Berrett and Mr. Nixon exerted themselves to the explanation. We were deeply impressed upon the active answer, and all attendants felt the blessing of the Lord was with us.

Hymn and prayer was by Mr. Nixon, and Mr. Berrett.

February 24th, 1946

Attendants: Mr. Richards, Mr. Kocherhans, Mr. Davis, Mr. Swett, Mr. Mellor, Mr. Shiga, Mr. Maki, Mr. Nakamura and his family (4), Mr. Horike, Satos (3)

We had Mr. Shiga and Mr. Maki who came from Okazaki as new attendants to the meeting. They are beginners to Christianity and Mr. Richards explained to them about the principles of Christianity. Mr. Horike presented a question about "resurrection" and Mr. Kocherhans answered the question earnestly. There were two middle school boys and one primary school girl. Though they can understand English very little, they can learn what is in Christianity, and . . . [about the] *faith of the members of the Church . . .* [and] *the expression of enthusiasm and earnestness in preaching . . . .*

On February 24th, 1946, Tatsui wrote a lengthy letter to Ray Hanks, who had returned to Utah and mustered out of the Army; Brother Sato discusses his trials as well as his gratitude for the gospel:

The letter that you wrote to our family reached me by courtesy of Mr. Davis and Mr. Richards. Reading your letter, first of all, we feel really happy that you arrived at your home in safety. How your family rejoiced at your coming back, we can easily imagine.

> May you and your family be happy and live in peace forever is really a wonderful thing, as I used to say, that you had started for Japan to fight by order of the Army, but on the contrary you fulfilled your duty not only for United States of America but also for the Lord in exerting yourself to win real peace, not a temporal peace but an eternal peace of both terrestrial and spiritual.[22]

Brother Sato then mentioned the difficulties of the final months of the war, the death of his daughter, and the continuation of Latter-day Saint meetings since Brother Hank's departure:

> As I have told you before, since the beginning of the last year due to the ever strengthened air raid we hardly could take care of our children, at length my children fell in the victim of bad disease and we lost our daughter on the 2nd of September, the memorial day of peace commencement. Being exhausted both spiritual and physical, my health failed and I could not get up from the bed of sickness together with Yasuo who was still suffering from malnutrition.
>
> But as I had to make my living I got up in spite of my weakness and went to the silk store—I think you remember that little silk store at the foot of the bridge—and begun to work as "English speaking clerk" relying upon my poor command of English, when you appeared before me as a "G.I."
>
> After your departure we, especially Yasuo, miss you very much, but Mr. Davis, Mr. Richards and their comrades that is Mr. Kocherhans, Mr. Nixon, Mr. Berrett, Mr. Swett, Mr. Miller, Mr. Gailey, Mr. Valleau, Mr. Flygare came in turn to my home. And we make it a rule to have a Christian meeting on every Sunday at my home with the members of L.D.S.
>
> They come to my home from their camp neglecting distance and inconvenience of traffic. We open our meeting with hymn and prayer, after that we discuss about topics in the "Principles of the Gospel" and close the meeting with our favorite hymn and benediction. Recently my neighbors and some new comers joined

> as attendants. The seed that you planted in Narumi has begun to sprout and members of L.D.S. are taking care of it with great enthusiasm and earnestness. But we were informed that they are going to other place evacuating their camp. We will again miss them very much. But I believe that the Lord is with us working wonderful things all the time. I believe we shall be able to touch with American missionaries before long and under their leadership we shall be more active and grow up.
>
> I am working every day except Sunday as a translator or an examiner of Censor Office in Nagoya, which is a part of the Counter Intelligence Dept. of American Army. I feel very happy that I am working every day acting my capacity in behalf of the United States of America. I have made up my mind to do my level best for the work. May the Lord protect your health and may your business become prosperous.[23]

Shinji Takagi discussed this in his manuscript on the early Church in Japan:

> At this time, Tatsui was using his English language skills to censor personal letters and possibly other materials written by Japanese nationals, as the Mormon soldiers had arranged a position for him in the civil censorship detachment in Nagoya in January.

Takagi points out that the operations were "massive" and kept track of "letters, calls, and even telegraph traffic along with monitoring publications, radio programs and the Japanese media." He concluded, "No wonder, through the intermediation of Mormon soldiers, Tatsui's English language skills were immediately put to work."[24] This experience certainly helped prepare Tatsui for his later calling as the Church's translator and interpreter.

The Camp Closes and Friends Leave

Tatsui's diary continues:

March 3rd, 1946

Attendants: Mr. Richards, Mr. Nixon, Mr. Kocherhans, Mr. Swett, Mr. Mellor

Opening prayer was by Mr. Nixon.

As we were told that members are going to evacuate the Dept. Sato told [of] his career . . . [in] life and asked Mr. Nixon to tell about his most impressive religious experience during his stay in South America.

Answering Sato's request, Mr. Nixon told two very impressive stories that he had experienced in South America.

We closed the meeting with a prayer and benediction by Mr. Richards.

March 10th, 1946

Mr. Swett came to my home. He is the last L.D.S. member who is staying at Uto camp, [he] told about the importance of genealogy (about the pedigree) and rebaptism and baptism of the dead. He had also heard that Brother Kocherhans was also transferred to Zama. Richards went to Zama on the night of the 4th and Mr. Davis went to Osaka on the 26th of February. On the 6th of March Mr. Mellor left the camp.

Sato closed the meeting by his prayer.

C. Elliott Richards Reflects on These Times

Richards records the details of his own involvement and the historical context in his personal history (he shared with me):

In the first of November 1945, I disembarked in Nagoya. Nagoya had likewise been leveled by our B-29 bombers. I was then transported several miles southeast to my assigned camp in

Okazaki. I was to be in the 11th Replacement Depot. My primary job was to be a Currency Exchange Officer, along with Lt. Phillips and Lt. Small. We roomed together, were issued Army .45 pistols, and each day would pick up $15,000 each. This we would exchange for the yen of the servicemen going home. At that time the exchange rate was 15 yen to the dollar. Often I would have to go back to the Finance Office for another fifteen thousand dollars. While at this camp I was made 1st Lieutenant and given additional duties in the Replacement Company. During free off-duty times, most of the cadre would go into Okazaki and visit bars. . . .

Shortly after my arrival at Okazaki, I found an LDS Branch of servicemen meeting in the camp. On my first visit to the Branch, I was impressed by an English-speaking Japanese man whom three of them (Ray Hanks, Reed Davis, and Mel Arnold) had met while souvenir shopping in the small town of Narumi (now part of greater Nagoya). They had been invited into a tea shop because the proprietor thought they looked so cold. He had invited them to have some hot tea, but they had refused, telling him that they were Mormons and didn't drink tea or coffee nor did they smoke. These three, and others of the LDS group, had been meeting once or twice a week with the Sato family, and they invited me to join with them. I was the only commissioned officer in the group and could occasionally obtain a jeep for our transportation. However, most of the time we would have to hitch a ride in GI trucks to get there, and ride the local train coming back. Tatsui knew the train workers and arranged for them to stop for us when they would see us by the tracks.

It was December when I joined the group going to Narumi to teach the Satos, and thus began for me one of the most memorable experiences in my life. I shall never forget my first night in their humble home, sitting on the floor with my feet under a quilt, absorbing heat from the single charcoal pot (a hibachi) in the center of the room. It was cold and snowy outside, but inside we were all burning with the Spirit of the Lord. Brother Sato had known of the LDS Church less than a month, yet the testimony he bore to us brought tears to my eyes—it was a testimony of thankfulness, humility and faith. He and his wife, Chiyo, are sure that their young daughter, who had died of malnutrition and dysentery in October, was on the other side helping to bring the gospel message to them and to open the way for them to receive these glorious truths and attain eternal life.

At the time of one of these visits, the heaviest snowstorm experienced there in 20 years had occurred. Also we stayed at the Satos too long to catch the train back to camp. What an unforgettable night we had, walking 17 miles back to camp in the beautiful moonlight, with snow piled up on the sides of the road, and our hearts so filled with the Spirit. Reed Davis had been a singer in the Tabernacle Choir and led us in singing carols and hymns most of the way. I'll never forget the feelings of that glorious night!

This was an extremely tough time for the Japanese people. Many were literally starving, because there were no food products available for sale in their stores. The economy was in shambles because of the previous huge war effort. I was able to help the Satos a little because I was Company Mess Officer and could salvage some of the "C" and "K" rations or other edible food about to be discarded, and give it to them. Six-year old Yasuo really went for the "K" rations—they were concentrated chocolate, and he thought I was the "greatest" because of this gift.

Servicemen went home based upon their number of months of service time, so over the weeks and months our LDS group changed regularly. Reed, Mel, Norton Nixon, George Swett, Lavor Kocherhans, Bruce Gailey, and many others came and went. When the 11th Replacement Depot was closed down in early March, 1946, I was the last one of our group still there. It was with a heavy heart that I said good-bye to the Sato family, knowing that no one would be nearby to continue the teaching and help them reach their goal of baptism.

I was transferred to the 4th Replacement Depot at Camp Zama near Yokohama. From there I wrote many letters to the Satos, explaining gospel principles and encouraging them to study, pray, and remain true. Already, Tatsui had organized his own Sunday School. Each Sunday he was teaching dozens of the neighborhood children the principles of the gospel as he understood them.[25]

Endnotes

1. Interview with Reed Davis, St. George, Utah, 25 July 2002.
2. Ibid.
3. Tatsui Sato, diary entries in English, 15 November 1945.
4. Ibid, 22 November 1945.
5. Tatsui Sato, "Watakushi no kaishu [my conversion]," *Seito no Michi*, December 1958, pp. 13 –15.
6. Tatsui Sato, entry for 18 November 1945.
7. Ibid., 3 December 1945.
8. Correspondence, Ray Hanks to parents, 5 December 1945.
9. Tatsui Sato, entry on 10 December 1945.
10. Correspondence, Lavor P. Kocherhans to the Satos, 22 December 1945.
11. Correspondence, Ralph Morley to the Satos, 22 December 1945.
12. Tatsui Sato, entry for 25 December 1945.
13. Correspondence, W. Richard Nelson to Tatsui Sato, 25 December 1945.
14. Tatsui Sato, entry for 30 December 1945.
15. Correspondence, H. Grant Flygare to the Satos, 9 January 1946.
16. Selections from correspondence: Reed Davis to Ray Hanks, 12 January 1946.
17. Correspondence, George E. Swett to the Satos, 20 January 1946.
18. Sato Tatsui Kyodai no ryakureki [a brief biography of Brother Tatsui Sato], dated 12 March 1987.
19. Correspondence: Norton D. Nixon to the Satos, 20 January 1946.
20. Correspondence: Max D. Mellor to Tatsui Sato and son Yasuo, 27 January 1946.
21. Correspondence, Ross Berrett to the Satos, dated ca. January 1946.
22. Correspondence: Tatsui Sato to Ray Hanks, 24 February 1946.
23. Ibid.
24. Shinji Takagi, "The Eagle and the Scattered Flock: Church Beginnings in Occupied Japan, 1944–48," manuscript copy, August 2001.
25. Selections from "C. Elliott Richard's Personal History," copy in possession of author.

Chapter 3

Joy of Baptism

ALTHOUGH HIS SERVICEMEN FRIENDS had disbursed after the closing of nearby Camp Okazaki, Sato continued to keep in touch and express his gratitude for their efforts in teaching him and his family. He wrote Brother Davis on 12 May 1946 about his family and his hope for baptism:

> I received very fine letters from Mr. and Mrs. Hanks the other day which were sent by courtesy of Mr. Richards. They wrote in their letters that you wrote to them about the Sunday meeting and appreciated it very much, but it is our family that ought to say many thanks to you for your special kindness and taking care of Yasuo. Above all, we must express our utmost gratitude for your wonderful introduction to the true Gospel of the Church of Christ of L.D.S. But for you and Mr. Ray I could not have been given the true information of the Gospel to which I was looking forward for a long time. Your coming to our town and to my home was truly a wonderful event. I believe that there is a special will of the Lord to select us as a first Japanese missionaries of the restored true Gospel in these district of Japan. I have made up my mind to study more about the principles of the Gospel and do

> good deeds worthy of the believer of the Gospel. I and my family are hoping that some day we shall be granted to be the members of the Church of Christ of L.D.S. if we deserve truly.
>
> Unfortunately, the living condition are getting worse and worse, people are all running after foods and only selfish people are getting rich and thrive, but the former are too stricken to listen to the voice of the Lord and the latter are too selfish to take care of the weak. Mr. Davis, please pray for us that we shall be able to tide over this plight of time and be able to build the true church in this district. Please tell Mr. Ray and his family that we appreciate the fine letters very much and I am making my best to get through this crisis of Japan, I believe that by your sincere prayer the Lord will always watch over our family. I wish you could find some good Japanese friends and have good Christian meeting as before. . . .[1]

The Satos continued to hold Sunday School at their home in Narumi on a weekly basis even though contacts with their military friends had diminished following their transfers. Children had heard about the Sunday School and as many as 30 came to the meetings during this time.

Brother Sato wrote Elliott Richards on 30 May saying the food situation was very severe, but acknowledged the protection of the Lord:

> I hope you have received my letter which I wrote to you about two weeks ago. Are you and you family well? We are all well, but Yasuo has become somewhat weak and is apt to catch diseases from his schoolmates. I am working as ever at the C.C.D. office in Nagoya and by the blessing and protection of the Lord we are barely escaping from the famine which menaces all over the country, though the living conditions are going from bad to worse as you see in Tokyo and its suburban districts.[2]

Chaplain Nelson had heard about Tatsui's interest in baptism. He stopped at Narumi on his way back from an appointment in Gifu on 27 June to talk with the family about receiving more instruction and being baptized. The chaplain suggested that this might happen after a servicemen's conference scheduled for July.[3] C. Elliott Richards, then at Camp Zama, had kept in touch with his many friends, including Ray Hanks and Reed Davis, who had returned home but were still writing to Brother Sato. Richards told his friend, Brother Hanks, that his wish was to see the Satos baptized before he left Japan:

> And it is our prayer that the Lord will open up the way for them to be received in the waters of baptism and receive the laying on of hands for the gift of the Holy Ghost. I know that . . . other teachers will come to complete the work you have started. They are humble people, and have a mission to perform here among their own people . . . .[4]

However, things were about to change for him and his family as contact was restored with the Church and he was able to get more assistance for his efforts.

It was at this time that Boyd K. Packer, fortunately, was transferred to the Army Air Corp Station at Itami, near Osaka. He had already heard about the Satos from his close friend Elliott Richards and had become involved in teaching them and preparing them for their baptism. Richards made a point to attend the baptism also—he was able to take a temporary leave to witness the happy occasion. The long-awaited baptism was held on 7 July at the pool at Kansai University (in Nishinomiya). The baptism was scheduled after a servicemen's conference in Osaka where about 150 servicemen gathered to strengthen their testimonies. Many of the servicemen then proceeded to the Kansai pool for the historic baptism. Brother Richards baptized Tatsui and Brother Packer baptized his wife, Chiyo.[5]

The Day of Days

This was a very special day for those involved. Brother Richards wrote a special letter to Brother and Sister Sato on that memorable day, one that had lasting meaning to the family:

> This is a Day of Days, and with open arms we all welcome you into the Church of Jesus Christ of Latter-day Saints. The joy that I have is inexpressible—I thank our Heavenly Father that He opened up your hearts, and opened up the way for you to be "born again" and receive the gift of the Holy Ghost. I thank Him for the privilege and blessing of being a witness to this wonderful ordinance before going home—and I thank Him for using all of us to give unto you the plan of salvation and eternal life. You are on the road now. You have passed through the gate. Brother Ray, Brother Reed, Brother Horshlaus, Brother Swett, Brother Mel, and all the others are rejoicing with us today—oh what a blessing this is! The Lord has opened the way and made all this possible—never fail to be faithful and rely on Him for all things. And I promise you Brother and Sister Sato that you will be able to "tide over" this time of famine and disease—just have faith and pray, and continue the fine work you have started. It is with sorrow that I leave—but we shall meet again!![6]

A week later, on 14 July, Brother Sato wrote a letter of thanks and an in-depth explanation of the baptism to Brother Hanks, who had done so much to help his family during their hard times:

> We received [your] fine letter on June 6 and June 25 and the first box. They are really wonderful; I thank for your thoughtful combination of the contents. They help us great deal. I shared them to Mr. Ito's family and Miyata, the good old widow near the bridge and to my wife's younger brother who fortunately came to see us from Tokyo. My family also thank for the good deed and deep sympathy of the deacons who are so kind as to help us out of

the difficulties. We shall keep their names and always remember their names and kindness.

Brother Ray and Sister Hanks, the 7th of July 1946 was the happiest and the most wonderful day for us. We were baptized in Osaka under the auspices of Chaplain Nelson and Brother Richards who came from Tokyo administered the baptism for me and Brother Boyd Packer for my wife. We have been born newly and have become the member of The Church of Jesus Christ of Latter-day Saints. We believe that it is the highest privilege and the highest honor for us to be baptized by the restored Priesthood. Chaplain Nelson came from Osaka to my home on the 27th of June, and he came to Nagoya taking my wife and Yasuo with him to see me. He said that I and my wife should be baptized so we had to come to Osaka with Yasuo. I accepted this proposal at once as a wonderful gift, for we had been praying for our baptism and becoming the member of L.D.S. since members of L.D.S. had left Okazaki camp. I accepted it with full thanksgiving for the Lord

We were very busy during succeeding week preparing for the happy journey. My wife made two robes of white silk for the baptism: it is a wonderful dispensation that this white silk material that had been bought and kept for the use of my departed daughter to become her parents' robes for their baptism. We believe firmly that everything has been prepared by the will of the Lord. We started at about noon on July 6th for Osaka from Narumi. It was fine day though we felt somewhat hot. We could get on 2nd class coach of express train thanks to Chaplain Nelson's good will. Now it is almost difficult to go by train with a child like Yasuo, as it is literally packed with people, except one can buy 2nd class ticket which cost one too dearly. Yasuo enjoyed the trip very much as it was his first trip to Osaka. On our arrival at Osaka station we were fully astonished and were moved almost to tears from an unexpected joy to see Brother Richards was waiting for us on the platform. Brother Ray you can easily imagine how happy we were, for I employed all available means to inform him of our baptism with no success. We met Chaplain Nelson,

Brother Boyd Packer who is one of the most intimate friends of Brother Richards and other brethren, and we were received warmly. On that night we slept at Mr. Kawabe's home.

Next day we fasted, after attending the special service and L.D.S. conference, we went to Kansai University, where we found a very nice swimming pool. There we were baptized and entered the gate to eternal life; the day was the best day for the baptism, a curtain of cloud was drawn under the severe sunshine and the weather was neither hot nor cold. After that we returned to Osaka and the sacrament was administered to which we were joined and many wonderful testimonies were made. On that night we had a fine meeting at Mr. Kawabe's home. Next day, though we had a good deal of rain, Chaplain Nelson came to take us to Osaka station and by his help we could only get on the train.

Next day I received your letter and the box safely in Nagoya. Opening your letter, strange to say, I noticed that you call us Brother and Sister for the first time in your letter. We believe that as you and Mrs. Hanks have been always praying for our family, the Lord informed you of our baptism before it was administered. We are very happy now, for Gift of Holy Ghost has been sealed; and we are always under the protection of the Lord.[7]

Brother Richards and Packer: The Story Behind the Baptism

In his personal history, Brother Richards provides in-depth background on his and Brother Packer's involvement in bringing the baptism to fruition even though he had been reassigned to Camp Zama in the Yokohama area:

I was made group leader of the Zama LDS Servicemen's Group which met each Wednesday evening for gospel study. On Sundays, we would go into Tokyo and attend a very large servicemen's sacrament meeting held in the auditorium of General MacArthur's headquarters building, across the street from the emperor's palace. On the first Sunday in April, a special conference was held to correspond to general conference at home. Nearly 500 GI's gathered from Japan, Okinawa and the Philippines. I sang in the chorus and was surprised to see a picture of us in the next edition of the GI newspaper, the *Stars and Stripes*, along with a positive article about the conference and the Church. The meeting was prepared and conducted by Chaplain Vadal W. Peterson.

In our Sunday meeting in Tokyo on May 26, 1946, my attention was riveted on one of the speakers. I don't remember what he said, but I remember the voice of the Spirit that came to me: "There is a man of God—get close to him." After the meeting, I introduced myself, invited him to our Wednesday night meeting and invited him to give the lesson. He was Lt. Boyd K. Packer, an Air Force pilot attached to Atsugi Air Base. He came to the meeting and taught a great lesson, then afterwards came to my barracks and taught me more.

On June 1st, my friends and I responded to an invitation from Boyd to meet him at Atsugi Air Base. We had a delicious steak dinner, and then he took us on a flight over Tokyo and Mt. Fujiyama in a large C-47 "Flying Fortress." It was exciting to be in the lower bubble under the plane with nothing between me and the ground but a bit of plastic. It was particularly exciting (and particularly scary) when we hit a thunderstorm and were bounced up and down and all around. I'm glad I had confidence in the man at the controls (and in the one really in charge "upstairs"), and we did live to tell the tale.

During one of our study sessions I let Boyd read a couple of Tatsui's letters that I had received including one dated May 30, 1946. In part it read:

By the blessing and protection of the Lord we are barely escaping from the famine which menaces all over the country, though the living conditions are getting from bad to worse as you see in Tokyo. Children the old and weak, die from hunger every day, and the morality of the nation are degrading rapidly . . . To my regret, almost all Japanese Christians are utterly ignorant of the Church of the Christ of LDS, still less the common people. Thinking of this fact, I always thank the Lord for my privilege of being informed of the true Gospel. Being selected, out of, truly, scores of hundred thousand people as a believer or a seeker of the true Gospel, I am always looking for a chance to do some good work that would be nice before the Lord. I make it a rule to read the "Joseph Smith Own Story" as it is my favorite story and I read it repeatedly and also I am reading the *Articles of Faith* which you left to me as your memorial book.

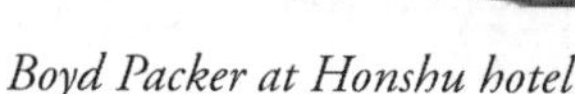

Boyd Packer at Honshu hotel

Boyd Packer

These letters so impressed Boyd that he suggested that we go up into our woods where we knelt in prayer and asked the Lord that the way would be opened for them to be received into the waters of baptism. As we were leaving, Boyd felt impressed to say that it would come about, and that we would see it! Shortly after this experience, Boyd was transferred to Osaka. In a letter to him I wrote:

I continue to stand all amazed seeing how the Lord works, His wonders to perform. He sent you to be my teacher, and through Him I bear witness that you have taught me more, done more to strengthen my faith and testimony of this glorious gospel than any other man on earth. Yet I know that the Father is my teacher, and that you who have done so much are an instrument in His hands. How can I merit all that He has given and shown unto me?

Soon after his arrival in Osaka, Boyd contacted Chaplain Richard Nelson who had met the Satos six months previously. The Chaplain told Boyd that he had felt impressed to make a recent trip to Narumi to visit the Satos. There, he had determined that they were ready for baptism, and he had made arrangements for them to come to Osaka to be baptized. Boyd was able to contact me to inform me of the good news and to let me know that the Satos really wanted me to do the baptizing! I was thrilled! But I had a problem. My time for departure had already arrived, and I was scheduled to leave on a ship July 5th, almost the next day. I talked to the camp commandant, and gratefully he finally understood why it was so important to me to stay (no one had ever made such a plea before). He allowed a week's extension and arranged for new shipping orders for me. He also gave me permission to ride by train to Osaka (GI's weren't normally allowed to ride the trains). So with a light heart I rode to Osaka and went out to the airfield to await Boyd's return from a flight. When he came in, he looked so sad—a fellow pilot had just been lost on their search and rescue mission.

On Sunday morning, July 7, 1946, he drove in his jeep to a servicemen's conference being held in downtown Osaka. We proceeded on to the conference. I now quote a letter I wrote to Ray Hanks describing the events of that great day:

There were about 60 in attendance in the morning session . . . as the speakers focused on the significance of the conversion and approaching baptism of this outstanding Japanese couple. We all fasted morning and noon, so right after the first session we piled into our caravan of jeeps and trucks and rode out to the chosen spot—an undamaged open air swimming pool on the bombed out and ruined campus of the Kansai University nearby Kobe. Brother and Sister Sato looked like angels dressed in their baptismal kimonos—made especially for this wonderful occasion from white silk belonging to their departed daughter. This helped them feel closer to her. As we sang "Oh, It Is Wonderful" with the Satos standing in the center of the semi-circle, I couldn't keep the tears from coming. I was so happy and thankful to realize that there they were, so sincere and faithful, about to be received into His kingdom. I can't describe how I felt as I baptized Brother Sato. I felt so filled with the Spirit and so far removed from this physical world. Boyd then baptized Sister Sato, and Chaplain Nelson confirmed and bestowed the Holy Ghost upon them.

Upon my return home to Salt Lake City soon thereafter, it was exciting for me to visit with Grandpa George F. Richards, then President of the Quorum of the Twelve, and with Elder Harold B. Lee to tell them of these wonderful events in Japan marking the unofficial reopening of the work there.[8]

Chaplain Nelson

Tatsui and Chiyo Sato

President Packer Recalls

I have always thought that Tatsui Sato was one of the most interesting men I have ever met. I treasure my memories of him. I first met him in Japan when we were there in the military in early 1946. We met him at the home of Dr. Kawabe, a university professor.

One of the brethren had obtained a Japanese translation of the Book of Mormon. As Tatsui thumbed through it, he said, "This is not right," then turning a few pages, "This is wrong. This is not right." I thought he just did not like the book. Then he explained, "The word for God used in this translation is for a fierce God, a vengeful God. You have taught me of a loving God. Either your book is wrong or you are wrong." I wrote in a little notebook that he would join the Church and be valuable as a translator for the Church.

He was baptized on July 7, 1946, in a swimming pool at the Kansai University. The university had been completely destroyed in the war, but there was clean water in the pool. C. Elliott Richards baptized Tatsui Sato, and I baptized his wife, Chiyo.

We met several times then and until I left Japan for home. I will never forget the night in the railroad station in Osaka when we were bidding one another good-bye. There were many tears from all of us. It was a sad parting.[9]

Chiyo Sato baptized by Boyd Packer

Tatsui Sato baptized by Elliott Richards

Lucille Tate, in her biography of Elder Packer entitled *Boyd K. Packer: A Watchman on the Tower*, mentions his close call as the B-17 they were flying landed on Tinian Island with its last drop of fuel. He felt it was an answer to his patriarchal blessing.

Brother Packer, ready to go home from his base near Tokyo, was very upset with an extended assignment to be operations officer for a search and rescue unit at Itami Air Base near Osaka. Despite his objections to his commanding officer, he was told: "Packer, you are still going!" He questioned the Lord as his greatest desire was to return home as soon as possible. He recalls:

Somehow, I don't remember how I took hold of myself, but looking back now, I can say the Lord was answering my prayers

> then. There came from that experience, from things that happened in those few months, lessons essential to the preparation for the calling that is now mine. I couldn't see that far ahead, but those tests or trials that we receive, oft times the Lord will prepare us for what He has in mind.

The biographer continues:

> As he filled new flight assignments, he became acquainted with an educated Japanese gentleman, Tatsui Sato, a Christian, who had been taught the gospel by Ray Hanks and C. Elliott Richards. Both Sato and his wife, Chiyo, knew what these men had taught them was true, and shortly after Boyd's arrival in Osaka they accepted the challenge to be baptized. A spirit of kinship immediately existed between Boyd and this man's family. Boyd felt the potential of Tatsui in service to the Church. The Satos' young son, Yasuo, told his father that Boyd would someday be a great man in the Church.[10]

Tate's account of the baptism follows:

> The Satos' baptism—the first in Japan since 1924, when the Japanese mission was closed—took place 7 July 1946, after the morning session of conference. About 150 LDS servicemen and a few Japanese came fasting to the meeting. At its close, they went out from the city of Osaka to Kansai Gakwin University, which had been largely destroyed by bombs. There stood what was left of a once-beautiful swimming pool and enough bathrooms intact for the participants to change into white clothing. After a poolside service, Elliott Richards baptized Tatsui and Boyd baptized Chiyo. From that time, the Satos always called Elliott and Boyd their sons.[11]

In his book *Memorable Stories and Parables*, President Packer explained the impact of his duty in Japan at that time:

> I did not serve a regular mission until my wife and I were called to preside in New England. When I was of missionary age, when I was your age, young men could not be called to the mission field. It was World War II, and I spent four years in the military. But I did do missionary work; we did share the gospel. It was my privilege to baptize one of the first two Japanese to join the Church since the mission had been closed twenty-two years earlier. Brother Elliott Richards baptized Tatsui Sato. I baptized his wife, Chiyo. And the work in Japan was reopened. We baptized them in a swimming pool amid the rubble of a university that had been destroyed by bombs.[12]

This poignant account from Elder Boyd Packer of his last day in Japan reveals the wretched conditions many Japanese faced during the post-war years:

> I boarded a train in Osaka for Yokohama and a ship that would take me home for separation from military service. Major Richard Nelson, one of our chaplains, took me to the train in a jeep. It was a very chilly night and Brother and Sister Sato came to the station to say good-bye. Many tears were shed as we bade one another farewell. The railroad station, what there was left of it, was very cold and forbidding. Starving children were sleeping in corners, the fortunate ones with a newspaper or a few old rags to fend off the cold. Tears shed as we bid one another farewell.
>
> I slept restlessly on the train. The berths were too short anyway. I heard a tapping on the window and raised the blind to see where we were. There, reaching from the platform, tapping on the window with a tin can, stood a little boy. An orphan and a beggar: this was always true if they carried a tin can. It was their plight. He might have been six or seven years old. His little body was thin with starvation.
>
> He had on a ragged shirt like a kimono—nothing else. His head was shingled with scabs and scales. His left jaw was grotesquely swollen—an abscessed tooth perhaps. Around it he had

tied a filthy rag with a knot on top of his head—a pathetic gesture of treatment.

When he saw that I was awake, he waved his can. He was begging. In pity I thought, how can I help him? Then I knew, I had money, Japanese money. I quickly groped for my clothing and found some yen notes in my pocket. When I tried to open the window it would not open. I slipped on my trousers and hurried to the end of the car. As I pushed at the resistant door, where he stood expectantly waiting, the train pulled away from the station. Through the dirty windows I could see him, the rusty tin can, and the rag around his swollen jaw.

There I stood, an officer from a conquering army, heading home to all of the material blessings—the warmth of family association, to opportunity. There I stood half dressed, clutching a handful of Japanese yen which he had seen but which I could not get to him.

I was impressed—perhaps scarred by the experience. Sometimes I wish I could forget that sight. Perhaps I need, greatly need, to remember. I wanted to help him, but I couldn't. The only comfort I draw is that I did want to help him.[13]

Endnotes

1. Correspondence, Tatsui Sato to Reed Davis, 12 May 1946.
2. Correspondence, Tatsui Sato to C. Elliott Richards, 30 May 1946.
3. Information in "Japanese Mission History 1945–52," as cited in Shinji Takagi, "The Eagle and the Scattered Flock: Church Beginnings in Occupied Japan, 1945–48," manuscript copy, August 2001, p. 22.
4. Correspondence, C. Elliott Richards to Ray Hanks as cited in Ibid, p. 23.
5. Ibid., pp. 23–24.
6. Correspondence, C. Elliott Richards to Tatsui Sato, 7 July 1946.
7. Correspondence, Tatsui Sato to Ray Hanks, 14 July 1946.
8. "Personal History of C. Elliott Richards," copy in possession of author.
9. Boyd K. Packer from Introduction in Watabe Masao, et al., *Ametsuchi o miyo*, i–ii.
10. Lucille Tate, *Boyd K. Packer: A Watchman of the Tower* (Salt Lake City, UT: Bookcraft, 1995, pp. 64–66).

11. Ibid., 64–65.
12. Boyd K. Packer *Memorable Stories and Parables* (Salt Lake City, UT: Bookcraft, 1997, p. 70.)
13. How to improve Our Ability, Individual & Organizational, to Reach the "Lost Sheep" given February 19, 1969 to the General Authorities and in Priesthood Board Meeting.

Chapter 4

Building the Kingdom in Narumi

FORTUITOUSLY FOR TATSUI SATO and the fledgling members of the restored Church in Japan, a new Latter-day Saint soldier named Dr. Thomas E. Bauman arrived on the scene to fill the void left when Brothers Hanks, Davis, Richards, and others, left to return to the States. Dr. Bauman would have many powerful spiritual experiences connected to Brother Sato, and these two men of God would remain lifelong friends. Brother Bauman was transferred from Fukuoka, Kyushu Island to Nagoya in the fall of 1946.

The following account is from Dr. Bauman's lively, lucid biography, detailing some of his encounters with the Satos in Nagoya and Narumi:

> On my first Sunday in Nagoya, I found our LDS meetings. There were about twenty in attendance, about half of them being Japanese. One of the families, a man and his wife and child, were introduced as members. The man's name was Tatsui Sato. I learned later that he was baptized a few months before under the direction of Brother Boyd Packer who, at the time, was an officer in the Air Force . . . It seems that I arrived on the scene in Narumi and met Brother Sato about the time I was needed.

Brothers Richards and Davis had both been transferred home. The group was dwindling. There were no group leaders at that time, but the Sunday services continued. We had an occasional Japanese investigator attend. I had access to a jeep when I needed it and would help with the transportation of Brother Sato and his neighbors on Sunday. Quite often I visited in their home during the week. My friendship and love grew rapidly for Brother Sato and his wife and child. Genuine love quickly occurs when the catalyst is the Church and its teachings. This love we felt for one another at that time has continued to this day.

In Narumi, Brother Sato had the missionary spirit. He organized the neighbor children into a group, and I went to his home and taught the children the best I could with Brother Sato as interpreter. I looked forward to the Sunday meetings and the trip to Narumi to transport the Satos and their neighbors to the meetings. During the week, I would also visit in their home and hold an MIA meeting with the older children. A few years later, I learned that quite a few of these children in Narumi were baptized into the Church. Christmas came, and we had a most enjoyable time sharing what food and candy we could buy from the PX. I also found an orphanage to help at that time. . . .

From left: Bauman and Swenson with gifts, December 1946

Considering everything, this was really a happy time of my army life. I looked forward to visits with Brother Sato and his neighbors. His home was very small. We would take our shoes off at the door. The floors in their home were covered with straw mats called tatami. Brother Sato's front room was only about ten feet square. There were no chairs in this typical Japanese home. They sat on the floor with their knees folded under them. The American soldiers could not do that for very long. I would find myself fidgeting my legs out and take up most of the room. We often laughed about my awkwardness in their home. The Satos had a pet we never saw, but we could hear it once in a while. They seldom saw it either, but they would feed it and seemed unconcerned about it. It was a rat. We could hear it running on the roof almost every time we went there. Their attitude was that if you fed it, it would not bother you.

One day when I was visiting, it was obvious that Brother Sato had a severe cold and a cough. I brought him some nose drops and cough syrup. They were in small one-ounce bottles and looked alike except for the labels. The next day when I was in my office, I received a telephone call from Sister Sato who said her husband was very sick and ready to die. He had taken the cough syrup and nose drops and got sick after that. Further questioning revealed that he was not sure which bottle contained the nose drops and which contained the cough syrup. As a result, he put a dropper full of cough syrup into his nose which he tolerated well. When he swallowed a teaspoonful of nose drops, however, it was a different story. That was enough stimulant medicine to elevate his blood pressure and cause his heart to pound and race. I got a jeep and hurried out to their home. By the time I arrived he was improving. His heart was not racing and pounding, and he was resting quietly. We still laugh about it to this day.

For some time, I had been thinking about asking for a transfer, but I kept hesitating because of my activities with Brother Sato. I felt that perhaps I was really needed there to give support to the little branch. One day, after I had been pondering this problem for some time and was feeling uncertain and agitated about my remaining time in Japan, I decided to make my problem of whether or not to ask for a transfer a matter of prayer. I did not want Brother Sato to feel that I was abandoning him, but I wondered if I were really needed in our branch. Instead of going to lunch that day, I went to my room and knelt at the side of my bed and prayed for guidance in trying to make a decision. After I had finished my prayer, I got into my jeep and was driving back to my office. While turning the corner at one of the busy intersections, I suddenly and unexpectedly felt something that is impossible for me to adequately describe. Suddenly, without any anticipation or warning, I was startled with a sudden exhilarating sensation that seemed to course though my whole body from my head to my toes. There was no discomfort associated with this experience. It was pleasant beyond description. It lasted only a second or two, and then it was gone. I noted immediate great joy that continued for several hours. The miracle of this experience was a message that was forceful and clear even though no words were spoken. I knew that I was to stay. With the events that occurred later to Brother Sato, I have felt that he and his family were being nurtured and protected for the important callings that would come to him both in Japan and in Utah. I shall be eternally grateful to the Lord for this experience. The realization that our Heavenly Father actually communicated with me for those few seconds from His exalted throne is almost beyond comprehension.

I was in Japan just a few more months. I received word from home that my mother was having more nervous problems and that she would have to spend some time in the hospital again. In fact, my father had contacted the Red Cross requesting that I be transferred to the States near his home. I suppose the doctor felt that if I were near, I might have a positive influence on her nervousness. I do not recall hearing much about Mother's problems while I was away. I knew nothing about the application that my father sent to the Red Cross for an emergency transfer home. Before I knew what was happening I was saying good-bye to the Satos and the office force with whom I worked. I will never forget the final parting from the Sato family in their home. Sister Sato

> had remained somewhat in the background during my acquaintance with them. She supported Brother Sato in all that he did for our little branch and for his neighbors who were investigating the Church. Suddenly this demure lady and I embraced with tears flowing down our cheeks. That was the last time I saw her.[1]

Bob Swenson was another influential friend Tatsui was privileged to meet. As a member of the 5th Air Force Band, Brother Swenson had fallen in love with and married Fumie Suzuki. It was not legal for either one to live in the other's country at the time, so Bob Swenson returned to Japan as a missionary, thus allowing them to be together.

At the start of his mission in February 1947, Bob Swenson was in Nagoya. He had many responsibilities immediately upon arrival, to which he quickly began to give his utmost efforts. On Sunday mornings, Swenson would drive his jeep 20 miles from Nagoya to Brother Sato's home, where neighborhood kids attended a weekly Sunday School meeting. Brother Swenson said that almost every child in the neighborhood would show up, and it's easy to picture the joyful spirit that must have pervaded the Sato family home on those days.

Part of Sunday School at Sato's home, 25 May 1947
Brother Sato at far right

Brother Swenson also recalls how the Satos would attend the Nagoya base military chapel to partake of the sacrament. The chapel was located inside the military hospital building, across from Nagoya Castle. One memory Brother Swenson cherishes in particular is attending Yasuo Sato's baptism, a moment that brought him indescribable joy. When the Sunday School had so many attendees that it no longer fit in the Sato's tiny living room, Brother Swenson helped the Satos rent a city hall used by local villagers, which was well suited for the burgeoning group.[2]

Brother Uetake gave a report on the progress of the work in Nagoya at the special Latter-day Saint Centennial Conference held in Tokyo on 19–20 July 1947:

> Shigeru Uetake of Honolulu, representing the group from Nagoya, Japan, stated the group was organized approximately a year ago. They had a Sunday School with 35–40 in attendance and an afternoon Sacrament meeting with 8 to 10 attending. They have a cottage meeting with their MIA the first of each month.

Part of a cottage meeting group at Sato's home, 25 May 1947
Far left: Bros. Whetten and Uetake Back center: Bros. Sato and Swenson

> Quite a number of Japanese people attend. Brother Robert Swenson of Salt Lake City acts as Sunday School Superintendent. They performed a baptism in June. This group has been doing some very active work with the Japanese, and their efforts are showing very splendid results.[3]

The Joy of Mingling and Protection of the Lord

Nagoya became the headquarters of the American 5th Air Force in late 1946. This brought more servicemen, including several Latter-day Saint soldiers. An adult Sunday School was organized in the Sato home in Narumi on Christmas Day, 1946. Wadsworth Shigeru Uetake from Hawaii was set apart as president. Thomas Bauman and E. Carling Whetten, both servicemen with the Air Force, also attended. Brother Bauman had access to a jeep and ferried people back and forth between Narumi and Nagoya where a group was now being organized.

Shigeru Uetake

Brother Sato felt that Dr. Bauman was "truly a God-sent distinguished Mormon missionary to my family" and "that his assignment to Nagoya was a definite plan of the Lord to save my family."[4] Takagi makes the point that the Latter-day Saint servicemen once again came at the right time to assist Brother Sato and to help get the work started in Nagoya. Brother Sato was not alone anymore and was able to get assistance. He concludes that as no organizational Church existed in Japan, except for the servicemen's groups, that much of what was happening was "self-motivated, and often unauthorized" as the servicemen tried to help however they could with the work in Japan.[5]

In a letter in late 1946, Brother Sato wrote to Elliott Richards noting that although their condition was difficult, he felt the Lord was protecting him and his family. He was greatly appreciative of the new group of servicemen whom it was a "great joy to mingle with," but he also had fond memories for those who brought him the gospel:

> It was a long journey since you left your home, but during the journey you did many good works and especially for us you did many fine deeds. They are not ordinary ones, but they are of divinity and of eternity. The plan of the Lord has been made clear by the coming of the members of the L.D.S. to our country. I believe it is a revelation that Brother Ray and his comrades came to me and informed me of the true Gospel.
>
> Brother Richards, though we have been missing Sunday meeting, thanks to Chaplain Nelson's good will, we could keep [in] touch with the members of the L.D.S. of 5th Air Force in Nagoya, and we have been attending the Sunday service and partaking the sacrament since three weeks ago. It is our great joy to mingle with the member and receive power and Holy Spirit through their Priesthood.
>
> I have many hopes and dreams for the future of the Church of Jesus Christ of Latter-day Saints in our country. When I think of it, they make me happy and encourage me. But the road to heaven is not an easy one; it is narrow and thorny, and one has to endure every suffering till one enters the gate of eternity. Brother Richards, the living condition is becoming more and more stringent, but we believe, yes we feel truly that we are under the protection of the Lord.[6]

Brother Sato Reports on Church Growth and Struggles to Reed Davis Family

Brother Sato wrote Reed Davis near the end of 1946 about his efforts with the Sunday School in Narumi and struggles during this difficult period of rationing:

> My dear Brother Davis: We were really thrilled to receive your wonderful letter and the fine photographs of you and your family. We are also very glad to hear that you are all right and busy in carrying out your business. I want to say congratulations to you, because you are going to be a papa of three children. I heard that Brother Ray became a daddy of four children and Brother Richards is a father of two children. It is very fine to hear that members of L.D.S. family are increasing. We missed you very much, because on August last year, there were only two Nisei (Japanese national born in the States) members of L.D.S. in Nagoya, and we were not able to receive Sacrament even on Sunday. Then we prayed earnestly for the Lord to send us L.D.S. members to Nagoya, and really our prayers were answered. Now we have 14 members inclusive of our family, and we go to Nagoya every Sunday to attend to the Sunday Service. We have Sunday School on every Sunday at my home, and last Sunday we had even 53 children. They come from my neighbor, even from next village, and they sing hymns, listen to the story from Old Testament, learn how to pray and learn some English. They are all eager to attend to Sunday School and are looking forward to "the party" that was promised to be given on some fine Saturday afternoon of this month. Also, we have Young People's meeting on every Saturday evening at my home, at the same place where you used to be, and we have about 12 regular attendants. They are all eager to hear the gospel and the doctrine of our Church and ask questions whatever they want to be explained. Lt. Savage (officer of 5th Air Force) takes care of Sunday School and Lt. Bauman (officer and doctor of 5th Air Force) takes care of Young

People's meeting. They are all members of L.D.S. and are always helping our family.

In the half period of last year, though it was difficult enough for us to make our living, Brothers in the States and in Japan gave us great help and encouraged us. Thanks to the warm heart and good will of Brothers we are getting along all right every day. So, we believe, that if we pray earnestly from the humble and true heart the Lord always answers for our prayer and indeed our prayers were answered. Closing this letter, may I ask you a favor of you? Could you send me several kinds of good seeds of pumpkin and watermelon, because these seeds have been degenerated in Japan and we can get only very poor crops if we can not get good seeds of them in this year? Next, I want to tell you that Mr. Albert Y. Suzuki is going to be transferred to some place very soon, so please write to me through Brother Bauman and please be careful enough not to mention my name in the package that you would send to me through Brother Bauman.

May the Lord always be with you and watch over you and your family. Mrs. Sato joins me to send best regards to you and Mrs. Davis. Yasuo goes to school, but sorry to say still he isn't strong enough, but the vitamin tablets that you gave to him helped him very much. We hope some day we shall be able to meet you and talk [to] each other about the sweet time that we enjoyed with Brothers. Mrs. Sato is learning English so that she might be able to speak and write in English.

Always your friend and Brother,
Sato Tatsui and family[7]

Timely Assistance from the Hanks and Richards Families

Brother Sato wrote a lengthy letter to the Richards family about the middle of November, thanking them for gifts and elaborating on the difficult situation in occupied Japan:

I received the fine letters that both of you wrote to us on the peaceful Sabbath Day. I can imagine by your letter how happy and peaceful your home is. How are you today? I hope you are all fine as ever and everything is going on all right. We are all well and I am glad to inform you that our living is getting somewhat better. We believe that these things all come from the earnest prayer of my true friends of L.D.S.

I received the dictionary and the Combination Reference that you sent to me. Thank you very much indeed. I am using the dictionary in my office every day and finding it very useful. The Combination Reference is a great help to us when we want to know something about Bible, faith, gospel and so on. We always thank for your kindness and help.

Brother Richards: A year and more than two months has passed since my daughter passed away. About this time last year I and Yasuo were both lying on sick bed; Yasuo had been sick since August and even in his recuperating time he could hardly walk due to the after-effect of his illness. Reminding of these things, we truly thank for the Lord's will that led us to this renewed life and saved us by the restored Gospel. He gave us my daughter. He took her from us and in the midst of the darkness of my spirit, He sent you from far away from U.S.A. to my home crossing the vast Pacific Ocean. Whenever we remind the facts we can see clearly His boundless grace in everything. His marvelous and wonderful plan that led us to the baptism and fullness of salvation.

Brother Richards: I am glad to tell you that this year's crops of rice and sweet potatoes are very good, unusually good, and from November 11 rice ration has been increased to 360 gr. from 300 gr. per person per day (for adults) though this quantity is not enough. From June to the beginning of September, it was the hardest time for us. On the 27th of June we were noticed that the days portion of rice ration would be cut off in a month owing to the absolute lack of rice stock. On hearing the notice my wife determined to give up one meal in a day and persuaded Yasuo who just came back from school saying "My good son, you know there are many people who are so poor that they can not take meals even twice a day. Your one meal can not be served from today because you took four times of meal in a day." Hearing mother's word Yasuo seemed to be very sad, but she sent him out to play. After a while, she intended to go out and was standing by the gate, when she heard a jeep coming and looked. She found Chaplain Nelson (we had been looking forward [to] his coming), Brother Romney, Brother Empy and a chauffeur in front of my house. They came to inform me about our baptism. After their talk they took lunch with Yasuo and my wife and they left more than two dozen of canned food for our meal. Since that day there has been no need of cutting off one meal in a day.

When the gift of Chaplain Nelson was over there came Brother Ray's gift box on the 10th of July for the first time. We shared our gladness with friends of mine and several friends of Ray in Japan. There were many nice foods that were never tasted before. The second big box with seeds and canned food came to me on the 30th of August from Brother Ray. There were many nice canned foods that were sent (4 from kind "Deacons of the Timpanogos Ward"). We used the food to make nice meal on the 2nd of September (the Memorial Day of my daughter). As we had no sugar ration in this year we flavored the cakes (that were made of flour sent from Brother Ray) by sugar given by Brother Brown. The cakes were highly appreciated by the little children (friends of my daughter). They said that the sugar flavored mush made of beans (sent from Brother Mel in Provo) were the sweetest. The second big box did not come after 70 days since its start, and we nearly gave up its arrival supposing that is was confiscated by censorship, but at last it came to us on the last of August when wheat was short and there was no sweet-potatoes. It came to us on the neediest time. We can see that there was a plan of the Lord in the long delay of its arrival. It was a marvelous thing.

Brother Richards: During the hard times as my salary (500 yen cash and 300 yen from my blocked deposit) was not enough to sustain our family, I had to sell my properties for necessary food. Now seeing the harvest of bumper crop of rice in front of my house am thinking that there will be no need of selling our clothing for food again. I suppose a great number of Japanese people are feeling the same and they cherish more or less peaceful mind in their heart. We are not worrying [about] tomorrow's food (Matt: 6–32, 33, 34) Our Father in Heaven has given us every necessaries. He gives us whenever we pray for, and He will give us. He is living and He is living with us.

We had only Brother Uetake as the attendant to our Sunday meeting in Nagoya Chapel but we were given two more members of L.D.S. that is, Sister Campbell and Brother Whitten, and Brother Whitten has been attending every Sunday with us. We are very glad to be given new members of L.D.S. for our prayers: asking to increase the number of member of L.D.S. was answered. You wrote to me about Sunday School text and Bible stories for children these are what we want for our work and were praying for since August. It is marvelous that you wrote to me about them before I mentioned.

Brother Richards: May I write to you the following letter that was written by my wife (originally in Japanese):

Dear Brother Richards: I sent to you several crochet pieces and pictures through Brother Uetake on 13th November. There are crochet and pictures for you and Brother Boyd Packer and Brother Nixon and Brother Romney . . . . The silk material for Marylee from me is the silk material that had been bought for my daughter. I think there will not be silk material with such beautiful bright color now in Japan. It had been bought before five years. Perhaps Marylee's mother will find the best usage of the silk material for her. The biggest crochet piece with paper written "for my tithing" is for sale. Brother Richards may I ask a great favor of you? Could you kindly enough to find some wealthy lady who wants to buy the crochet piece at a reasonable price for my tithing? It took six reels of thread and 70 days from the 10th of August. I spent on for one hour and half to make it every day. Whenever I was making it I always prayed that "Our Father in Heaven, may the owner of this crochet be blessed by the Lord, and if the owner is not righteous before the[e], may the blessing be back to me." Some flower of the piece has more than three prayers and whenever I began to work I always prayed for the blessing without fail. Would you please buy for me, with the rest money of tithing, 6 reels of crochet thread, crochet needles (No 12 and No 14, three of them) some needles for cotton thread and needles for sewing machine, Baking powder and dry yeast, may I ask your help?

Brother Richards: I received a postcard and a parcel from Brother Boyd through Japanese Post Office (packed with candy and food) . . . . Please tell him that we are thanking for his kindness very much and we are ready to share our gladness with Yasuo's little friends who is wanting sweaters. We are always speaking of you and your family.

Be always happy and well. May the Lord always be with you and watch over you.

Sincerely yours,
Chiyo Sato and Family[8]

Sister Chiyo Sato wrote a letter in English (likely translated by her husband) to Brother Davis shortly thereafter expressing her thanks to both Reed and his friend, Ray Hanks, for mail they had received:

Dear Mr. Davis,

Today I have received a parcel and two post cards from you and your Japanese friend Mr. Kiyota Seido. In the parcel five beautiful English books which were sent from Mr. Ray and his family for Yasuo were found. They are wonderful books both interesting and instructive for English beginners such as Yasuo and Mrs. Sato, they are really what we wanted. I want to express my heart felt gratitude for Mr. Ray's kindness and consideration as well as your kindness. I should be very much obliged if you would [be] kind enough to send our best thanks to Mr. Ray and his family, and Yasuo is now attending to school but he got whooping cough and chickenpox from school friends in April, so he got shots every day by our doctor. We were troubled very much but he feels very well now.

I am doing farm now. I planted potatoes, green peas, spinach in my garden west side in March. It's growing so fast that I am running after to take care of them. I have a plan, that I will plant sweet potatoes and soy beans, for we have little food. In April we got ration about 1000 calories for one day a person. (P.T.O.) I would like to see you one more time in Japan. God be with you always and keep you from all harm and danger.
Sincerely yours,
Chiyo Sato[9]

The following letter to Brother Hanks from Brother Richards written in May 1947 illustrates the compassion and concern the two had for the plight of the Satos during this difficult period, and the joy they shared over the success of the Sunday School in Narumi:

Dear Ray & Family,

It has been a mighty long time since I last heard from you & don't fall over from the shock of receiving a letter. Seriously, I am sorry for the lapse of time and we hope that our letters will become more frequent.

We have been hearing from the Satos somewhat regularly and with each letter our hearts "melted" all the more. To be here in this land of plenty and then to realize the conditions surrounding the lives of such people as the Satos in a country where food, clothing and the necessities of life are at a premium, really does humble us. And I'm sure that you, Ray, haven't forgotten the tough times they were having when you were there, and they aren't getting better. Little Yasuo has intestinal worms and has been sick all winter, being able to go to school only ten days—Sister Sato and Brother Sato are both alternately up and down from their beds. I don't know, Ray, if you have heard from them recently, at any rate I'd like to tell you of their present circumstances and activities.

On the cheerful side of the picture, the meetings the Satos are holding in their home are growing. On Sunday morning they have over 60 children out to Sunday School, and on Saturday evening they have about 20 young people attending class. In this they are receiving a big thrill. They have obtained an organ somewhere. A high school teacher plays it for them, so they really must be having quite the meetings. Remember those wonderful nights?[10]

Hanks also wrote Elliott Richards on 29 May regarding the Satos:

Thanks so much for your letter of May 11th, please excuse the delay in reply. We have been rather busy here in our business and in Church activities, but surely that is no excuse for not replying sooner.

Since receiving your letter my thoughts have gone out to the Satos and our prayers have been for them, and I felt guilty in praying for the Lord to bless them when I knew that I could help in this blessing by sending something to them. My wife has truly the Spirit. When she heard of Mrs. Sato losing her kimonos she said, "Ray, the kimono which you brought me is a luxury to me. To them it is a necessity. We shall send it to them." I have quite a nice overcoat that I do not use that I will send to Mr. Sato. Also I will try and find a coat and something for our dear little Yasuo. The deacons brought over a few beans and canned goods and we shall send them also. Truly there is a greater blessing in giving than receiving when analyzed in its true light.

The Satos have brought something into our lives that is great and wonderful. Such faith and humility are virtues from the Heavens. Your love and kindness to them will last eternally. I am grateful that their good lives brought us together, even though that was a long evening until 3 a.m. the morning after our visit with them in Narumi. Isn't it gratifying to hear of the wonderful work they are doing? Think of that, sixty out to Sunday School! Little do we realize that our small visits led to the furthering of our Heavenly Father's work in the great land of Japan.

Truly there are many wonderful people there who are hungering for the blessings of the gospel. Wouldn't it be wonderful to return again and see the Satos and do nothing but labor with them in missionary endeavors? Do you think it would be possible for us to plan such a dream? One never knows, do they? I'll surely have to brush up on my ten-word Japanese vocabulary.

We hope you are enjoying your wooden palace in Stadium Village. I am sure you would make it a palace. You and your wife and your lovely family would make any place a palace.

Now as to the sending of goods to the Satos. Will you write me by return mail exactly how to reach them? You say it is possible to send the package direct to them. I will send quite a good size box, and you say this will reach them directly? Any information you can give me as to the packaging, shipping, etc., and the correct address, I will appreciate. Thanks again for your remembering us, and we shall look forward to seeing you soon.

Truly yours,
Ray E. Hanks[11]

Reed Davis, concerned, wrote the Sato family a very long letter on 6 June thanking them for the priceless gifts of a spiritual nature he had received while in Japan and shared the joy of success of the Church in Narumi; he also continued to provide wonderful counsel to the family:

Our thoughts and prayers and kind wishes have always been for you since that wonderful apprenticeship we enjoyed with you in your wonderful land of Japan. Yesterday we sent you all a little remembrance, a few items of food and clothing. With it comes our love and appreciation of you for the things which you gave to us while with you across the waters. You gave to us something greater than can be packed in a box. You gave us a richness of faith that you knew that your Heavenly Father lived and that He would preserve you in all of your difficulties. This faith is one of the greatest gifts that one can have because truly it is from the Divine. You gave to us a spirit of humility and humbleness that characterizes a true member of the Lord's Church. You gave to us consideration and thoughtfulness and politeness that was deeply appreciated, and so in return our little bit is nothing of the richness which you gave to us.

My good wife, upon hearing from Brother Richards that Sister Sato had lost her kimono by someone who does not understand the gospel, her heart went out for her and so the kimono which I brought from your town of Narumi she is sending to Sister Sato. I hope the coat that we sent to you, Brother Sato, will be appropriate and give warmth this winter to your good soul. Our boy, Charles, who is 13 years of age sends a pair of Levis to Yasuo. I hope they will fit.

It was a thrill to hear of your wonderful work in the Sunday School and that over 50 kiddies attend it. Surely the greatest joys that come to any man are the joys which he gives to another. As we help one another our joys doubly increase because we have our own personal joy plus the joy that is received by another who receives the help, and so truly the Master was right when He said, "He that would be the greatest among you, let him be the servant of all." Another has said "that which we keep, we lose. That which we give away we keep; for the one who receives that which you give away keeps it eternally in an appreciative heart."

It is good to know that you have some fine young couples interested in the MIA work. I admire you greatly, Mr. and Mrs. Sato, for your living the Word of Wisdom even before you knew the teachings of our Church on the Word of Wisdom. If you can encourage the young people to discontinue the use of tobacco and explain to them the harmful effects of nicotine on their bodies and can encourage them in the abstaining of liquor and harmful drinks, you will have done a great mission.

Teach them the first principles of the gospel as found in our fourth article of faith: First, faith in the Lord Jesus Christ; second, repentance; third, baptism by immersion for the remission of sins; and fourth, laying on of hands for the gift of the Holy Ghost. These principles are eternal. The time that you take to explain them to another will be well invested. What greater blessing could we bring to any man or woman than to develop within them a deep faith that our Heavenly Father lives. How wonderful is our blessing, we are told, if we but bring one erring soul to God, so the second great principle of repentance is a wonderful principle. If we can but cause people to change from sin and sorrow to virtue and happiness, what a wonderful thing. When the Lord finds a person that has faith and has changed from erring ways, he is then entitled to take membership in His Church, the Church of Jesus Christ of Latter-day Saints. He is taken to the waters of baptism and there he is immersed, symbolizing a death to sin and a resurrection to a new life of service, humility, and purity and fineness of living. This is a physical ordinance which is part of the earth which we live in. Man's body is physical, but he also has another side of life, the spiritual, for he is part of the eternal heavens, and so there must be a spiritual ordinance made to consummate a full acceptance in God's Church, which brings in the fourth principle of the gospel, the laying on of hands for the gift of the Holy Ghost. Truly this is a gift from the heavens, for one who has this gift is able to understand more clearly the workings of God. He is able to explain more clearly to others the great plan of the Lord. The receiving of the gift of the Holy Ghost, which is a comforter and an influence that leads to all truth and knowledge connects with heaven.

May you have joy in explaining to others these beautiful truths, for truly they are eternal and they are true. I bear you my testimony that I know that they are true. You, too, may bear your testimony to others that they are true. We trust that all is going well with you, that you are able to make a living and that you are able to gain food for your family. Surely the Lord will preserve you because of your faithfulness. Write us at your earliest desires and let us know exactly your conditions, and if we can help you further it will be our joy to do so.

Our business here has been rather quiet. As you know, we are in the real estate and insurance business. Prices have been high for real estate, and people's finances are not as much as they used to be and so we have had a little lull in our business; but yet our business is growing. We have a nice little office in a good location in Provo which is a lovely little town of about 20,000 people. Here we have the Brigham Young University that has a membership of around 4,000 students. It is growing and students are coming from all parts of the country and different parts of the world. How wonderful it would be if some day Yasuo could attend this wonderful university where principles of the gospel are taught, as well as the sciences.

Mr. Sato, did you not get a degree in a chemical engineering college? I would enjoy very much for you to give me a little sketch of your life's history telling about your boyhood days—where you were born, some of your thoughts, and impressions, the education which you have received, and some of the jobs which you have worked in, and how you took an interest in Christianity and learned to speak and write the English language so well. Also, it would be very lovely to have something similar of Sister Sato's life.

Do you remember the night that we sat on your floor and you told us how you had prayed that God would send someone to comfort you in the departure of your little daughter, and how you told us that you thought we came in answer to your prayers? I assure you that it made us feel very humble, for truly I do believe the Lord sent us to you. And that, in another way, makes us feel very humble and very grateful to think that the Lord would be so kind to us to let us get acquainted with you.

There is no doubt in my mind that when we lay our mortal remains down that our spirit goes back to the God who gave it life, and that in due time our physical remains will be resurrected to unite itself again with our spiritual soul. The great prophet Alma, in the Book of Mormon, makes this clear to us as he wrote in the 40th chapter of the book of Alma. In the little box which we sent, you will find a few copies of the Church section of the *Deseret News*. They have many wonderful articles that you may enjoy, especially the one by our Prophet George Albert Smith, in his talk which he gave to the great congregation of Saints when he became President of the Church of Jesus Christ of Latter-day Saints. While in Japan, I received this Church section and I never had an article such as this quite impress me so much, and so when I discovered it at home I thought you might enjoy it very much.

I must close for now and will be looking forward to hearing from you soon. Brother Elliott Richards sends his love to you. I have on my desk a letter from him telling of his correspondence with you and his love of you. I think Brother Richards is truly a servant of the Lord and was also sent to assist you in being baptized in the Church. Siyonara. Excuse my spelling. In other words good-bye.

As ever your friends,
Davis Family[12]

Continued Efforts in Narumi and Appreciation for Assistance

Tatsui Sato wrote the Richards a letter dated 12 June 1947:

I thank you for your writing two letters (through Brother Uetake) and a letter through Japanese post office. Especially I thank you for sending me the precious medicine by air mail. Truly we can not thank too much for your kindness and help for our family.

The number of children coming to our Sunday School has become almost constant (about 30). We started a story from Old Testament, beginning with "the creation of the universe" using "the second intermediate Sunday School" which you sent me as a text. We shall continue the story from the beginning to the end. We are studying "the article of faith" (that you left for me before you left for home) at the Saturday evening meeting with young folks, and I started "Wednesday evening Bible class" since June 4, having 6–7 young folks to come and study Bible in English. We had rainy Sunday every week except the last Sunday but about 30 children came. They are learning how to pray (I help them how to pray opening and closing prayer) and how to sing Sunday School hymn. They can sing "Jesus Wants Me" and "Merry,

Merry Children" pretty well. They listen to the story that Brother Uetake tells them (I interpret the story). We would like to give picture card (for Sunday School children) to diligent children. How do you think of it? If you approve, would you kindly send me some picture card for them. You can imagine how they feel happy when they could get it.

We would like to go to Salt Lake City (if it would be permitted) in order to study more about Holy Scriptures and the fullness of Gospel. We are speaking of the dream if it would be realized.

Brother Romney wrote to me the other day, saying he was graduated from the university. Have you ever seen Brother Bauman? He was very kind to us when he was staying in Nagoya. We are always thankful for his guidance to living in Gospel and deep sympathy for our livelihood. Brother Bauman is a young doctor graduated from the same university you are studying and his home is in Salt Lake City. I hope he will be a good friend of you. Brother Bauman left for the States about the middle of March, but he is still in service at the camp hospital in Colorado Springs.

I received the receipt for the tithing and the money order ($5) you sent me through Brother Uetake. I thank you indeed for your taking care of the matter, and we sent the money ($5) to Central Pacific Mission as our tithing through Brother Uetake, for it is our prayer to offer all of the money as our tithing to the Lord.

Brother Richards, thank you very much for the medicine. We will give them to Yasuo with great care, as you said. Doctor said even 1/3 tablet of "Santonin" will be sufficient as a dose for Yasuo. As for "Gentian Violet" [our] doctor never saw it before, and he said he must consult with a text book before he can determine the dose. We do hope Yasuo will be healthy in this summer taking good care of his health.

Food condition is not good. We got 20 lbs of rice, 15.5 lbs of whole wheat flour, 6.7 lbs of whole wheat grain, 15.5 lbs of corn flour, 6.7 lbs of maize flour as food ration for May.

Total 64.4 lbs = 2.14 lbs for 1 day for 3 persons = 0.71 lbs per day per person. That is a little more than 1,000 calories for a person. Flour was given as main food we used up the baking powder. It was excellent to make bread. If it would not bother you much, could you kindly send us the baking powder? We made excellent bread with the baking powder and the nice flour you [sent] me, it was indeed excellent. Yasuo was very much pleased with it, and our friends were too. We shared the pumpkin and squash seeds with my neighbors. The seeds were planted and many have put forth their leaves. We are expecting abundant crops of them.

That your family is always happy and is always amply blessed by the Lord

This is our sincere prayer. Brother Richards we are making our best to work [for] the Lord and to study, to live in the Gospel. . . . We send our best thanks and our best hearts to you and your family.

Sato Tatsui, Chiyo, Yasuo

[P.S.] We are sending more stamps to Dick, the larger ones are memorial stamps for the New Constitution of Japan, smaller one is ordinary 1 yen and 30 yen stamps.[13]

The genuine feelings of compassion and love that Brothers Richards and Hanks had for the Satos is expressed in a letter dated 14 July 1947; this letter to Richards from Hanks is regarding a letter delivered by mistake:

Dear Elliott,

A letter of yours from the Satos came to me by mistake. It had your name, but was addressed to me, and I thought that perhaps it could have been a wonderful letter that I couldn't help reading it and sharing with you some of the heartfelt feelings of the Satos. I trust that it meets with your approval that I retain a copy of the same. I hope by now the folks have received the little box of remembrances that we sent better than a month ago. You surely have been thoughtful of them, Elliott, and I know that the Lord loves you dearly for your kindnesses to them.

I know that the Lord loves them for their humble and sweet life they are living, and their desire to further His work in their land. Express our kind regards to your good wife, and to your family. It is always a pleasure to hear from you.[14]

The Lord is Always with Us

Brother Sato wrote a detailed letter to Reed Davis on 20 August 1947, in which he congratulates the family on the birth of a son, reports his son Yasuo's baptism the previous month and mentions his continued efforts "working for the Lord":

My dear Brother Davis

Congratulations! I congratulate you upon the birth of your baby. It is really happy news for us to hear that your family was given a boy baby. Our family sends our best love and prayers to him that may the Lord give ample blessing to him and always watch over him. I wish your business is always going well and your family is getting along happy days. Please pardon me for my delay of my answer. Your gifts arrived to us in safety and some kind of seeds came out already, even they bore good fruits. I am sorry that pumpkins, squashes and cucumbers were somewhat seasonal in this land of Japan, and they could not bear fruits. On the other hand, beans gave us abundant crops, and they helped many people of my neighbors when there was scantiness of vegetables in this early summer. I gave the seeds of tomatoes and water melons to the Prefecture nursery, and they found, after they cultivated, the seeds have wonderful qualities. Good seeds can help many people. I am thinking if I could carry on the business of seed dealer. Yasuo was much pleased with the gift you sent him. Thank you very much.

He was baptized on the 5th of July at Ohama beach, about 20 miles south east from Narumi, and Brother Uetake (Sgt.) administered the baptism. On the next day, special Sunday service was held at the little chapel in Nagoya, and I was conferred the Aaronic Priesthood and was ordained as Deacon. It is our greatest joy that the baptism for Yasuo was administered so successfully and he has become healthy and strong since the baptism.

The Lord is always with us. He gives us ample blessings that we never dreamed of. When you were at my home with Brother Ray, Brother Richards and other brothers, my family was the only one that were listening to the true gospel of your church, but now I have a Bible class on every Wednesday night and a Sunday School on every Sunday morning. More than ten investigators come to my home to study the Bible in English, at the same time they learn singing in chorus. One night, I and my wife were thrilled with joy when we heard someone was singing our favorite hymn with beautiful soprano in beautiful moonlight, yonder on the river bank. Tears came out when we were listening in the rhythm. When we work for the Lord, He always helps and He gives a reward more than we expect. Though the living condition is adverse to even our struggle, I am working for my family and for the Lord. We salaried class men are miserable and there is the likelihood of us being ruined by the inflation, but wonderful helps came in time when we were needy. I believe that the Lord is living and working among us.

My wife is very well and she wishes to send her best love to the newly born baby, and also she wishes to send her best regards to you and Mrs. Davis. We think that now we have to work all the time only for our living, but sometime we shall be able to come to Zion, our life's destination, and shall see you and your beloved family again. May your business become prosperous and may your family be always happy is my sincere prayer. Best love to the baby and to you all.

Always yours,
Sato Tatsui, Chiyo, Yasuo[15]

A few weeks later, on 5 September, Brother Sato wrote a letter to Brother Boyd K. Packer congratulating him on his marriage and reporting on the progress of the work in Japan. He also thanks Brother

Packer for his role in his baptism and mentioned why the gospel appealed to him:

> Dear Brother Boyd Packer,
>
> How are you? We are very glad to hear from Brother Richards that you were married to your fiancé. Congratulations! Congratulations! My wife, Chiyo, also sends her best congratulations to you and to the bride. We imagine how wonderful was the ceremony in the temple, and how warmly your friends celebrated the wedding reception. It is very glad for us to hear of our Brother's most happy affair.
>
> Though we are struggling for our living, as a little flower and nameless weed can be welcomed by desert travelers, so every kind thing sinks to our heart and it lightens the darkness of our life like jewels. We want to hear good things and to learn good things. When Brother Richards were at my home there was none but my family who was listening to the true Gospel of your church, now we have Sunday School, cottage meeting and Bible class at my home. Children and young folks come to my home gladly. If you were here you would be deeply impressed on hearing the innocent children sing the L.D.S. hymns in good English. They also gladly listen to the story from the Old Testament. The seeds that were planted by Brother Richards have come out and growing up. I watch over them, giving nourishment, and dreaming of the time when they will thrive and bear good fruit. It is really marvelous and wonderful thing that the Lord guided you to Japan across the vast ocean. I firmly believe that there was a definite plan of the Lord for sending you to ordain the baptism for our family.
>
> It is a wonderful thing that the Lord has already opened His mission in this land of Japan. We have to only work for Him. The doctrine of the Church of L.D.S. is really wonderful. If it be allowed for us to go to Zion, I would like to go there and study all about your Church.
>
> There are many points in the doctrine of L.D.S. Church that are easily understood by the oriental way of thinking. That is the main reason why I was attracted by the doctrine and have a firm

faith in it. The truth is revealed when good conduct (body), good preaching (mouth) and good will (heart) harmonize, according to oriental scripture. As there are still many survivors who are believing that John the Baptist is the Messiah, and do not believe in the Gospel of Jesus Christ, so there are many people in Japan who believe the salvation by Buddha and do not know the true Gospel. I believe that Buddhism in Japan has acted its role, just as John the Baptist acted his mission in the land of Judea. Luke 3: 4, 5, 6, I am trying to do my best to explain that it is not the first time we are listening to the true Gospel, but we had been listening to the Gospel long ago, we have only forgotten the fact that we had been brothers and sisters, and once before we had been listening to the preaching of Jesus Christ. Though I am poor and powerless when I work for the Lord He always helps me sending the Holy Ghost. What a privilege!

We are always talking of you and thinking of you. May the Lord be always with you and watch over you, and May the Lord give ample blessing to both of you, is my sincere prayer. My wife Chiyo and my son Yasuo send their best love and best thanks to you all.

Always yours,
Sato Tatsui, Chiyo, Yasuo[16]

A Treasure to Each Soul

Tatsui Sato wrote Elliott Richards a very sentimental letter on 10 October 1947 in which he shared his feelings on testimony and faith; he also discusses the work in Japan and the difficult conditions at the time:

I am very glad having received your letter and the gift package you send to me, which arrived in good shape. Yasuo and my wife were very glad when they received the package from postman and found such wonderful gifts you sent for us. Tears come out when I think of your love and help for my family. It never can be thanked too much. I owe my family's clean and healthy living solely to your great help to my family's welfare.

I am very glad to say that Yasuo has become healthy and he plays outside all day long. Now the hot summer days have gone and cool autumn day is here. We had rather little rain in this summer and some place in Japan crops have been burned dry, but in some district a heavy rain caused flood, and it swept away wide fields. However, in general, this year's rice crop is hopeful and I pray that the food condition might be bettered.

We had the Christian college meeting on Tuesday evening, but it has been discontinued because of the difficulty of transportation for Bro. Uetake. We [have] more than twenty young people who were studying on the Gospel and seeking after truth. We studied about "The Articles of Faith" with them.

Faith can neither be explained by words nor be acquired by discussion. I believe it is a treasure that is given by God to each soul. I really thank God that He has given me the treasure, and also I thank that He has given me the privilege to bear the testimony that I have it. As gems have its luster, so faiths enlighten our life. As gems without luster is not true one, so faith without exercise is an incomplete or an inactive one. Faith itself and its exercise makes a faith complete.

I want to do good works, and I want to help other people, but to me [I am] sorry what I can do is only to tell the true Gospel to other people and give what little thing I have. My wife shared the clothes that you sent, to my neighbors. They were very much pleased with them and thanked for your kindness to sent the clothes for us. At present we are so short of textile materials that any kind of old clothes will be a great help for the people here. I should hate to trouble you, but if you could send some more for us I should be very thankful for it.

Due to the shortage of coal, electricity is not plenty enough to give us light it is cut off several times in the evening, and often we have to have a Bible class under candle light. I wrote a letter to Bro. Nixon, if the letter reaches you please give it to him. My wife gets up before 5 o'clock in the morning and prepares meal and

> lunch for me, and after supper she has to arrange food and fuel for tomorrow. In the day time she has to go out to buy things that I am selling as my side work. Her only recreation or consolation is to learn music by organ and to attend to Sunday service.
>
> However, the little chapel in Nagoya has been transferred and to my sorry the Sunday service has been discontinued. Bro. Richards, we are not discouraged. We have countless blessings that the Lord has given us. He is always with us and helps us.[17]

Concerned about his friend and no response, Brother Sato wrote two months later, on 10 December, telling Brother Richards about Yasuo being baptized and about receiving the priesthood. He continued to mention his efforts in teaching the young people in Narumi and wanted to express his thanks for a welfare box he had received, which he felt the Richards' family had a hand in:

> Are all of you well? It seems to me I have not heard from you for a long time. I am anxious to hear of you. I wrote two letters to you. Have you received them? I believe it takes long time before they are delivered to you. This time I am going to mail this letter by air mail so that this may go faster than ordinary one.
>
> Now it is getting colder and colder every day. Winter has come here already. I wish all of you will enjoy good Christmas and a happy new year. When I count the blessings given from on high in this year, in reality they are countless. First, it is the most precious blessing of the Lord that Yasuo was baptized and became one of the members of L.D.S. Second, I was conferred Aaronic Priesthood and was ordained to be Deacon. These blessings are the most precious one and the highest privilege for us in this world. Third, I believe it is our Lord's blessing that I could keep the Bible Class for young people and the Sunday School for children through this year. Some time it was hard to keep the class and the school regularly, but I took up courage when I saw children and young people enjoy and welcome what I teach. Forth, I am poor in material and weak, but by wonderful help

that came from Brothers and Sister in L.D.S. church, I could tide over the plight up until now. I am feeling that my family is under the protection of our Lord, etc.

Bro. Richards, please tell General Church Welfare Committees that I received the welfare box in good shape, and I feel exceedingly grateful for their kindness. I was surprised at what is contained in the box. Cans of good food: bars of fine soaps. May I express my best thanks for their kindness through you? Really it was a question that what can I do for children on this year's Christmas day. Last year it was rather easy for me to give something to children from my own pocket, but this year it is pretty hard to make them happy within my power. I really thank for the kindness and help by the Welfare Committee, and I want to send my best thanks for my Sunday School children. May I add, I believe that the welfare box came through the good offices of you and your family including your parents. Thank you very much.

The clothing which is sent from your family was distributed among some of my neighbors who are in needy. I believe you would join me to enjoy happiness that I feel when I see children and people are enjoying to wear the clothing that I shared. I am sorry to tell you that things for us have not been bettered yet, and living conditions are getting harder and harder.

In these days the welfare box from the committee is a great help for me to live in Gospel. As my income became so small sum of money by inflation that I have to carry on some business for myself, but it is hard to find good one in these days. In closing this letter I am glad to tell you that my wife and Yasuo are very well and they are expecting a good Christmas and a happy new year.

May the Lord give full of blessing to all of you and watch over you. Always thanking you and your family[18]

Brother Thomas Bauman, who had returned home to Salt Lake City, also sent a Christmas letter to the Satos:

> It is with great joy and humbleness that I have been privileged to gain the friendship and brotherhood of you fine people. I am so thrilled that the Lord provided a means whereby you were privileged to hear the gospel, and I am even more thrilled that you understood and accepted it. I am sure that you and your family will receive the Lord's blessings in great abundance. I know you can and are doing a great work in teaching others of the gospel. On this Christmas Day, when peace and good will prevails throughout the lands, I want to express my thanks to God for the fact that there are still fine, good people on the earth like you are. Through the efforts of you and all good people who embrace the gospel, lasting peace and good will eventually come to the earth when Christ returns to reign. May God bless you all—
> Sincerely,
> Your Brother[19]

In a summation of this period, R. Lanier Britsch, the eminent authority on the Church in Asia remarks: "Brother Sato, who remained faithful to the Church until his death in Salt Lake City in 1996, organized a Sunday School in Nagoya in 1946 [Narumi is a suburb] and conducted it almost single-handedly until missionaries were sent there in October, 1948."[20]

Indeed, the level of Brother Sato's commitment to the gospel and his conversion, despite difficult circumstances, is shown in his heroic efforts to build up the kingdom of God in his native Narumi.

Endnotes

1. "Personal History of Dr. Thomas E. Bauman," 1993, pp. 85–88.
2. Interview with Bob Swenson.
3. "Tokyo L.D.S. Centennial Conference:" copy of report, 19–20 July 1947, courtesy of Alma Ogata of Honolulu.

4. Shinji Takagi, based on letters from Tatsui Sato to Thomas Bauman (7 March 1949) and Reed Davis (20 August 1947), "The Eagle and the Scattered Flock: Church Beginnings in Occupied Japan, 1945–48," manuscript, pp. 26–27.
5. Ibid, pp. 48.
6. Correspondence, Tatsui Sato to C. Elliott Richards, about December 1946.
7. Correspondence, Tatsui Sato to Reed Davis, probably early 1947.
8. Correspondence, Tatsui Sato to C. Elliott Richards, about November 1946.
9. Correspondence, Chiyo Sato to Reed Davis family, May 1947.
10. Correspondence, C. Elliott Richards to Ray Hanks family, May 1947.
11. Correspondence, Ray Hanks to C. Elliott Richards, 29 May 1947.
12. Correspondence, Reed Davis family to Tatsui Sato family.
13. Correspondence, Tatsui Sato family to C. Elliott Richards family, 12 June 1947.
14. Correspondence, Ray Hanks to C. Elliott Richards, 14 July 1947.
15. Correspondence, Tatsui Sato family to Ray Hanks, 21 August 1947.
16. Correspondence, Tatsui Sato family to Boyd K. Packer, 5 September 1947.
17. Correspondence, Tatsui Sato to C. Elliott Richards, 10 October 1947.
18. Correspondence, Tatsui Sato to C. Elliott Richards, 10 December 1947.
19. Correspondence, Thomas Bauman to Tatsui Sato, 25 December 1947.
20. Internet entry, R. Lanier Britsch, "Part 7, History of the Church in Japan," www.ldsworld.com/gems/history/0.2631.html.

Chapter 5

Arrival of Missionaries

In so many ways, one can see the hand of the Lord working in the lives of Brother Sato and the American servicemen who brought the gospel to him. Brother Sato's faith and dedication to the restored Church in Japan was overwhelming, and no power could keep the seeds that the elders planted in Narumi from flourishing under his inspired care. With prayer and faith as his tools, Brother Sato built a sturdy, unshakable foundation for the Lord's Church to take hold. But for it to continue growing, missionaries were needed—clearly the Lord responded to Brother Sato's unflagging conviction.

A Plea for Missionaries

Because of his remarkable success and enthusiasm for the gospel, Brother Sato decided to write Church headquarters in Utah. He addressed his letter to Elder Harold B. Lee of the Quorum of the Twelve. This letter, as cited earlier, told the story of Tatsui's encounters with Christianity and conversion to the gospel of Jesus Christ. President Lee answered his concern for the need for missionaries in Japan with the following personal response, dated 29 December 1947:

It was a delight to receive your lovely letter so full of thanksgiving and appreciation for the little help the Church has been able to give to our faithful people in Japan through the General Welfare Committee. I am sure you will be glad of the news that a mission is now being opened by the Church in Japan with President Edward L. Clissold from Honolulu, Hawaii, as the President. President Clissold during the war was trained to speak Japanese and spent some time in Japan in the service of the country. He therefore is prepared to understand not only the language but something of the people. Unfortunately, military restrictions forbid the sending of more than the mission president at this time but President Clissold by himself intends to do everything possible for the benefit and blessing of Church members in Japan as well as our friends who are interested in learning more of the gospel. I am today sending your letter and address to him so that you might have an opportunity of working with him in an attempt to do all possible for the advancement of the work of the Lord. We assure you that our desires are to spread the gospel wherever conditions permit and as rapidly as missionaries are available for this work.

With kindest personal regards,
I am faithfully, your brother,
Harold B. Lee[1]

A Year of New Hope

Ray Hanks wrote the Sato family in January 1948, praising them for sharing the gospel and promising continued help with their needs. In wishing "new hope" for 1948, he had no way of knowing the impact of the new mission and the changes that were to occur in the lives of the Sato family later that year:

We received your good letter of December 12th, truly we all have many wonderful blessings and I know the Lord loves one with a grateful heart. Our Heavenly Father is very kind to us in the blessings he showers upon us in our weakness. Truly today there is need of strong courage. I am sure that the Lord led us to find you because you had prayed for help. We all need help, each day of our lives and when we have been blessed it is our duty to share with those who are less fortunate than we. You have received the gospel, which is a true plan of God's way of life and there are many in your land who are less fortunate than you, and how wonderful to know that in your humble faithful way you are sharing your blessings by teaching others the true plan of life.

Yesterday morning I was reading in the Book of Mormon in the 4th chapter of Mosiah and he was telling how we are all beggars, begging constantly for His blessings, and how we should help one another that we are not the ones to say who is worthy and who is not worthy. Truly the Book of Mormon is the word of the Lord, spoken through ancient American prophets. Many of the worlds are beginning to realize this and also, Brother Sato, what you and your good wife and Yasuo can do to further its cause will bring you blessings today and eternally, for it is God's work and His work is eternal.

I often tell my friends about you good people, your faith and your sincerity. Though many miles lie between us, your good influence lingers close. There is no distance that separates this grand spirit of yours. I was happy to know that the Church Welfare sent a box to you. Our Orem Junior Chamber of Commerce is going to help out also. I know they would appreciate a letter from you telling about your civic conditions and how the young men between the ages of 20 and 35 look to a peaceful, prosperous life. I'm enclosing the names of a number of our boys in the Chamber of Commerce who send greetings to you, also an article of interest. Will you inform us the items that you need most, the kind of medicine, seeds and food. We wish to assist you in your needs. We know the Lord will continue to bless you as you continue to bless those about you. We trust you had a very Merry Christmas and may 1948 bring you new hope, new joys, that will make you happy now and forever.

Ray E. Hanks[2]

Brother Sato wrote to Brother Packer on 17 January mentioning the response to his letter from President Lee and the news of President Clissold's coming. He shared his feelings about the need for the gospel among his people and his testimony of the truth:

> How are you today? I hope all of your family is well and getting on all right. I received the gift parcel that you sent in November 1947, on 10th January 1948. Thank you very much. I would like to tell you how it gave hope and courage for us to tide over this inflation. Also, I received your wonderful letter. I hope you had a splendid Christmas last year. We had a wonderful Christmas too. Sunday school children made a Christmas decoration by themselves. They brought together paper, cotton, colored thread etc. from their home, and finished a Christmas tree. On the day before Christmas day, Sister Bock in Nagoya came to my home by car with plenty of wonderful Christmas gift for the children. On the next day, after celebrated Christmas, all of the children, ninety three in all, received wonderful Christmas gift. It was really wonderful. I thank God that He remembered my prayer and gave such blessings to all of the good children.
>
> Last December I wrote a letter to Apostle Harold B. Lee who answered me a wonderful letter telling that Japanese mission is being opened with President Clissold of Hawaiian Mission. It is really good news, and I am looking forward to his coming here. People in Japan need a real religion, the truth on which the Kingdom of Heaven is built. It is my greatest Joy to work with him hand in hand for building up the Kingdom of Heaven in this country. Truly, Jesus is the foundation stone and love is the fundamental principle to rule over the Kingdom. I understand that the spirit world is not another world, but it is merged into this world to be one and to be real existence. I am seeing it, living in it and shall be living in it forever.
>
> I learnt by an Oriental scripture that to do good deeds is to adorn or to beautify the Heavenly world; I believe this corresponds to the Holy words in Epistle Titus, (Titus 2:10).

Furthermore, the scripture says that when we are making our efforts to do good works, flowers in the Heavenly garden increase their fragrance and beauty, on the contrary, when we are reluctant in doing goodness flowers there will be withered away. Brother Packer, if I could ask your favor, I would like to read book of Moses and The Pearl of Great Price, for I have never read them before. I have The Doctrine and Covenants and I am reading it now. It makes me surprise that there are so many characteristic doctrines in it which corresponds to my personal faith that had been formed under the influence of the Oriental thoughts. This is the most important and essential fact that the L.D.S. Church must be established in the Oriental countries.

In closing this letter I would like to say many thanks for your warm heart and deep sympathy toward my living condition.[3]

President Clissold Opens the Mission

Edward L. Clissold of Honolulu, Hawaii played a large role in bringing the gospel to the Japanese people, both in Hawaii and later in Japan. Clissold had a long history of involvement with the Japanese saints in Hawaii. He was instrumental in founding a Japanese Sunday School in Honolulu in 1934. This led to the reopening of the Japanese Mission (it was closed in 1924 in Japan) with headquarters in Honolulu in 1937. Clissold, who had a strong interest in the language and people, received more training during World War II as he served in the U.S. Navy during the war. With the sudden death of President J. C. Jensen of the Japanese Mission, he became acting president of a mission that baptized far more members (over 200) in five years than the previous mission in Japan (1901–24) did in 23 years.

Also, because America was fighting Japan at the time, and because of the feeling that other Asians should be included in proselyting efforts, the Japanese Mission became the Central Pacific Mission. Also, because of the war, it was difficult to find replacements for missionaries, and the work was handicapped. Nonetheless, Hawaii provided a foundation for learning the Japanese culture and language, and many of the converts would go to Japan later as missionaries. Clissold, despite his concurrent naval duties, was officially set apart as mission president at April Conference in 1944. In May 1944, Clissold was ordered to duty outside the mission and was, therefore, replaced by Castle H. Murphy, who was also president of the Hawaiian Mission. However, after the war, Melvin A. Weenig became president of the Central Pacific Mission so the missions would have separate leadership.[4]

Because of his language expertise, Brother Clissold was transferred to Tokyo with the Supreme Command of Allied Powers (SCAP) under General MacArthur as part of the occupation of Japan in September 1945. He placed notices in several Japanese newspapers inviting members from the early mission to "call on him in his quarters at the Dai Ichi Hotel." Several Japanese members heard and did, in fact, call upon him. They became the foundation, along with servicemen, for a group of Saints in Tokyo.

Clissold was released from the Navy in February of 1946 and returned to his home in Honolulu. The following year in the spring, he accompanied President Weenig of the Central Pacific Mission to meet with servicemen and members and to determine the procedures required to enter Japan again. According to the early mission journal, letters of application for a permit to enter Japan were sent by those brethren to the War Department in Washington in May of 1947. The permit was refused on the ground that the Church had not been active in Japan immediately prior to the war and consequently could not send operating missionaries back. There was, however, a provision for sending one missionary representative of churches not active before the war to Japan, and the brethren appointed Eldward L. Clissold as president of the new Japanese Mission. He was officially set apart on 22 October 1947, but it was several months before the necessary arrangements could be made for him to return to Japan.

Meanwhile, Harrison "Ted" Price and Wayne McDaniel were called as the first missionaries to Japan, but were sent to Hawaii to labor in the Central Pacific Mission until they could be cleared for transfer to Japan. Interestingly, Paul V. Hyer, then a missionary in that mission, created the first missionary language training program to train the first few groups of missionaries that were to arrive. Elder Hyer had studied Japanese in the military and in college, and was able to provide missionaries with a basic foundation while they were awaiting transfer to Japan. He went on for a doctorate at Berkeley and to be a distinguished professor of East Asian history at BYU. He was a close friend of Brother Sato for many years.[5]

With great fanfare, President Clissold had his farewell testimonial on 22 February 1948. He sailed from Honolulu on the President Cleveland for his new assignment in Japan that same day. Arriving on 6 March to a small reception of servicemen and old members, he attended a group meeting in Gotanda at a house made available by a friend of the Church. There, he spoke of his calling to reopen the mission in both English and Japanese.

President Clissold found a Japanese Sunday School conducted by Brother Fujiya Nara at Shimo Kitazawa with nearly 50 children in attendance. The servicemen with Brother Sato had also helped Brother Nara with materials and direction. On 8 March, Clissold visited with SCAP authorities to try to get a permit to bring in missionaries that were waiting in Hawaii. He already had connections as a former member of the staff. "He was informed that he would have the privileges of Occupation forces for 60 days and was billeted at the Dai Ichi Hotel, which incidentally was his former residence." He immediately opened an account for the mission (which included donations from servicemen) and met with several important contacts. Clissold spent the next month trying to find a residence for the mission office. It was a difficult search in Tokyo, where housing was scarce, because much of the city had been burned by incendiary bombs during the final year of the war.[6]

Mission Home and Future Site of Temple

Through his contacts, President Clissold was finally able to find a suitable property, though the building was abandoned and in need of considerable repairs. The former home of the Minister of Welfare, the residence had been hit by incendiary bombs in May of 1945 and had to be completely rebuilt. The property, located across from beautiful Arisugawa Park and near foreign diplomatic missions, also included a detached house where the Satos were later to live for a time when they moved to Tokyo.

The Mission used the detached residence as its headquarters until the home was completed that fall. Sister Clissold arrived on 4 September, and the home was completed enough to house a new group of missionaries that arrived in October. By November the landscaping was completed, and the residence became an important landmark and center of the Church in Japan. Later, because of its prime location, it became the site of the first temple in Japan.[7]

Missionaries Enter Japan

On 26 June, the first four missionaries were finally allowed to enter Japan—Elders Harrison "Ted" Price, Paul C. Andrus, Raymond C. Price, and Wayne McDaniel. These men were veterans of the war and also had spent a few months in Hawaii waiting for permission to enter Japan. According to historian Lanny Britsch, 17 missionaries were to arrive by the end of the year. Besides the mission president and his wife, nine were *Nisei* (including two sisters) and seven were Caucasians.

The elders did have some prewar missionary material, including the 1908 Alma O. Taylor translation of the Book of Mormon, collections of songs and a few tracts. There was also much interest in having missionaries teach English and Sunday School classes. Although President Clissold hoped to have more missionaries and Church literature, he found them hard to come by during these difficult times.[8] Housing was especially scarce, and living conditions in Japan were very difficult. Those who did come paid a great price to build the kingdom in what was becoming more and more a Buddhist country.

Paul C. Andrus with Tatsui Sato

Clissold Visit and Missionaries in Narumi

The missionaries initially went to Tokyo, but President Clissold was very aware of Brother Sato and his efforts in Narumi. Clissold was determined to visit Narumi and meet Brother Sato; this was arranged in August. He promised a set of elders, and within a month, Elders Harrison "Ted" Price and Kojin Goya were given the assignment.

Brother Sato wrote about the Clissold visit and the passing of his father in August (in a letter dated 22 September); he also discusses the conditions in Japan:

> How are you Brother Richards? Is all of your family all right? I do hope all of them are very well and enjoying daily life in peace and in righteousness. Hot summer day is gone and it is now already September; the autumn season is here. I trust that you will

pardon my long silence since May. I am sorry to let you know sad news. My father passed away on August 17th. He had a stomach trouble since the end of the last year. We did all we could, but his sickness became worse. I consulted with three doctors one of whom was my brother in law, but they said due to old age his recovery would be hopeless. He was given shots of vitamin and glucose solution every day, but he became weaker. It was very hot and sultry summer this year, and but though it was favorable for rice crop, yet it was unbearable for the sick. We prepared for him whatever he wanted to take, but he could take only very small quantity. He could take fresh tomato juice, milk, soft boiled rice, soft fish meat etc. Milk was good for him, but it was hard to get. On August 16th his condition became very bad; returning from my job I felt that the day was the last day we could talk together. At the midnight he fell into coma; I grasped his hand and counted his pulse to the last one. It was early in the morning of August 17th. He was 74 years of age.

Though I lost my father, whom I was unable to convert, I have a great consolation that I shall be able to be baptized for him so that he may be entitled to eternal life and salvation. It is my utmost happiness that you preached me true Gospel and made my eyes opens to the fact that there is a way to salvation for the dead. I do hope someday I shall be privileged to receive baptism for my father.

This time I have happy news to tell you. Brother Clissold, President of Japanese Mission came over [to] Narumi, on the beginning of August. It was a big day. We were very glad to have long waited missionaries with us. Sunday school children welcome him singing "Jesus Wants Me for a Sun Beam," "Merry, Merry Children" and "Love at Home" in English, and this pleased him very much. He told a story for children in excellent Japanese language which surprised us very much. It was really wonderful. Two weeks after he sent two young missionaries to Narumi, and again we had a big Sunday school and Bible class too, told stories for children and members of Bible class in very good Japanese language. I was very glad to find them blessed with gift of tongue.

I hope they will make a good progress in language during their stay in our country. I have found a good room for rent in my town for missionaries. When President Clissold approves, missionaries will come over and begin the work for the Lord. What I have been praying for the Lord for a long time is going to be realized. Seeing the "minutes" written by the brothers when they held a cottage meeting at my home, President Clissold said that it would become a precious historical record of Japanese Mission of L.D.S. Church in Japan.

Last Sunday we had more than 70 children at my home. I am sorry that my room is getting narrow for the children. I have Sunday school children from 5 up to 14 or 15 years old, so that it is necessary to divide them into two groups, but at present it is hard to have two classes. However, I am glad to see my Sunday school is growing up. What children's parents desire strongly is of course to teach children the true way of living taught by Jesus Christ; but at the same time, they want to have us take good care of their children while they are out to work. There are many children who are left without care while their parents are out to work. Many times I think that if I were able to have a wide and good house for the children, how people would understand well the true meaning of our Church's teaching.

I believe if I continue the work and pray for the Lord, be sure my prayer will be answered. Brother Richards, do you remember the hill and the paddy field around my home? Due to the good climate of this summer a good rice crop is expected in this harvest time. You brothers of L.D.S. Church came across the Ocean by the divine Will and planted seeds of beautiful flowers of Mormonism. Many seeds have come out and they are growing. I am expecting the time when they will bear good fruits.

Yasuo asks me to say hello to Uncle Charly. He is now third grade in primary school. When you came to my home he was just a little weak kid, but he became healthy; rarely ill since he was baptized. My wife is always busy with home work; even she has to stand in line to get ration still now, but she is sticking to organ. I think if she continues to stick to organ she will be able to play hymn within a few years. Yasuo also learns music and English. My wife has a firm belief that someday we shall be gathered to Zion. I pray also that her prayer be answered and we shall be able to meet you at Zion.[9]

Shortly thereafter, on 25 September, Brother Sato wrote Reed Davis a similar letter, also talking about his father's death and Clissold's visit:

How are you? Is all of your family very well? I hope they are all well and enjoying daily life in peace. I received your letter and read it with many thanks and happiness. I am very happy that you always remember my family and think of our welfare. Knowing that you are working as a missionary for the Lord, I am very glad and would like to know your wonderful experience about your missionary work.

Brother Davis, I trust you will pardon my long silence. My father has been sick for a long time, but he passed away on August 17th. He was 74 years of age. I consulted with three doctors and we did all we could, but due to his old age there was little hope for his recovery. He became seriously ill on August 16th, and passed away in the early morning of the 17th of August. Though I lost my father I have a great consolation that I shall be able to be baptized for him so that he may be entitled to eternal life and salvation. I feel very happy that you preached me the Gospel and opened my eyes to the truth that there is a way to salvation for the dead.

Do you remember the hills and paddy fields around my home? We used to go up and down the hill and told bout the time when missionaries will come over [to] Narumi for missionary's work. What I have been praying for the Lord for a long time is going to be realized. Brother Clissold, President of Japanese mission came over [to] Narumi on the beginning of August, and we had a big Sunday school. Sunday school children welcomed him singing "Jesus Wants Me", "Merry, Merry Children" and "Love at Home" in English which pleased him very much. Two weeks after he sent two young missionaries to Narumi, and again we had a wonderful Sunday school and Bible class. I have found a good room for rent in my town for missionaries. When President Clissold approves, missionaries will come over and begin the work for the Lord. I had 72 children at my home last Sunday. Can you imagine how many children can take their seats in the little room (where you used to be)? I had more than one hundred children last Christmas, and I can expect more children on this year's Christmas. I am sorry that my room is becoming narrow for children, but I feel glad to see my Sunday school is growing larger.

Brother Davis, Yasuo and my wife say many thanks for your wonderful gifts. Also I thank you very much for your warm heart and kindness. Yasuo was just a little kid when you came to my home, but he is third grade in primary school now. Once he was very weak, but he has become healthy since he was baptized. We speak of you always and remember your kind heart. We want to hear from you. I sincerely pray that the Lord may bless you and watch over you . . . .

And as a postscript:

I am very glad to know that my letter to Apostle Harold B. Lee was printed on the issue of the *Deseret News*. President Clissold kindly sent me the script of the magazine.[10]

Elder Harrison "Ted" Price and Elder Kojin Goya from Hawaii arrived in Narumi to assist Brother Sato with the work in October. Interestingly, the place they had finally found to rent was formerly part of an old inn owned by the mayor. The elders found it somewhat dark and depressing and wanted to paint it white. However, when the landlord heard about their plans, he was upset, as a former emperor had stayed there.[11]

One of the early important baptisms was Toshiko Yanagita, the daughter of Brother Tomigoro Takagi, who lived in Nagoya. She was baptized in August 1949 and, along with her husband, later assumed important leadership roles in Nagoya. Sister Yanagita was involved later in translating the Church hymnal used in Japan until the 1980s and served as Relief Society president in the earlier mission.

Elder Price Recalls Narumi and the Sato Family

Elder Harrison "Ted" Price, at his home in Murray, Utah, related the story about his life and mission call to Japan. He remembered President Heber J. Grant, who, ironically, closed the mission to Japan in 1924. "He spoke as a prophet of God," that some of the youth in attendance at the time (in the old Salt Lake 11th Ward around 1937–38) would be going to Japan, and predicted great things for the Church in Japan. Ted's brother, Ray, a deacon, was two years younger and sitting on the front row where President Grant pointed. Perhaps this had something to do with the success of the Japanese Mission in Hawaii, opened in 1937.

Then Pearl Harbor happened, and Ted found himself fighting the Japanese as a marine in the Pacific. He had returned from the service, was awaiting his mission call, and was shocked to be called to be the first missionary to Japan. In fact, he thought they had made a mistake. When he found out that it was for real, after rereading the letter from the First Presidency, he said to himself, "For three years the Japanese have been trying to kill me, now they are getting another chance." He initially went to Hawaii to wait the final approval and, after several months, was able to join President Clissold in Tokyo. He and Kojin Goya from Hawaii were sent in August to help Brother Sato in Narumi.[12] Interestingly, his brother, Ray, was called to Japan only a few months later.

Arriving in Narumi was a great shock to Elder Ted Price. He was very impressed with Brother Sato's knowledge of the gospel and his great faith. In Narumi, Tatsui was extremely popular and had many connections. Brother Price remarked that Narumi was still very rural and a feudal village at that time. He considered it a "real introduction into the Japan of old." He remembered meeting many older Japanese in the cemetery and appreciated the great hospitality of the people of Narumi. With Brother Sato's help, the missionaries were able to find housing from the mayor, Mr. Shinzato.

The house was very old and dingy, and rats were a serious problem for the elders. They decided to get some white paint, but Shinzato was horrified that they wanted to paint a former Japanese inn—a place where the famous Japanese poet Basho had actually written a poem and other important guests had stayed. In fact, Brother Price has a picture of Tatsui holding a box that contained one of Basho's poems. It was several months before the elders were able to get a kitchen cabinet that could keep the mice out. Life was difficult during that time because the elders were limited to food rations, the same as the natives. They felt fortunate to get their rations, which included rice, tofu and sweet potatoes. Brother Sato, who had problems feeding his own family, tried to help wherever possible.

Brother Price told of a miracle that happened that made a difference in their lives. He found a 100 yen note in his scriptures, which at the time was a considerable amount of money. He felt prompted to go to Nagoya, though he was greatly tempted to use the money for food. There, he and his companion met a Latter-day Saint serviceman who had a year's supply of food and was going home. This new cache helped immensely, and they were able to share some of it with the Satos.[13]

Elder Price remembered how kind and compassionate Tatsui was towards everyone. Tatsui was extremely well grounded in the principles of the gospel and had the ability to organize concise interesting lessons that related each principle to his own culture. Initially, Brother Sato provided simultaneous translation of the elders' talks, but gradually the elders became more independent as they learned the language.

Members of the branch decided to hold a street meeting in front of the Nagoya Train Station. Tatsui made lanterns a couple of feet in diameter to attract attention. They sang Church hymns, and Tatsui and the elders took turns speaking. They had to be very careful, as street meetings were illegal in those days. They were able to meet a brother from the early Church and make some good contacts.

Elder Price remembers that over a dozen people were baptized from the Sunday School Brother Sato had started almost two years earlier. He called Tatsui "a truly inspired leader and great pioneer of the gospel in Japan," and considered him a truly remarkable man and a lifelong friend. Elder Price recalled Brother Sato talking about losing his beloved daughter and that he carried her picture in his pocket. Tatsui's son, Yasuo, was still quite young, but he had memorized many scriptures; and that was very impressive to the elders. Elder Price felt Yasuo was extremely bright, and mentioned his later contribution in developing Japan's famous Shinkansen "bullet train" railroad system.[14]

Tatsui was friends with community leaders, Buddhist priests and neighbors alike. In fact, the community provided the branch with a community center that held around 200 people. They used this to hold their enormously popular Sunday School. Elder Price was amazed as Tatsui drew big charts, using both, Japanese and English, to explain gospel principles. It was some sight to see so many shoes at the entrance to the hall. When Elder Price arrived, he could not speak a word of Japanese, but with Tatsui's encouragement, he became very fluent within the year he was in Narumi—he felt "blessed with the gift of tongues." Elder Price was surprised when suddenly he received a call from President Mauss to open the Fukuoka mission. He had spent a year working closely with Tatsui, and it was difficult to leave such a wonderful friend. He had formed a friendship that was to last a lifetime with Brother Sato, whom he considered a "uniquely spiritual man." [15]

Tatsui Writes about Missionaries in Narumi

Brother Sato described his joy, to his friend Ray Hanks, of having missionaries come to Narumi. This letter, written around January

1949, describes their activities and challenges in Narumi at the time:

> How are you, are you very well Brother Ray? Is everything going on well? I have heard that even America is under the menace of high commodity price and difficulty of living. I must thank you very much for your wonderful gifts to my family, thank you very much Brother Ray. My wife and my son Yasuo, who are both very well, happily join me to say many thanks for your gifts and to send their best love to you and to your beloved family. I hope all of your family is very well and living happy life.

Kojin Goya and investigators in Narumi

> I am glad to tell you that the long waited missionaries came to my town and settled here in Narumi since November last year. They are Elder T. Price from Salt Lake City and Elder Goya from Hawaii. I am happy to say that I have a privilege to work with them and have an opportunity to offer help for them. It was rather hard to find a good shelter for missionaries in such small town like Narumi, but fortunately I could borrow 3 rooms for them, and installed furniture and commodities for cooking, bath

and warming etc. Fortunately this winter is extremely mild, the mildest winter that I have ever experienced.

The sign hanging in front of the gate to Brother Sato's residence

Last Christmas Day I had more than 250 children at my home. Many of them could hardly enter the room and the rest of them had to stand in the garden. Fortunately it was fine weather. Sunday school children cut out a Christmas tree from my garden and they made Christmas decoration by themselves, and installed it in my living room. All of them, who attended Sunday school, received wonderful Christmas gifts sent by Church and its members. We had such a wonderful Christmas. As our Sunday school is growing larger we divided children into three groups, and Sunday school is held at two places since the 2nd of January. M.I.A. meeting on Tuesday evening and Bible class on Saturday evening, both are held at my home. Relief [Society] club has been organized, and the members, chiefly are young girls, distributed many clothes and food to the needy people in this town. I am feeling happy that we can help the needy first, because we have been blessed so much. All these information will gladden your heart. Furthermore, Boy Scout is going to be organized under the supervision of missionaries. Missionaries are doing a grand work to propagate the True Gospel to the country people who is still living in superstitions and feudalistic ideas. As time goes on, I am convinced that you are truly a distinguished Mormon, missionaries whom God sent to me in order to save my family. I am sure that there was a definite plan of the Lord that He sent you to Japan in order to meet my family. I will work for the Lord who sent you to me and made my eyes open to the Truth of the universe and clearly shown me the way to salvation. Brother Ray, whenever our Church became prosperous there was always a opposing influence, and there is too. I am thinking of difficulties that I have to meet face to face in future, though nobody is aware of it now. Please pray for me that I may stand upon my own feet and that I can help, encourage and lead the "God chosen people" to "the promised land."

Brother Sato's residence, where meetings were held

Brother Ray, I make it a rule to invite missionaries once in a week for supper, on Saturday evening. I feel happy to have an opportunity to make them happy. They are fine young men, and they are busily engaging in their grand work of preaching Gospel and organizing bodies. I hope they meet plenty of wonderful experience while they are doing their good work, and after they fulfilled their missionary work, I really hope that they may go back for home with good impressions. I sincerely pray that may the Lord pour blessings upon you and give health and happiness so that you may enjoy the earthly life in righteousness. Please remember also our prayer to your family.[16]

Children on their way to attend Sunday School

Brother Sato wrote a similar letter the following month to his friend Reed Davis and credited the servicemen for planting the gospel seed that was beginning to take hold:

Please pardon my long silence since I wrote you last. I thank you very much for your sending the best poster and crayons to Yasuo as a Christmas gift, and also I thank you very much for baking powder and other things that you sent for my family. The crayons had arrived just two days before a picture contest for which Yasuo was praying for "Father" that he would like to have good crayons. We were very glad, because we could bear a testimony that "Father" will surely answer for children true prayer. Yasuo's painting was selected as one of the best, and is being posted up at his class room. He is very fond of painting; also he is learning [to] play my organ and on 5th of March to come, he is to play organ accompanied with dancing, performed by ten school girls, at the talent contest at his school.

I am very glad to tell you a happy news that two missionaries, Elder Price from Salt Sake City and Elder Goya from Hawaii, have been settled in my town since November last year. I was glad to have a privilege to arrange a room for rent in my town and accommodations for them. I have been helping and working with them by keeping, Sunday school, M.I.A. meeting, Bible class and by visiting patients and needy people in my town. Our Sunday school is growing larger, and we had to divide children into three groups according to their age; up to 10, up to 14, over 15. My wife teaches the class of the youngest. M.I.A. meeting is held on Tuesday evening, from 7 to 9 o'clock, and usually we have about 50 attendants. My living room has become too narrow for the attendants; so that I and my wife are praying together for larger meeting place. We are praying that may the Lord help us and give us more strength to meet every difficulty. Since the missionaries coming our work has become active and investigators and children to come to Sunday school are growing larger in number Relief [Society] Club has been organized since investigators, helped making Christmas decorations, sang a chorus on Christmas day, made cakes for children and distributed clothes and food came from Hawaiian Church to the needy people in this town. Last Sunday afternoon, we had a meeting and had a talk with Mother's Day (6th of March). A play, singing song is to be staged and flowers will be presented to mothers. Girls sing the hymn "God Be with You" very well; even they are able to sing in chorus.

A seed that was planted 4 years ago and has been fostered by the "Three musketeers": that is Brother Ray, Brother Mel and you, and other Mormon brothers, is growing up. I really hope the seed will bear rich fruits before it is harvested. My living room has already become too narrow for attendants to the meeting.

In spite of the fact, I feel very happy in my mind because the Lord will be sure helps me, so long as I remain righteous before him. My wife is using every day the sewing needle that Mrs. Davis sent for her. She wants to say many thanks for the kindness. Some day, we would like to be gathered to Zion and we would like to have an opportunity to talk you at there about God's blessing. If you allow me to ask you a favor, please kindly send me the M.I.A. song with music. As time goes by, I am convinced that the Mormon brothers who came to my home and preached me the true Gospel of Jesus Christ were truly God sent, and especially distinguished missionaries of the Lord. May the Lord help you and protect you in every condition. May His abundant blessing be poured upon your family forever and ever.[17]

A little over a week later, on 7 March, Brother Sato wrote to Brother Bauman about the missionaries and progress in Narumi. He asked for prayers on behalf of his family and the work, and said his ultimate goal was to be "gathered to Zion":

How are you? Please pardon my long silence, I have not written to you for a long time. Are you very well and as busy as ever? I hope you are all as fine as ever are very good doctor in your city. I hope too that all of your family is very well and happy. First of all I thank you for your wonderful gifts to my family, thank you very much. It was really a surprise for us, and we were very happy and proud of having such wonderful gifts. As time goes by, I am convinced that you are truly a God-sent distinguished Mormon missionary to my family, and I am sure that there was a definite plan of the Lord to save my family. I sincerely pray that God protect you and let you make wonderful work as a doctor and missionary.

Brother Bauman, the long waited for missionary came to my town, and has been settled here in Narumi since last November. It was rather hard to find a good shelter for missionaries in such small town like Narumi, but fortunately I could succeed to borrow 3 rooms for them, and installed furniture and commodities for cooking, bath and warming etc. Fortunately this winter has been unusually mild, the mildest winter that I have ever experienced. Last Christmas Day, we had more than 250 children at my home. They could hardly enter into the room, and many had to stand in the garden. Sunday school children made Christmas decoration by themselves, and installed it in my living room. Children, every one of them who attended, received Christmas gifts, were sent from Church and its members. We had such a wonderful Christmas. As our Sunday school is growing larger, we divided children into three groups and since the 2nd of January, Sunday school is held at two places. We have M.I.A. meeting of Tuesday evening and Bible Class on Saturday evening, both at my home. Relief Club has been organized, and members, who are chiefly young girls, distributed many clothes and food to the needy people in my town. There are poor people who are suffering from T.B. My wife visited them with clothes and good food and told them "Good Tidings of Jesus Christ" which is gradually going into their heart.

Boy Scout is going to be organized under the supervision of missionaries. All these information will tell you a promising future progress of our Church and gladden your heart. However, whenever our Church becomes prosperous there was always an opposite influence, and there is too. I am thinking of difficulties to come, that I must meet face to face in the future, though nobody notice it now.

Brother Bauman, please pray for my family and ask God that I can stand on my own feet and can help encourage and lead the "God chosen people" to "the promised land." I make it a rule to invite missionaries to come my home for supper on Saturday evening, and I feel very happy to have an opportunity to make them happy. They were very much pleased with the peanuts butter and homemade cakes—which were made of the good flour and baking powder you sent to me. Brother Bauman, I was very busy since last year, so busy that I had to work on Sunday, which

I hated so much, and one of my clerks resigned to get better job, and another clerk entered hospital due to nervous break-down. My ultimate hope, also my family's hope, is to be gathered to Zion, and I am happy to find an article in a newspaper saying that they are going to revise emigration law there in the States. I do hope that there will be opened a channel for gathering to Zion for members of our Church here in this country. I sincerely pray that the Lord may help you in your good work and protect you from evils. May you and your family is always healthy and enjoy earthly life in righteousness. My wife and my son Yasuo, both are very well and happily they join me to say many thanks.[18]

More Missionaries Arrive

Chiyo Sato wrote to Brother Davis on 29 May and mentioned that Narumi now had more missionaries. She also mentioned "Relief [Society] Club" gatherings in Nagoya, charitable activities and Yasuo's growth:

How are you? Are you very well? Please pardon my long silence. I am very well. Now, I am going to write you about my "work". This morning I paid a visit together with 3 members of the Relief Club on a poor young lady patient who suffering from tuberculosis. One of her kidney has been taken away by an operation last year and also one of her rib bone was taken, and another has become ill. We call on her with flowers and fruits juice.

In the afternoon at the mission home I helped missionaries with getting ration food and frying fishes for their meal on Thursday every week. I go to the mission home for sweeping house with some of the young girls of Relief Club, sometimes with Yasuo.

Today I saw an article in the *Church News* describing of two missionaries in Nagoya and our family (April 15th edition). The two missionaries are Elder Price and another is Elder Goya who is now working in Tokyo. In the morning of 30th the April, two more missionaries came to Narumi and we have four missionaries now. Every Sunday, we have a Sunday school for children under 10 years old and we have about 100 of them, sometimes 120. We borrowed a small house on a hill. I am praying for special blessing of the Lord, so that we might be able to attend the meeting. On Saturday evening this week, the first party of L.D.S. members in Nagoya was held at Sister Bock's. I suppose it was held because Brother Swenson and Sister Bock are both going to leave for home. December last year, the Relief Club was organized. Since then I have been doing many works. Usually on Sunday, Monday and Thursday I work for the Relief Club. I call on patients, bring clothes and salt to the needy people, sometimes I make cakes and bring it to the needy. The other day, I made some cakes and brought it to a poor family in which they have a leper boy, who is 9 years old, and who goes to a leper house in Okayama Prefecture. This mother died of the same sickness about 5 years ago, and is survived by 3 children, 14, 12 and 9 years old each. His father is a carpenter. I also gave the boy some old clothes of Yasuo. When I was going home and said good bye to the 12 year old little girl she replied and said, "Would you come again?" It sounded so sad and tears came out. Next day I called on the house with Elder Price and I went there several times. People are afraid of them and would not call on them. There are many poor people.

Before long, it will become the "rainy season" and as I have no rain shoes and rain coat it is hard for me to go out in rainy days, but I am doing my "missionary work" diligently, as it is Lord's work. There are many poor families, grandfather is a sufferer of alcoholism and sells everything for liquor; father died in the battle front surviving many children and the bereaved family is at a loss. I call on these poor families. I help the parent and teachers association. I help with making meals for school children, and I feel very happy, but all members of my family is very well.

A picture contest which is held two times a year was held last week. At the contest Yasuo's painting was selected. Every time his painting was picked up among the contestants. He is now in the fourth grade and he is the tallest of them and has become healthy, but sometimes he is a naughty boy. Please remember that I am praying for the Lord that may He give many blessings to your family and watch over you.[19]

Vinal Mauss replaced Edward L. Clissold as mission president in August 1949. President Mauss was one of the last missionaries in Japan before the closing of the mission in 1924. He put more emphasis on language training and was determined to organize the mission into districts throughout Japan. Initially Elder Harrison "Ted" Price was in charge of the district covering Aichi Prefecture, including Narumi and the larger Nagoya area. Elder Price stayed there until November 1950, when President Mauss had a vision to send him to Fukuoka, where he stayed with an influential Japanese woman and Diet member. Through the contacts he was able to make, he made many converts and friends for the Church in Fukuoka.

After Brother Sato moved to Tokyo in January 1950, a branch was opened in Nagoya. The Narumi branch finally became part of the Nagoya Branch in March of 1956.

Endnotes

1. Correspondence, Harold B. Lee to Tatsui, 29 December 1947.
2. Correspondence, Ray Hanks to the Satos, January 1948.
3. Correspondence, Tatsui Sato to Boyd K. Packer, 17 January 1948.
4. Manuscript copy of "Japan Mission Journal," dated May 1948, pp. 1–2.
5. Ibid., Hyer paper on language training, Japanese Centennial papers.
6. "Japanese Mission Journal," 6–21 March 1948, copy courtesy of Alma Ogata.
7. "The Japanese Mission Home," 1948 paper, copy from Alma Ogata.
8. R. Lanier Britsch, *From the East: The History of the Latter-day Saints in Asia*, 1851–1996, pp. 88–91.
9. Correspondence, Tatsui Sato to C. Elliott Richards, 22 September 1948.
10. Correspondence, Tatsui Sato to Reed Davis, 25 September 1948.
11. Information from Ray Price: Lanai City, Hawaii, telephone interview with Greg Gubler, 10 June 2004.
12. Interview, Greg Gubler with Harrison "Ted" Price, Murray, Utah, 15 August 2004.
13. Ibid.
14. Ibid.

15. Ibid.
16. Correspondence, Tatsui Sato to Ray Hanks, about January 1949.
17. Correspondence, Tatsui Sato to Reed Davis, 29 February 1949.
18. Correspondence, Tatsui Sato to Thomas Bauman, 7 March 1949.
19. Correspondence, Chiyo Sato to Reed Davis, 29 May 1949.

Chapter 6

Translation Time in Tokyo

After his ordination as an elder in the Melchezidek Priesthood on 12 June 1949 by Elder Matthew Cowley—the first ordination among the Japanese in several decades—Brother Sato was set apart in August of 1949 as the first official translator and interpreter for the Church in Japan. At that time, he was closing in on his 50th birthday. He continued in that position until 1965, when he reached retirement age and was called to translate the temple ceremony in Hawaii. In that calling, he performed a great mission for the entire nation of Japan. This powerful deed has reverberated through the succeeding generations, impacting members of the Church abroad, as well as in Japan.

The correspondence in this chapter gives insight into the turbulent times in which this crucial work of the Lord was being performed. It certainly was a time of despair and hardship for many. But the fiery aftermath of World War II also forged the spirit of men such as Brother Sato. He turned his love for peace and the Church into producing astounding works to glorify his endless love for our Savior. Though the years continued to pass, Brother Sato maintained correspondence with his servicemen friends and felt greatly indebted to them for bringing him the gospel. These letters, though personal, reveal the struggles Tatsui and his family faced, as well as the special feelings of friendship they had for each other.

The visit of Elder Matthew Cowley in 1949 included the many missions and branches of the Church in the Pacific and Asia. The Apostle visited Japan soon after it had been reopened, and found "several thriving branches" that had resulted from the "combined efforts of missionaries and Latter-day Saint servicemen stationed in Japan." He noted that the people were enjoying religious freedom and, for the first time, were being "proselyted by hundreds of missionaries from many different denominations."

After meeting with Church members in the branches (including Brother Sato), Elder Cowley remarked that the new members were "some of the grandest people I have ever met."[1] John Clawson, a missionary at the time, remembers Brother Sato translating for Elder Cowley. At one point in the speech, Elder Cowley said, "Japan is a beautiful country without any weeds." Brother Sato translated everything to that point and then suddenly stopped and asked Elder Cowley, "What are weeds?" Elder Cowley laughed and said, "Since there are none he doesn't know the word for weeds." Everyone laughed.[2]

Brother Sato wrote of his ordination, his position as a translator and of Elder Cowley's visit in a letter to C. Elliott Richards, dated 4 August 1949:

> How are you and how is all of your family? Is all of your family very well? It is August and real summer is here. Strong sun shine, hot air, high moisture content etc. everything is summer like and really summer is here. This year we were visited by several typhoons; they were Dera, Gloria, Fay and Hestar. Some of them brought heavy rain with strong wind, but our district . . . suffered only very little damage. This year's crop is promising, and we must endure a little hot weather. Yasuo and my wife are enjoying this summer.

I am very glad to tell you happy news. When Elder Clissold came to Narumi with Apostle Cowley two months ago, we had wonderful Sunday school, and I had a privilege to talk [to] him about how the gospel was brought here by the three service men after the War, and how cottage meeting was opened at my home by Brother Richards and others. It was my great joy to tell him the brief history of our Church in Narumi. In the afternoon we went to Nagoya chapel for sacrament service. After that I was ordained by Apostle Cowley to Elder. Isn't it wonderful? I believe you will surely be glad to hear this news.

I attended the first conference of our Church held in Tokyo on 16 and 17 July. About 27 or more missionaries assembled from various parts of Japan. There were about ten representatives of Japanese members [who] came from Hokkaido, Osaka, Nagoya etc. It was really a thrill to see members of our church for the first time. The first day was opened by a session, when district records were read by missionaries, and after that a testimony meeting was held. Next day, on a fine Sunday morning, the first conference was opened at a Japanese Girl's High school near mission home. It was a wonderful meeting and we had more than several hundred attendants. Church activities of various parts of Japan were reported by Japanese representatives, and I also had an opportunity to report the Church activity and brief history of our Church in Narumi, and I had a privilege to be an interpreter for the speech addressed by Apostle Cowley and Sister Cowley. Next day I enjoyed an excursion to Nikko with missionaries.

Brother Richards, I am going to quit my present job, and become "official interpreter and translator of Japanese mission." The job was given by President Clissold to me. I shall work in Tokyo part of the month for the time being; my family will stay in Narumi till I can find a house in Tokyo. A great chance to work for our Church and gospel is waiting for me. Isn't it wonderful? I believe the Lord wants me to be an instrument in His hand to bring about the gospel in Japan. I will work for our Church and the gospel as long as I can; for this is the best thing in the world.

> Please give our family's best love to your family. I sincerely pray that may the Lord be with you everyday and watch over you, may He protect you and your family from all evil thing of the world and may He keep you healthy and happy. I pray also that may the Lord guide your intelligence and knowledge so that you may be an excellent doctor to take care of the sick and the needy.
> Sincerely, your brother in Church.
> Tatsui Sato[3]

The following letter is from Brother Hanks. Dated 1 September it congratulates Brother Sato on his official calling as translator and interpreter for the Church in Japan and acknowledges this great service:

> Truly it was a joy to receive your letter as of August 4th, wherein you related that you had just been ordained an elder by Apostle Cowley. Yes we are very happy about this great news, it is not everyone who has that privilege of being ordained by an Apostle, but we know that you are truly worthy of the blessing . . . .
>
> It is a great joy also to know of your new position as an official interpreter, and translator of the Japan mission with President Clissold. You have been called to be of great service to our Heavenly Father in furthering the great cause of the restoration of the gospel. It will be through you that many people will be blessed; as you are a blessing to others great blessings will be returned to you.
>
> We are enclosing with the rain coat to Sister Sato, a book of the sermons of our general conference. Also a box of candy for Yasuo. May the Lord bless you and yours, and all who are engaged in His cause . . . .[4]

Encouragement and Gratitude Expressed

Brother Hanks wrote a special letter to Sister Sato on 2 September encouraging her in the work and congratulating her for her service and support. Sister Sato was a great support to her husband, a nourishing mother to Yasuo, and she had a strong testimony of the gospel:

> This is in reply to your good letter. It was a pleasure to know that you are well. We are happy that the little Xmas remembrance found you. We are pleased to know you are doing a good work in your Relief Club and that you are working with the missionaries. It is also a great deal of joy to know that you have four missionaries in your town. My how wonderful it is to hear of nearly 120 children attending your Sunday School and that nearly 50 of the older folks meet in other classes. I am sure that little children enjoy hearing the stories of the Old Testament from you. I know your husband also is a good teacher for the older group.
>
> Your home shall always be a sacred home to us for there we caught the sweet spirit that you and Brother Sato and Yasuo have. It is a joy to know that the missionaries are teaching in your home the beautiful writings of our Book of Mormon and that your people are learning the English language so that they might more clearly understand the beautiful truths of the gospel. You spoke about your rainy season, and that you have no raincoat or rain shoes. We are sending to you a raincoat and I shall look to see if I can find some rubbers. If not the raincoat will soon be sent on its way.
>
> It is said that "He who would be the greatest among you let him be the servant of all." You have explained how you are helping many of the poor families. Truly this is a real spirit of the gospel and our Heavenly Father has promised rich blessings to those who have the spirit of helping others.
>
> May we congratulate Yasuo on his fine painting and winning the contest! If he ever has an extra picture sometime we would be very pleased to have him send us one if it was not too much trouble. We are pleased to know that he is healthy and getting along nicely. We know that now that he has been baptized in the Church that he will be a good boy and be a great source of joy to you and Brother Sato. Tell Yasuo we are proud of him and know that he will be a real and true member of our Heavenly Father's Church which he now belongs to.

> May the Lord bless you in health, strength and spirit that the good things of life that you stand in need of may come to you for the good things that you are doing for others. This is the sincere wish of your brother in the faith. My wife and family extend kind wishes to you also.[5]

Sister Chiyo Sato graciously expresses her gratitude for a thoughtful gift from the Davis family and responded immediately with a letter; she was deeply touched by the death of a friend and shares her testimony:

> How are you getting along? We are all well. It is now hot mid summer. We are getting along in a really [hot] summer under strong sunshine. Yesterday [the] thermometer stood at 95 degrees F. Today I received the gift parcel you sent me. I have never dreamed of having such a wonderful rain coat and rubber shoes. I was so much pleased with your warm heart, and I was moved to tears. I will enjoy the rain coat and shoes as long as they last.
>
> The young lady whom I mentioned in my previous letter, passed away yesterday. I am ashamed of my weak faith to hear her speak, when I remind her words that "I believe I shall be able to return to Father; may be said I am confident of too much." Nonetheless, God always give me wonderful blessing for which I am thanking always.
>
> Thank you very much for your kindness.
>
> Yours sincerely,
> Chiyo Sato[6]

Assignment to Translate Book of Mormon

Paul C. Andrus, who was among the first group of missionaries to arrive in Japan in 1948, was assigned to the mission home during this time. In an interview, he noted that, "I had the privilege of associating with Brother Sato on a daily basis after he moved to Tokyo from Narumi." He continues:

> One of my earliest memories of Brother Sato is his translation of the sacrament prayers. When President Clissold assigned Brother Sato to retranslate the Book of Mormon, he asked him to first translate the sacrament prayers which he promptly did. President Clissold then formed a committee to review Brother Sato's translation. This committee consisted of President Clissold as chairman and Brother Sato, Sister Fujiwara and me as members. I have fond memories of the meeting with Brother Sato and this committee in the front room of the mission headquarters.

This procedure set the pattern, he noted, for later approvals from the First Presidency for Tatsui's later translations.[7] President Clissold had used his former military connections to obtain the necessary legal approval to preach the gospel in Japan and, as he was promised by the Brethren, would be replaced once he had established the work in Japan. After 18 months, he was replaced and was able to return in late August 1949 to his home in Honolulu. After only a few short weeks working with President Clissold, Brother Sato was to work with the next mission president, President Mauss, for over three years.

President Mauss came to Japan on 20 August, replacing President Clissold as mission president. He had served as a missionary in Japan just before the mission was closed in 1924. He was to serve until October 1953, and he relied considerably on Brother Sato in the conduct of the mission and translation work. President Mauss also worked very hard to increase the missionary force, but the breakout of the Korean War in June of 1950 made this goal more difficult to achieve.[8]

In the following letter to Reed Davis about October 1949, Brother Sato, writing from Narumi, discusses his assignment to translate the Book of Mormon and his health struggles at the time. As always, he was grateful for the offer of assistance:

> I am very glad to inform you of another glad news that I was assigned to a big job. I was set apart to revise an old Japanese

translation of Book of Mormon to a good modern Japanese language, and translate it if necessary, and to translate [the] Pearl Of Great Price and some of the Church booklets. Isn't it a wonderful job? I believe you will be very glad to hear this news.

Book of Mormon is truly a wonderful book. As I was reading the passages from this book, I found my faith was strengthened tremendously. This book must be printed in Japanese as soon as possible so that the people in this country may read it in their own language.

However, Brother Davis, I found it is true that when one is engaging in a sacred work, there is always evil spirit to destroy the Lord's work. I found my health rather failed, and I had to come back to Narumi to recuperate [from] my sickness. Doctor says it is "Beriberi" with heart weakness, but having rest[ed] about a month I feel almost all right and I am going to Tokyo soon to take up my job. I am working in Tokyo 2 weeks in a month and the rest of the month I work in Narumi. But at any rate, I must find my home in Tokyo and move to there. It is a kind of difficult task under present condition, but I believe the Lord will always open a way for those who work a sacred work for Him.

My address in Tokyo is c/o: President Vinal Mauss, Japanese Mission of L.D.S. Church, Tokyo, Japan. When I told of you to President Mauss, he said he would willingly take care of anything that might help me. If you would kindly allow me to take advantage [of] your kindness to help me financially, please get in contact with President Mauss of Japanese Mission. He will take care of me.

My wife and Yasuo are very well, and my wife wishes again to say many thanks for sending the fine raincoat for her.

I sincerely pray that may the Lord watch over you and bless you for many good deeds you have done. All of our family sends best love to you and to your family.[9]

On 16 November 1949, Mission President Vinal G. Mauss responded to a letter of concern from Brother Davis and states how "fortunate the mission was to have a person" with Sato's "qualifications."

President Mauss concurred that they should cooperate in helping the Satos and relayed the reason the Satos were struggling at the time:

> Thank you very much for your letter of October 28 regarding Brother Tatsui Sato. At the present time, Brother Sato is engaged by the Church in translating Church literature into the Japanese language. I was not aware of his circumstances that you referred to in your letter and shall be happy to investigate further. Would you be kind enough to advise me when he wrote to you regarding his finances?
>
> Brother Sato has been hoping to dispose of his property in Nagoya in order to buy a home in Tokyo where he would be nearer to the mission home and his work. So far, however, he has not been successful and it may be this he has had reference to. At present, he comes into Tokyo with his sister two weeks each month to carry on his translation work and then returns to his home in Nagoya for two weeks.
>
> I appreciate your interest and the generous offer of the priesthood brethren there to assist him. Would you be kind enough to advise me somewhat regarding the need that he expressed in his letter to you?
>
> He is doing a marvelous work in his translation, and I am sure that we are fortunate to have a person with his qualifications to do this work, and we will do all that we can to cooperate with him in helping him overcome his financial difficulties.
>
> Again thanking you for your letter . . . .[10]

The Move to Tokyo

Brother Sato thanked Brother Davis for his concern and offer of help and tried to "ease" his mind regarding his situation in a letter dated 2 December. He told Brother Davis of his intended move to Tokyo and a pending job for his wife cooking at the mission home:

> How are you Brother Davis? I know that you wrote a letter to President Mauss in Tokyo and kindly proposed that you would

help me if I am in distress. Thank you very much. I truly appreciate your kindness and friendship, to help me financially and spiritually as well. You are always very kind. I am very happy to tell you that President Mauss is very kind and [willing to] take good care of me. I am not in distress at present, so please ease your mind and don't worry. My family is going to move in Tokyo in January next year. My wife will work as a cook at the mission home of our Church in Tokyo. The address is: c/o Vinal Y. Mauss, President of Japan Mission 2–14 Hiro-cho Azabu Minato—ku Tokyo, Japan

Brother Davis, I have a strong testimony that God is living and is with us as long as we seek for the gospel He taught. Joseph Smith is a true prophet, because he restored the True Gospel and taught it to his followers. I am very glad that I can bear these [this] testimony in the name of Jesus Christ.

Merry Christmas and Happy New Year to you and all of your family. I sincerely pray that may the Lord be with you and watch over you.[11]

Tatsui had commuted back and forth on alternate weeks during the fall until the family finally moved into the detached house next to the mission home in Azabu in mid-December. President Mauss had made it available as temporary quarters until the Satos could find a home in Tokyo. The Sato family soon became active in the Aoyama Branch and settled down for their first Christmas in Tokyo.

Just after Christmas in 1949, Sister Sato wrote a letter of gratitude for the special presents sent by the Davis family, and mentions the interruption of Sunday School classes and progress of the Church at their new branch in Aoyama. She also expresses her thanks for the gospel:

How are you getting along? I have not written for so long time but I don't forget about you. Always we talk of you. First of all, I must say thank you very much for your sending a lot of Christmas presents. It made us very happy. Especially, the beautiful slipper made me very happy and it keeps me surely warm. Yasuo, how he was glad when he found the ball and the glove. He was very anxious for [a] glove [for a] long time, but I couldn't buy it for him because it is very dear in Japan. Now he is playing with it every day.

We have about 20 members in Aoyama. It is not so many but we are enjoying Sunday school and Sacrament every Sunday. We missed Sunday school about one month, but from next week we can have them as usual. About thirty or more investigators came and had good senior Sunday school at Aoyama Ladies sewing school last year, but we couldn't borrow that house from the beginning this year, but now we can borrow another school and start it again in February. Now we are missing Junior Sunday school, but it will soon be able to start again, because we are looking for the class rooms.

It snowed last night, but it became a very warm sunny day this afternoon. I am very happy that God always blesses us and I can study wonderful gospel. I pray always May God be with you and watch over you.[12]

Yasuo also expressed his appreciation to "Uncle Reed" Davis, who at the time was living in Susanville, California. He made a minor request for a replacement item:

How are you Uncle Reed? I painted a picture with the crayon that Uncle Ray gave to me and I got first prize at the contest. As the crayon was over will you please send me a set of it? I became third grade and I was elected as a monitor.

I want to see you again.

Yours,
Yasuo[13]

Brother Sato, likely busy with translation work, did not write again until he wrote Brother Davis a brief letter on 13 March 1950 from his new address in the mission home. The situation had improved greatly for the Satos. He also mentioned his calling in the Aoyama branch, using his priesthood, and his nostalgia for Narumi:

> How are you Brother Davis? Now I am in Tokyo living in mission home with my family. My wife and Yasuo are very well [and] enjoying Tokyo. They wish to send you their best wishes. I am working as a translator and at the same time I am helping Church work. I am in charge of Sunday School at Aoyama, Tokyo. The other day six people were baptized and I baptized three of them. It was my first experience to practice the holy priesthood that I hold. How wonderful it was!
>
> Sometimes I miss the little Sunday school children in Narumi, and also I remember life in Narumi. However, I am happy helping Church work here in Tokyo.[14]

War Clouds Near Japan

After a "long silence," Brother Sato again wrote Brother Davis the following November and told of the growth of the Aoyama Branch. Tatsui was also excited to relay news of the continued growth of the branch at Narumi. He saw much potential for the gospel to heal and felt "many people" were "searching after the truth." Tatsui hoped for a quick resolution of the Korean conflict now occupying the news because of the closeness of the war to Japan and because of his own difficult wartime experiences:

> How are you my dear brother Davis? Please pardon my long silence, for I did not write to you for a long time. Since my family moved to Tokyo, I had to start everything newly, but we got used to the living in the city and we are happy now. May I tell you about the Sunday school in Tokyo? When I was appointed as a superintendent of Aoyama Sunday school in Tokyo, we had only a few members and about fifteen Sunday school children. I had to work hard to build up the Sunday school, and after 10 months work now we have 25 active young members and about

50 children who regularly come to Sunday school. During the past month, I had many wonderful opportunity to baptize people who became the members of our Church. I am thanking for the blessings of the Lord who guided me to the true Church.

Both my wife and Yasuo are very well now, though my wife was ill several months ago. We are enjoying our life in Tokyo. Yasuo has become a boy, he has grown up to be a boy and he is in the 5th grade of the Primary School. He likes Tokyo very much.

Recently I received a letter from Narumi, my native village, telling that they have 20 members over there. I was very much thrilled to hear that, for all of the members were my pupils of my Sunday school in Narumi.

Brother Davis, there are millions of people in Tokyo, who are suffering from diseases and want of necessities. There are many people who are seeking after the truth. As I am feeling it very necessary to tell them of the true Gospel and salvation by living in the Gospel. I have cottage meetings as we had in Narumi when you stayed in Japan. It is my great joy and pleasure to tell the truth to the Japanese people and lead them to our Church.

As you know there is a war going on in North Korea. I am praying from the bottom of my heart that the war may cease and peace be established lest we should experience the miserable condition again. I had enough sad experiences during the past war.

A little Japanese doll is on its way to you, I hope it will reach you in good shape with our best love to you. I pray that the Lord always bless you and watch over you.[15]

Brother Sato also wrote that same day to Brother Bauman regarding the progress of the work, his family situation and his efforts to spread the gospel:

I am very glad to know that you are very well and your family is growing. Please pardon my long silence, for I did not write to you for a long time. Since my family moved to Tokyo I had to start everything newly in Tokyo, but we got used to the living in the city by and by, and we are happy now. I am glad to tell you about our Sunday school in Tokyo. When I was appointed as a superintendent of Aoyama Sunday School in Tokyo, there were only a few members and about fifteen Sunday school children. Therefore, I had to work hard to build up the Sunday school, and now we have 25 active members and more than 50 children. During the past months I had many thrilled experience to baptize people to become the members of our Church. I am thanking that the Lord gave me such a wonderful opportunity to save God's children's soul.

Both my wife and Yasuo are very well now, though my wife was somewhat ill several months ago. Yasuo has grown up to be a boy, and he is in the 5th grade of Primary school. I have been working for the translation of the Doctrine and Covenants, and I have finished the preliminary translation, and I am going to write it fair for better translation. As you know there is a war going on in North Korea and it has influenced great deal on the economic and political condition in Japan. I pray from the bottom of my heart that the war may cease and we may never experience the miserable condition that we experienced in the past War.

I have enough sad experiences in the past. Now I have cottage meetings where I am trying to find good peoples who have a humble heart to accept the true Gospel. In Tokyo there are millions of people who are seeking for the salvation. I am making my efforts to approach these people that they may have the opportunity to hear the Gospel. I feel always a great happiness in trying to do so; for I believe it is our Father's will. I am always thanking for the blessings of the Lord who guide us and watch over us, at the same time my family never forget your kind and generous heart that helped our family in our distress.

A little Japanese doll is on its way to you as a remembrance. I hope it will reach you with our best love.[16]

Thanks and Remembrances

Another year passed, and Brother Sato again thanked the Davis family in this letter written from Tokyo on 30 January 1951. Tatsui mentioned that he continually told the story of his conversion in Narumi and reported on the rapid growth of the Church in Japan:

> Thank you very much for the wonderful Christmas presents you sent to my family. We were all surprised when we opened the big package and found the contents. You can hardly imagine how Yasuo felt happy when he found the baseball gloves in it. The baseball gloves, which was his long dream, and it was realized! Thank you very much Brother Davis. I am very glad to say that your kindness and love for my family make my testimony stronger. I always bear my testimony before people that the restored Gospel is true and our Church is the only one that has the fullness of the Gospel. I repeat my story of meeting you at Narumi and being enjoyed the cottage meeting with other brethren at my home, and after that I always add my testimony that the strong testimony of these three GI's made me believe that there is the true Gospel which was restored in this latter days. In Narumi, where my mother is still living with my brother, though my father passed away 4 years ago, there is our Church organization which has about 20 members of our Church and is growing larger. I hope you will remember the paddy fields in front of my home and the muddy road which leads you to the foot of the little bridge. All of them are the same as ever. I can recollect the deep impression when you visited me at my home, and the sorrow when I heard that you were going to move [to] another camp. It is my family's desire that sometime we may be able to go to the States and enjoy the Temple work. If it be realized how great our happiness would be!
>
> Brother Davis, as you mentioned of Chaplain Nelson in your previous letter, so I inquired of it with Chaplain Curtis who is serving as a Chaplain in Tokyo and one of the members of our Church, but no information could be got. If you would let me know in what member of the Church section it was described I will appreciate it very much.
>
> It is very sad to hear the rumor of War again, so I sincerely pray that may the Lord help us to overcome the difficulties that

> would come and may the Lord help us to bear it to the end.
>
> Our Church in Japan is growing larger and I am very happy to tell this to you. My wife and Yasuo also join me to say many thanks.
>
> May the Lord watch over you and may His Spirit be with you.[17]

Shortly thereafter, on 10 February, Brother Sato wrote Brother Boyd K. Packer and thanked his family for their kindness. Tatsui realized that the Church was "truly one family" and made the point that Elder Paul Andrus of the mission home, who was soon departing, knew Brother Packer well:

> Thank you very much for the wonderful Christmas present you sent to my family. It arrived safe to my home. It is very kind of you to remember my family and send many wonderful gifts that we never can enjoy. Yasuo was very happy when he found many good things that he had hoped for. My wife also wishes to say many thanks for your kindness.
>
> We are very happy since we moved to Tokyo. We are living in the home which is in the site of the Mission Home in Tokyo. This year on finishing their missionaries work about 20 missionaries are going for home. Brother Paul Andrus is one of the missionaries who came to Japan 3 years ago. My family had a farewell dinner at my home last evening, when he mentioned that he knows you well. I was impressed by his words and realized that our Church is truly one family. I have many things to do, which are very important work for our Church in this country. I really wish that you would pray for me that I may be able to accomplish these works for which I was called of God.
>
> My family sends their wishes and heart to your family. I pray that may the Lord be always watch over you, and may His spirit be with you. Please give my family's best wishes to Sister Packer and our little friends.[18]

Because the number of missionaries was cut back due to the Korean War, Mission President Mauss had to consolidate some of the branches. In September of 1951, two larger branches were created in Tokyo, with Tomigoro Takagi called as president of the Tokyo First Branch, and Fujiya Nara (a convert who remained faithful after the mission was closed in 1924) as president of the Second Branch. Brother Sato was called as a counselor to Brother Nara in addition to his Sunday School teaching and full-time translation duties.[19]

Interview with John Clawson

John Clawson is a longtime friend of Tatsui and a former missionary in Japan. He originally went to Japan in the 5th Air Force in December of 1945 near the beginning of the Occupation. He was originally stationed at Yokota, but spent the last 10 months at Tachikawa. After his discharge, he went to Weber College briefly and then was among the first missionaries called to the new Japanese Mission in January 1948. He went to Hawaii to study the language until visas could be arranged for entry. He finally arrived in the summer of 1948. He said in those days, language study was "very primitive." The missionaries relied on the members, and he felt that many of the missionaries "must have sounded like a bunch of Swedes as their pronunciation was far from perfect."

He was helping in the mission home and doing missionary work in the Tokyo area the first two years of his mission. He mentioned that Brother Sato came to the mission home in the fall of 1949 on an alternating basis and finally moved there in December. He was very obliged to Tatsui for teaching him about the language and culture. He remembers Tatsui telling him that "three women talking together became the [Chinese] character for noise." Brother Clawson also talked to Brother Sato and learned how he thought in terms of gospel principles. He explained the three degrees of glory from a Japanese viewpoint and told of his strong feelings that the "lost ancestors of the Japanese had to be restored."[20]

Tatsui told Brother Clawson about the trauma of the war. He explained how he had become a professor of metallurgy and had become involved in helping to develop special metals to improve Japanese cannons and bombs. (This had been in 1937 when Japan invaded China and moved into a wartime economy.) During World War II, it became increasingly difficult to obtain the materials to make cannons and aircraft parts. It was very difficult as well, because the industry was heavily bombed. After the war, Tatsui's expertise was useless, as there was little industry and use for a professor of metallurgy. That is when he had to use his English skills to survive—selling trinkets to GIs.

Tatsui liked to tell the story of his conversion and the importance of standing up for your religion. He was so impressed by the Latter-day Saint servicemen saying "No thanks; we are Mormons" to the offer of tea. He was receptive and was presented the Book of Mormon the next week. That and learning about the gospel from the soldiers changed his life. Brother Clawson felt that Brother Sato "was indeed a chosen man for the job" as translator/interpreter for the Church. He really was impressed by his simultaneous translations, and later with what he had heard about the translations of the standard works. Most of all, he was impressed by how kind and thoughtful Brother Sato was to everyone he encountered. Interestingly, after a year and a half, Brother Clawson was transferred to Narumi, which he said by then was "all swallowed up by Nagoya."

He realized the huge impact Tatsui had made in the village and was a beneficiary of Tatsui's hard work in building the kingdom. The meetings were still in the City Hall and the children's Sunday School was very active. Community leaders supported learning values and even some English. In the summer of 1950, he remembers a baptism where they had six candidates for baptism. Miraculously, amidst a huge rainstorm, the heavens closed up until the baptism was finished. He noted that several of those who were baptized at the time played an important role in the Nagoya area later on, and he credits

Brother Sato for being a true pioneer and a really "marvelous man." In closing his interview, Brother Clawson said that "Brother Sato is on the other side, and he is extremely busy with all the Japanese over there."[21]

Moving Out of the Mission Home

Sister Chiyo Sato mentioned in this letter to the Reed Davis family, written on 23 July 1952, that her family had to move from the mission home to a small house. She was hoping to sell silk paintings to supplement the family income, as the move was expensive:

> How is all of your family? I have not written for a long time, please pardon me. It is very hot summer in Tokyo, but we are all well. I heard this morning by radio that a strong earthquake was experienced in California. I wonder if any damage was suffered about your town.
>
> About two weeks ago I sent you ten silk paintings by mail. May I ask favor of you about this silk paintings, which are the same kind of picture I sent you before. Until November last year we had been living in a house in the site of mission home, but Brother Almond [Armond] Mauss, the son of President Mauss, wanted to live in the home where we had been, and we had to go out. We built small house with one room and a kitchen and living there since. But as we are poor and could not afford money borrowed yen 300,000 [those days, $1.00 was 360 yen, so about $800] and with all money we had saved we could have the house built.
>
> The Economy has become dull recently and prices of food getting high when we moved to Tokyo from Narumi. The price of the main food is 40% up that is the price of rice was 50 yen for one kilogram before, but now it cost 90 yen and the price of bread also became 30 yen from 20 yen. My husband salary is the same as that of three years ago and we find our living difficult.
>
> I have to help my family's finance by working something, but it is very difficult to find out a job, and I can not work out of

my home—so the more it is difficult. Brother Heater in Tokyo, he was selling the silk painting to the service men. So I also wish to sell the picture for my finance. Would you kindly look for some art shop that would like to buy this kind of silk painting for even a small amount each month? If they are sold at 80 cents for one, I shall be very happy, and please send the money ($8) to me by money order, subtracting any expense for sending.

We have been looking for if there is any good job and we explained our condition to Chaplain Nelson who came to Tokyo and asked for his help, but I don't know where he is now.

All are willing to serve the Lord. I pray that our Church may make a big progress. I also pray may the Lord watch over you so that all of you may be very well and happy.[22]

Brother Davis, always very generous, was willing to help and responded by asking Sister Sato to send more silk paintings as he could find buyers:

We are very sorry to have been so slow in answering that wonderful letter that you wrote to us. We have been very busy this summer and yet more busy today as we are leaving on a trip to Chicago tonight. So if you will excuse me then I will write when we get back from our trip.

Enclosed is a check for $35 that I received for your paintings. You can send another group of them because I have a number of orders for them. Send about 25 more in the next group and make about 6 of the tiger.[23]

Progress in Translations and Need for Repentance

The next letter to Ray Hanks, dated 6 September 1952, reports on the progress of Tatsui's translation work. He notes the circumstances in Japan and the influence of the nearby war. Tatsui also expressed the need for the Japanese people to repent:

I hope all of your family is very well and happy. Time passed by very quickly and it is almost Fall in Japan, though the sun shines hot. I have been working hard on my job translating scriptures and texts for Sunday school and other auxiliaries etc. I have finished the translation of Doctrine and Covenants, Pearl of Great Price, 1st Nephi of the Book of Mormon . . . [in] modern Japanese, *Joseph Smith Tells His Own Story*, etc., and I am typing them in Romaji that any one who can read and understand it may get in touch with the truths in them. When I finish typing and stenciling them I will send one of the copies to you one by one.

Since the opening of the Japanese Mission many missionaries came to Japan and many of them have finished their work and have already returned to their respective homes. From Tympanogas [Timpanogos] ward Sister Walker came to Japan and worked for a couple years. When I spoke of you she said she knew of Brother Hanks. I suppose she is now in her native town and is engaging her previous job. When you have an opportunity to call on the ward and see her please mention that I am "working as ever" and still studying and studying on the scriptures as ever.

Mr. Hanks, I sent out a bundle of silk paintings to you and they are on their way to you. They are the same kind of pictures that I sent to you before. Now I have a great favor to ask you about this. I believe Mrs. Sato also will write a letter about this, but Mrs. Sato has planned to sell these silk paintings and she is asking the amount be small. Since the breaking out of Korean War living has become more and more difficult though there are many who are making big money taking advantage of the situation. We have to do some side work in order to cover the expense we have to pay for.

Yasuo grew up to be a big boy and he is even taller than his mother. He is a first year boy of the middle school and has to learn many things he did not learn in the primary school. We intend to make a doctor of him, because we have many doctors in [among] my relatives.

> When I look at the situation of Japan, I feel something serious which will bring disaster to this people unless they will . . . repent [of] their wickedness. I believe in the prophecy told by "the mouth of God" in the scriptures both in former times and in latter days. Mr. Hanks, . . . [I think people] here are by far more austere than . . . [people in] America. We should be always sober and respect the word of God, otherwise terrible punishment of God may come upon us.
>
> I and also all of my family shall feel exceedingly happy if you would understand the situation in which we stand and would help us. I pray that may the Lord give many blessings to your family and watch over you.[24]

Brief Tenure of Hilton Robertson

President Mauss served from August 1949 until October 1953, a period of over four years. He was replaced by Hilton Robertson, who had served as president when the mission was closed in 1924. Robertson also had the distinction of being the first president of the Japanese Mission in Hawaii (1937–40). Interestingly, Robertson was called by President McKay to open the Chinese Mission in Hong Kong in 1949. However, the Chinese Mission, centered in Hong Kong, was moved first to Honolulu and then to San Francisco in 1951. Due to political tensions, only seven months after his release in California in February of 1953, Robertson was on his way to Japan. When he arrived in Japan, Robertson was concurrently the mission president for the Japanese Mission, the Chinese Mission and also for American servicemen in Asia.[25]

Tatsui Sato was heavily involved in translating the standard works and many Church manuals during the tenure of President Hilton Robertson (1953–55). Britsch, in his history, records the following:

> He [Robertson] supported and helped Sato Tatsui with his retranslation of the Book of Mormon—a project Sato began while President Clissold was still in Japan—and with his translation

of the Doctrine and Covenants and the Pearl of Great Price, which he worked on concurrently with the Book of Mormon. While President Joseph Fielding Smith was in Japan, he spent considerable time with Brother Sato, explaining difficult passages and helping him with interpretations of meanings. Brother Sato had worked carefully on this large assignment, since Presidents Robertson, Mauss, and Clissold all encouraged him to take whatever time was needed to do the job right.[26]

President David O. McKay believed very strongly in the international Church, was very interested in expanding the missionary program and was excited about the potential of the Church in Asia. He sent Elder Harold B. Lee to Asia in 1954 "to survey the progress of the mission and study the possibilities of growth." President Lee also visited Korea with President Robertson and was impressed with the enthusiasm among the servicemen to open up Korea. There were still lingering problems from the devastation of the Korean War, which officially ended in June of 1953 with a truce and a divided north and south. Elder Lee reported on his tour with a ringing endorsement in a speech in October conference. He said, "The signs of divinity are in the Far East. The work of the Almighty is increasing with a tremendous surge."

In July of 1955, President Joseph Fielding Smith arrived. He divided the mission into the Northern Far East Mission (now to include Japan, Okinawa and the opening of Korea) and the Southern Far East Mission (Hong Kong, Taiwan, the Philippines and Guam) as a replacement for the Chinese Mission. President Robertson continued on and assumed the presidency of the Northern Far East Mission while H. Grant Heaton became president of the Southern Far East Mission. President Smith also dedicated Okinawa, South Korea, the Philippines and Guam for the preaching of the gospel.[27]

President Edward L. Clissold, who had reopened the mission to Japan and was living in Hawaii, wrote the Satos on 19 December 1955 about his involvement with a new Church college in Hawaii.

He also had heard from departing President Hilton Robertson about the progress of the mission and expressed his deep feelings for the Japanese people:

> It just doesn't seem possible that another year has rolled around and we are celebrating Christmas again and looking forward to a new year. 1955 has been a very busy year for us. Along with the usual business and Church work, we have established a Church college in Hawaii. This was opened on September 26th with a faculty of 21 and a student body of 153. The Church has appropriated $2,000,000 for a complete set of buildings and work is beginning on them immediately. Until the new buildings are finished, the college is housed in temporary buildings at Laie.
>
> My family is all well. I suppose the most important event of the year in the family was the birth of our grandson on November 15th to our son, Richard, and his wife. The new baby will be named Edward Matthew Clissold. Our daughter, Carol, is in her last year at the University of Utah. She will graduate next summer. Otherwise, our children and grandchildren are well and happy.
>
> We saw the Robertsons for one day when they came through here on their way home. They spoke in glowing terms of the progress of the work in Japan and we are happy, of course, to learn of the success attained. We are sure the members of the Church in Japan will be pleased with the appointment of Paul Andrus and his wife, to succeed President and Sister Robertson. They are well qualified, are young and energetic and we are sure the work will grow under their direction.
>
> We think often of Japan and remember as always with gratitude, your many kindnesses to us. We are looking forward to the day when we will be able to visit Japan again. Until then, we do hope and pray that you and your family will be preserved in health and happiness.
>
> We wish you the season's best greetings and success in the new year.[28]

Paul Andrus Returns as Mission President

Paul Andrus, whom Brother Sato had worked closely with in the mission home—in the Clissold and Mauss eras, while he was a missionary from 1949–52—returned to Japan again in December 1955 as president of the Northern Far East Mission. He was only 31 years of age, unlike his predecessors who were in their sixties, and was to serve a lengthy mission (until 1962). Thus, he had a close and lengthy relationship with Brother Sato.

President Andrus, who was known for his excellent Japanese, spent considerable time with Brother Sato during his mission, working with Tatsui on improving missionary language and translations. The retranslation of the Book of Mormon by Brother Sato and new translations of the Doctrine and Covenants and Pearl of Great Price were completed in late 1955. President Andrus organized a translation committee, with the approval of the First Presidency, including himself, Tatsui Sato, Tomigoro Takagi, Elder Ben Oniki and Elder Don Lundberg. They were charged with readying the manuscripts for publication. The first press run of 10,000 copies of the Book of Mormon (printed by Sanseido Press) "were delivered to the mission home a day or two before Christmas 1956. The Doctrine and Covenants and Pearl of Great Price came off the press about a year later."[29]

Besides these monumental contributions, Andrus also credits Tatsui with much more:

> Another fond memory of Brother Sato is of his work in supervising the translation, typing, printing, and distribution of all Church materials. In those years, from 1955 to 1962, all of the priesthood and auxiliary manuals and materials for all the branches throughout Japan and Okinawa were translated, typed, printed and distributed from the mission headquarters in Tokyo. In addition to Brother Tatsui Sato, we had just hired one more full-time translator, Brother Hiroshi Sato, two full-time typists, and one full-time printer, Brother Kazuo Imai. Even working full time throughout the year, it was difficult for this staff to translate,

> type, print, and distribute all the manuals and materials we needed. Brother Tatsui Sato did a great job of supervising the translation, typing, printing, and distribution of all these materials.

Along with this, and related to it, was the monthly Church mission magazine. Originally started as a mission messenger in ditto form, it became the Japanese equivalent of the *Improvement Era*:

> It was during these years that we began to publish the monthly magazine *Seito no Michi*. Through the hard work of Brother Sato and many others, the *Seito no Michi* grew into a respectable monthly publication and filled a great need to supply current Church news and information to members throughout Japan and Okinawa. The *Seito no Michi* was also published at the mission headquarters in Tokyo, and Brother Sato served as editor.[30]

President Andrus remarked that he "worked very closely with Brother Tatsui Sato and came to know him very well." He considered him a "great man" and an accomplished translator. He also noted his service as "my Counselor in the Mission Presidency and my personal confidante and guide in dealing with the Japanese government and with the Japanese Church members." He also gives much of the credit to Brother Sato for the increased success of the mission:

> Brother Tatsui Sato also made a great contribution to our proselyting success in Japan and Okinawa by translating into Japanese the missionary teaching plan we developed in 1956 and the missionary teaching plan placed in effect worldwide by the Church in 1951. Converts baptized by the missionaries in Japan in 1955 totaled 55 and in 1956 totaled 141. During 1956 we developed and placed into effect in Japan and Okinawa a six-lesson teaching plan which we named *Teaching and Conversion Principles*. Brother Tatsui Sato translated this teaching plan into beautiful and effective Japanese. Using the teaching plan, our

> missionaries baptized 588 converts in 1957, 735 converts in 1958, 596 converts in 1959, 927 converts in 1960 and 1,290 converts in 1961. At the worldwide president's seminar in Salt Lake City in the summer of 1961, the Church introduced the *Universal Plan for Teaching the Gospel* to be used in all missions throughout the world. Again, we called on Brother Tatsui Sato to translate these lessons into beautiful and effective Japanese. Using this plan our missionaries baptized over 1,500 converts in 1962. Brother Sato's translations played a vital role in this substantial and unprecedented proselyte success in Japan and Okinawa.[31]

Though he was employed primarily as a translator, Tatsui helped the Church in many ways with his expertise. President Andrus said that Brother Sato was often taken "for granted" as he was called on to help with transactions and translations of every kind. Andrus traces these contributions and their importance:

> One of my fondest memories of Brother Tatsui Sato is of his great work in bringing the Church into full compliance with the Japanese government requirements for "Religious Judicial Persons" *(Shukyo hojin).*

Tatsui had originally registered the Church name as Corporation of the President of The Church of Jesus Christ of Latter-day Saints. However, when President Andrus became mission president in 1955, Tatsui recommended the name be more appropriately changed to "Matsu Jitsu Seito Iesu Kirisuto Kyokai" (the name of the Church in Japanese). Andrus recalled: "Brother Sato called my attention to the fact that our Shukyo hojin was not complying with the requirements of Japanese law." During the American Occupation, the Ministry of Education had been "lax in enforcing the legal requirements of Shukyo hojin" but Sato suggested the Church needed to come into "full compliance with the law." Andrus continues:

> Accordingly we began to make serious effort to bring our Shukyo hojin into full compliance; and well before my release in 1962, the Church Shukyo hojin had been renamed as Matsu Jitsu Seito Iesu Kirisuto Kyokai and was in full compliance; with the law. This extremely important accomplishment was brought about by Brother Tatsui Sato's years of working with the Mombusho (Ministry of Education).[32]

Andrus noted that during this time, the ministry "shocked us by announcing that each one of our Church branches must form a separate Shukyo hojin . . . to fulfill the requirements of the law with regard to record keeping and financial reporting." Andrus further noted that:

> This would have been impossible to do and would have effectively shut our Church operations down in Japan except in Tokyo. After numerous meetings with the Mombusho extending over several months, Brother Sato succeeded in convincing the Mombusho that all our Church branches in Japan were actually part of one operation and therefore the one Shukyo hojin we already had met all the requirements of the law. Brother Sato's heroic efforts at the Mombusho saved the Church from a disaster.[33]

In addition to his yeomen work working with the Japanese government, Brother Sato played a large role in helping the mission acquire real estate and shepherding these complicated transactions through to conclusion. President Andrus said he had a "multitude of memories" in this regard:

> While I was mission president, I bought 23 meetinghouse properties for the Church: 19 properties in Japan and 4 properties in Korea. Brother Sato working with real estate companies searched out many of these properties in Japan and participated in the negotiations for purchase. Once a purchase was finalized,

Brother Sato translated the deed into English. One copy of the English translation was filed with the original Japanese deed in mission headquarters and one copy of the English translation was sent to Church Headquarters in Salt Lake City.

President Andrus recalled the most memorable transaction working with Brother Sato was the "Omote Sando property." The story follows:

> Working with Japanese real estate companies, Brother Sato searched out and called to my attention the Omote Sando property. When Elder Gordon B. Hinckley, who was at that time an Assistant to the Twelve, visited Tokyo in 1960, Brother Sato and I showed him this property and recommended the Church buy the property. This property increased very rapidly in value and a few years later was sold for a huge profit to the Church. The money the Church gained from the sale of the Omote Sando property made possible the purchase of many meetinghouse sites and the construction of many meetinghouses throughout Japan.[34]

President Andrus also stressed that besides all of this, Brother Sato should be remembered for "his excellent service in his Church callings." Andrus expounded, "He served as a Branch President and later as a counselor in the Mission Presidency. At that time most of the active members of the Church were quite young and Brother Sato filled the need for maturity, wisdom, and dignity in leading and counseling these young members."

Another relatively unknown contribution during this time was Sato's recommendation of a cemetery site near Tokyo "so that the Church members could be buried there." Tatusi had carefully searched for a site. Andrus noted that this purchase was in process when he was released, and the land was developed shortly thereafter. Andrus felt that this was a great contribution by Tatsui, as it was a great blessing to the members. President Andrus pointed out that Brother Sato was a key person in the mission and "one of our dearest friends." He said, "We are looking forward to meeting him again and continuing our friendship forever."[35]

Continuing Letters of Friendship

In a letter to the Satos dated 11 December 1956, Brother Hanks shared the great promises to those who assist in the work and also added some words of advice to Yasuo:

> How are you all? I talked with President Robertson a short while ago and he spoke of your spirit to live the gospel. If we can live each commandment we then are in harmony with God's laws and are in a position to receive all His wonderful blessings. My testimony has grown as I have read the scriptures in the Book of Mormon. This verse found in 1 Nephi and 13th Chapter and 37th verse is truly a very wonderful one of promise to those who help in the work of the Lord as you all are trying to do. May I quote it for it is a true promise! "Blessed are they who shall seek to bring forth my Zion at that day, for they shall have the gift and the power of the Holy Ghost; and if they endure to the end, they shall be lifted up at the last day, and shall be saved in the everlasting kingdom of the Lamb, and whoso shall publish peace, yea, tidings of great joy, how beautiful upon the mountains shall they be."
>
> What are you all doing now? Are you still in the Sunday School work and doing translating work at the mission headquarters? I know you must all be doing a good work. Yasuo you are a fine young man by now, I know. Stay true to the faith, keep the Lord's commandments, study the scriptures, as well as all truth . . . and you will be like the magnet that drew the steel marbles to it, you will draw righteous men to you, to bless and help them.
>
> Sister Sato, a young man asked if I would write you and have you send a Japanese doll to his daughter who is ill. She is

> about 10 years old. This young man is getting dolls from different parts of the world. He would like to pay you for the doll, or perhaps he could send you something from America you would like—anyway let me know the cost. May our Heavenly Father bless you all and further the missionary work in Japan.[36]

Brother Richards wrote the Satos that same month, after many years, and inquired about their health and situation. He expressed his nostalgia for the meetings at Narumi and gratitude to the Satos for their kindness at that time. He mentioned how busy he was in his occupation as a medical doctor. Part of his letter follows:

> It has been a long time since I have written to you and although it is almost midnight, tonight, I want to send this letter. It is something that I have wanted to do for a long time. I have often wondered how you are getting along and how your health is. I hope that the years have been good to you and Sister Sato and Yasuo. I suppose that Yasuo is about 17 or 18 years old now, isn't he? I know that you have remained faithful to the Church all these years, and have brought Yasuo up to receive the priesthood. With the opening of the Japanese mission your opportunities to help with the gospel work must have increased. I still remember the meetings in Narumi, the Sunday School, and the many fine visits we had in your house, and the hospitality that you always were so kind to give us.
>
> I have met a Brother Reed Davis who now lives near us. He says that he knows you well. He spoke about you in our church service about 6 months ago. He states that he still remembers with gratitude the experiences he had in Japan with you and your family.
>
> We now have four children, and I am still working hard as a doctor. I have spent four years with further study and have specialized in orthopedic surgery or bone surgery. My oldest child recently got sick. She developed Poliomyelitis. She is getting better but she is partially paralyzed in one leg. We are grateful that her life was spared for us.[37]

Brother Reed Davis also wrote Brother Sato (on 4 January 1957) a similar letter about his memories of Narumi and gratitude for the influence of the Satos on his life. He expressed hope that the Satos could someday come to America:

> I am ashamed of myself for my long silence to you wonderful people, but if you will forgive me I should like to spend a few moments in talking with you. It has been several years now, since I left Japan but the wonderful memories still remain with me. Today as I reread one of your letters it caused a large lump to come in my throat. God was truly good to me and our other GI friends when he led us to meeting with you. The testimony of the gospel that I now have is due mostly to having met with you, your wife and Yasuo. So, forever I shall be grateful to you.
>
> Here in the United States we live a very busy life and it seems that when we are active in the Church, time is very precious. At present I am the mutual superintendent of our ward. We have a membership of 1180 people so you can see that we also have a very large Mutual. Since I have not heard from you in such a long time, I too am wondering what you and your family are doing and how you are getting along.
>
> I think I wrote and told you that we are now living in Salt Lake City and are very happy here. Lula, my wife asks if she still owes you for any of those paintings that you sent us. It has been so long that she wanted to know if we still owed for any. If so please let us know and we will send you the money.
>
> With this new year we wish you the best of everything and pray that we may have the joy of seeing you again, maybe it could be arranged for you folks to come to this country. If this would be your desire, maybe it can be done. You have done so much good for your fellow men I am sure the Lord will fulfill your desires.
>
> How is Yasuo? Is he still going to school? How big is he? Could you send us a picture of yourselves? May the Lord bless and keep you with good health and the necessities of life is my humble prayer.[38]

Brother Sato immediately responded (10 January 1957) to the Davis letter and talked of translating the standard works. He thanked Brother Davis for helping him in his time of need:

> I am very glad to receive your two letters from Salt Lake City after a long interval. It is I who have to apologize for my long silence. Brother Bauman who lives near to you wrote me a letter saying that he met you at the Mutual and heard you spoke of me. Brother Bauman is my friend and helped me very much while he was in Nagoya, Japan, and also after he went back home.
>
> I am very happy to have two of my best friends in the same ward. I am also very grateful to be the member of the same church and have the privilege to call each other brother or sister. Just before I received a letter from Brother Bauman I received a letter from Brother Hanks saying that he met you sometime ago and talked of me. It is really happy to hear that you brothers always remember me and are reminded of the fine experience we had in Narumi. I have been engaged in the work of translation of Book of Mormon, Doctrine and Covenants, and Pearl of Great Price, since 1950, for our Church. The translation was all completed and the new translation of Book of Mormon is to be printed and published sometime around this April. This new translation will greatly help the increase of faith and activity of Japanese Members. I am now engaged in the proof reading of the manuscripts feeling very busy all the day.
>
> I am happy to tell you that my wife Chiyo and my son Yasuo are all well and celebrated Christmas and a bright new year. Yasuo is a young man of 18 years of age and is in the second year of a college. He has a desire to be a medical doctor as Brother Bauman, and is making the preparation for the entrance examination of Tokyo University.
>
> Brother Davis, you mentioned about the money for the silk paintings, but I already received enough money for them. I should have told you that the money helped me very much when I was in need. Probably I and my wife may have opportunity to

go to the place where my friends live and be able to perform the important work for ourselves and also for my ancestors. May I have the opportunity and enjoy the sacred work!

I am sending little Japanese toys to you in token of my friendship. If your family be interested in them I shall be very happy. My wife and Yasuo join me to give our best regards to your family.[39]

Contributions to Mission Genealogy Work

President Andrus remembered that Brother Sato made a great contribution to genealogy and temple work by searching out available sources of family history information. And he collaborated with Sister Joyce Worthen in compiling the first handbook of instructions for doing family history work in Japan (1957).[40]

Brother Sato at this time was translating genealogical materials and guidelines. Brother Archibald F. Bennett, General Secretary of the Genealogical Society in Salt Lake City, responded to questions asked him by Tatsui in a letter dated 20 July 1959, to instruct him on the finer points of names submission and genealogy work:

> I was delighted to hear from you in your letter of June 20th, and to learn that genealogical work in the Northern Far East Mission is making a great progress. I was pleased to learn that your members are learning the steps to take in tracing their ancestry, and in preparing genealogical record sheets for temple work. . . . May the blessings of the Lord attend you in your activities in this important field.[41]

By helping the Japanese Saints and translating and learning the procedures from the experts, Brother Sato prepared himself for his next career as a specialist on Japanese genealogy.

Recognition for Completion of Standard Works

After the standard works were completed and published, Brother Sato received considerable attention for his years of effort and the beauty and authenticity of the translations. For example, Brother Clissold, who hired him as a translator originally, commended Brother Sato in a letter dated 21 January 1958 on his years of service and great contributions to the work in Japan. He was extremely impressed with the new triple combination, and wished he could read the kanji characters better:

> You, no doubt, have seen a copy of the *Church News* containing an article on the publication of the standard works of the Church in Japanese. I cannot tell you how thrilled I am in the completion of this monumental work. My heart goes out to you in deep gratitude as I think of the long years of painstaking labor on your part. Surely, the Lord raised you up at the right time to perform this important mission. After this long period of study and work, there are probably few men in the Church who have a better understanding of the gospel than you.
>
> President Andrus sent me a copy of the triple combination, and it is a handsome book. I can read the "hiragana" and some of the "kanji," and I regret that I did not persevere in my study of the Japanese to the point where I could read freely. Nothing would please me more than to be able to go through the standard works in Japanese. I am afraid, however, that would prove an impossible task for me at this age and with the other responsibilities which I have.
>
> Sister Clissold and I are looking forward to the time when we can pay a visit to Japan. It is nine years since we left, and we are eager to see you again.
>
> Please write and tell me about your family and what you will do now that this great work is accomplished.[42]

Passing of Chiyo and Railroad Engineering Studies for Yasuo

Tatsui's wife, Chiyo, passed away on 8 October 1958 after a sudden stroke. She had declining health in her last few years on earth. She was buried the next day in Ota Ward, Tokyo. She was only 55 years of age at her death. Her passing was very difficult for Tatsui and left him and Yasuo feeling very lonely. She was a faithful and dutiful wife and was much loved and admired by all who knew her. Yasuo was just entering college when she passed on.

The following year, on 20 July 1959, Yasuo wrote a special letter to the Davis family reporting on his studies in engineering and upcoming student employment in railroad design and construction. He also mentioned his father's and his own interest in ham radio and the sad passing of his mother, Chiyo:

> I fear that you can not remember my name, for our silence in corresponding with you continued so many years, but it is our great joy to tell that the Lord blessed every time during our silence.
>
> Tonight I found your letter which you entrust Brother Duckworth in my father's desk, and I am writing this letter remembering the time when you and your nice Brother visited our cottage in Narumi. We spent more than twelve years since you left Japan, and you would find in my enclosing photograph which I took at Nagoya station this spring that the time made many miracle change but the God's hands never changed this long time. My father still working in Church as interpreter and now he is Tokyo West Branch President, but I am working in Tokyo Central Branch as president of Genealogical Committee of Northern Far East Mission.
>
> Every Sunday morning we hear Tabernacle choir on AFRTS network, and talk with my father that you must be in the member of this beautiful chorus, we very often have heard Tabernacle choir on disk, Japanese broadcast and so on, it became very famous choir in Japan now.

Did brother Duckworth and his nice family return to Utah? I met them at Building Fund Dance Party this spring; it was much unexpected meeting and was surprised. They were good family and told me about you and your family.

How are Uncle Charlie, Brother Richards, and Uncle Ray and Brother Hanks, and Brother Boyd and many other Brothers in old days? Say, I was only 7 years but now I'm 21 years old, of course three times taller than I was . . . Now I go to the Tokyo Metropolitan University, third grade special study of civil engineering, and I want to become a railroad engineer, as you know, Japanese railroad is behind far from your country's one, and want to know any investigation of civil engineering of contribute to some Japanese civilization. This summer vacation I'm working Japanese National Railroad and making some design of concrete piles and concrete Bridges, it is in the Shiohama rail Yard near Tokyo Port. If possible, I wish to study any modern technique and learning in America.

My father and I have a hobby of Ham radio and have a license of Amateur Radio station, JALAVS is the call sign, if there were some responding direct through on the Air . . . I have 40m and 10m license and on 40m we shall be able to contact this autumn or winter. In Tokyo West Branch, there are two hams Mormon and often make a special meeting on the air, to contact America Ham Mormon is our desire now.

It is a sorrowful fact to tell [I] lost my mother, Sister Sato. It was November of 1958 and she had a stroke on that night, and went paradise, I believe expressly, very peaceful not being in pain.

To work God is a splendid thing and He gave us strong faith and Testimony and Hope of prowess [progress], He told us every time that our brotherhood was unforgivable [unforgettable]. He does not forget even this little island in the Far East and also our little family. It is a wonderful thing, and to tell these facts is always my gracefulness.

We have about two hundred members every Sunday and [I] meet forty to fifty every Sunday, but almost [all] of them are new member and young member. But I can tell you that the land of the Zion become [larger] steadily on this island in the Far East.

This Saturday we have special MIA meeting, contest of chorus and drama, and the other is Japanese children's song. I will be the pianist of the night. We are making a radio drama for November and I am composing some of the drama music, it is my hobby, but these are very interesting, and we have many other talents in our branch.

Next Sunday we have a Genealogical Public meeting and brother Fukazawa, secretary, and I will make a speech of a pedigree of ancient Japanese clan, Heike and Genji, who struggled many years which is similar as the War of Roses in England of York and Lancaster. It is very interesting fact, and probably all members will hear with interest.

Brother Davis, in closing my letter I will ask again your forgiveness for our long, long silence, but I remember every time when we heard and thought lovely old days and our brother in America.

I pray that you may have health and The Lord bless you and your nice family always. Thank you very much for your kind letter again. Sincerely yours

Yasuo Sato [address] Tatsui Sato and Yasuo #3 Takagi-cho, Akasaka P.O.Tokyo, Japan[43]

President Andersen Pushes Building Program and Temple Preparations

By the time he left in 1962, President Andrus had seen the Church grow to 7,000 members and 180 branches. The number of missionaries had grown from 66 in 1953 to 180 in 1962. However, in order to have wards and stakes, there was a great need to develop leadership and to find even more members. Dwayne Andersen, who had served in the mission office in the Mauss era, was called as the new mission president.[44] He had a master's degree in counseling and was accompanied by his vivacious wife, Peggy, whom many called

"Mrs. Mission President."

Elder Gordon B. Hinckley first visited Japan in 1960 as an Assistant to the Twelve. The following year, he was given the assignment to be supervisor of the Asian missions. From that time on, he was to have an enduring interest in the Saints in Asia. It was during the time of President Andersen that, under the direction of Elder Hinckley and Building Committee Chair, William B. Mendenall, an ambitious building program began in Japan. Brother Sato and Kazuo Imai, working as a printer in translations, continued to help in the transactions and negotiations.[45] Building missionaries were called among local members to help in these construction projects. President Hinckley took a personal interest and made many trips to Japan to mark the progress. He dedicated chapels and inspired the Saints at many conferences.

In one particular conference, at the Tokyo Area Conference on 22 November 1964, Elder Hinckley used Brother Sato as an example to the assembled priesthood brethren:

> Now it is the same with us. The Church offers you an opportunity to grow. The job you are given may seem very unimportant. But as you do it you will grow in strength. Brother Sato is an experienced translator. When he first started, he wasn't very good. And as he has worked, he has grown in ability.[46]

This was certainly a good example, as by this time Brother Sato had the reputation of being a translator and interpreter *par excellence.* Nearing retirement, he was now training a whole new generation of translators. Where initially he was the sole translator, the Church now had formed the Translation Department, and a number of people were involved. This was no longer a one-man operation but had now become part of a large organization. President Andersen and other leaders decided in 1964 to charter a plane for a Hawaiian Temple trip. This required great personal sacrifices and, of course, involved Brother Sato once again.

Continued Edification and Admiration

While the letters had decreased in volume, Sato's many friends continued to vividly recall the special experiences involved in their meeting and to recognize Tatsui's special calling in Japan. They felt a special kinship with what was happening. Brother Ray Hanks cited his mother's relative, who had originally translated the Book of Mormon, and the relationship he had had with both families. He continued to bear testimony of the gospel and was delighted that Brother Sato was recognized in the *Church News* as the translator for President Andersen of the Northern Far East Mission. Apparently, still keeping in close touch with the other servicemen, he relays their congratulations, as well, for all that Brother Sato had accomplished over the years:

> I have thought of you often, but have been a bit negligent in writing. I was happy to know that our son-in-law, Leo Grant, was able to see you around May of this year. Leo mentioned about Yasuo and his special radio. Give our love to Yasuo. I guess he is quite a man now. May things always go well for him and you! I look back over our experience and privilege of meeting you and Sister Sato in the fall of 1945. Eighteen years have passed since those pleasant days of visiting you good folks. I believe the Lord in his love for you and you fine people was very kind to us to let us meet you and share His gospel with you. I remember the evening Mel Arnold, Reed Davis and I visited you, and you mentioned about the passing of your little daughter. You stated that you and Sister Sato had prayed that God would send someone to comfort you, and you felt we had been sent to give that comfort. I too feel that our Heavenly Father was good to us to send us your way. Perhaps there was another influence that also directed us your way to bring about your great work in the kingdom of our Lord. My mother's cousin, Alma O. Taylor, with others helped President Heber J. Grant to open up the Japanese Mission around 1900. Cousin Alma O. Taylor translated the Book of Mormon

> into the Japanese language. Unknowingly, his influence may have directed us servicemen your way.
>
> I have a testimony that the Church of Jesus Christ of Latter-day Saints is the true Church, that Joseph Smith was a true prophet of the Lord. I believe that President David O. McKay is a true prophet today. I believe the Book of Mormon is a true book revealed to us through the hand of the Lord. Happiness came to me when I saw your picture in the *Deseret News* Church Section November 3rd, 1962. It read as follows: "President Dwayne N. Anderson of Northern Far East Mission addresses Tokyo members on chapel building, Tatsui Sato, translator." Congratulations Brother Sato we are all proud of you for the wonderful work you are doing in translating the Holy Scriptures into Japanese, your native tongue.
>
> Our good friends, Reed Davis, Mel Arnold, Elliott Richards and LaVor Kocherhans, I know would wish to join with me in sending their congratulations and love and kind wishes. Did Elder Boyd Packer visit you after I left? About two months ago I was called to be a high councilman in the BYU 2nd Stake. I am enjoying my calling very much. What is Yasuo doing in the Church? I am sure he is doing a good missionary work in his own way.
>
> Well Brother Sato, I will say good-bye for now, and I will look forward to hearing from you soon. I shall be pleased to know about your health, your work, the economy of your people, how the missionary work is coming, and all about Yasuo, and any other information you wish to send.
>
> Merry Christmas and Happy and Successful New Year, with love and kind wishes. My wife joins me in sending same, together with my family.[47]

These contacts with the servicemen, who first met Brother Sato in Narumi and taught him the gospel, lasted a lifetime. The correspondence is also very valuable in tracing the life of Brother Sato and his family during this busy time as a translator/interpreter for the Church in Japan. With his translations, Brother Sato made a contribution that has touched the lives of many thousands of Japanese and missionaries to Japan.

Endnotes

1. Henry Smith, *Matthew Cowley, Man of Faith*, p. 162.
2. John Clawson, Video interview on "Tatsui Sato," Bountiful, Utah, 12 July 2001.
3. Correspondence, Tatsui Sato to C. Elliott Richards, 4 August 1949.
4. Correspondence, Ray Hanks to Tatsui Sato, 1 September 1949.
5. Correspondence, Ray Hanks to Chiyo Sato, 2 September 1949.
6. Correspondence, Chiyo Sato to Reed Davis family, September 1949.
7. Paul C. Andrus, "Memories of Tatsui Sato," revised copy, 23 August 2004, p. 1.
8. Regarding President Mauss' tenure, refer to R. Lanier Britsch, *From the East: A History of the Latter-day Saints in Asia, 1851–1996*, pp. 91–96.
9. Correspondence, Tatsui Sato to Reed Davis, October 1949.
10. Correspondence, Vinal G. Mauss to Reed Davis, 28 October 1949.
11. Correspondence, Tatsui Sato to Reed Davis, 2 December 1949.
12. Correspondence, Chiyo Sato to Reed Davis family, early January 1950.
13. Correspondence, Yasuo Sato to Reed Davis family, early January 1950 (likely sent with above).
14. Correspondence, Tatsui Sato to Reed Davis, 13 March 1950.
15. Correspondence, Tatsui Sato to Reed Davis, 8 November 1950.
16. Correspondence, Tatsui Sato to Thomas Bauman, 8 November 1950.
17. Correspondence, Tatsui Sato to Reed Davis, 30 January 1951.
18. Correspondence, Tatsui Sato to Boyd K. Packer, 10 February 1951.
19. R. Lanier Britsch, *From the East: A History of the Latter-day Saints in Asia, 1851–1996*, p. 94.
20. Video interview, John Clawson on "Tatsui Sato," Bountiful, Utah, 13 July 2002, interview by Brian Gubler.
21. Ibid.
22. Correspondence, Chiyo Sato to Reed Davis family, 21 July 1952.
23. Correspondence, Reed Davis to Sister Sato, August 1952.
24. Correspondence, Tatsui Sato to Ray Hanks, 6 September 1952.
25. R. Lanier Britsch, *From the East: A History of the Latter-day Saints in Asia, 1951–1996*, pp. 97–101, 231–35.
26. Ibid., pp. 100–01.
27. Ibid., 98–101.

28. Correspondence, Edward L. Clissold to Tatsui and Chiyo Sato, 19 December 1955.
29. R. Lanier Britsch, *From the East: A History of the Latter-day Saints in Asia, 1951–1996*, pp. 104–05.
30. Paul Andrus, "Memories of Tatsui Sato," Revised version, 25 August 2004 (e-mail copy), p. 2.
31. Ibid., pp. 1, 4.
32. Ibid., pp. 2–4.
33. Ibid., p. 4.
34. Ibid.
35. Ibid., p. 5.
36. Correspondence, Ray Hanks to Tatsui Sato family, 11 December 1956.
37. Correspondence, C. Elliott Richards to Tatsui Sato family, 14 December 1956.
38. Correspondence, Reed Davis to Tatsui Sato family, 14 January 1957.
39. Correspondence, Tatsui Sato to Reed Davis, 10 January 1957.
40. Paul Andrus, "Memories of Tatsui Sato," Revised version, 25 August 2004 (e-mail copy), p. 5.
41. Correspondence, Archibald F. Bennett (Managing Director, Genealogical Society) to Tatsui Sato, 20 July 1959.
42. Correspondence, Edward L. Clissold to Tatsui Sato, 21 January 1958.
43. Correspondence, Yasuo Sato to Ray Davis family, 20 July 1959.
44. R. Lanier Britsch, *From the East: A History of the Church in Asia, 1851–1996*, pp. 114–15.
45. Ibid., 118–19.
46. George McCune, Testimony, p. 101.
47. Correspondence, Ray Hanks to Tatsui and Yasuo Sato, 16 December 1963.

Chapter 7

Special Calling in Hawaii

PRESIDENT EDWARD L. CLISSOLD, in an oral interview in October 1969, talked about Tatsui's translation of the temple ceremony and Elder Gordon B. Hinckley's role in helping the process along. It is a very inspiring story and speaks to Tatsui's superior abilities as a translator. Of course, Brother Sato would give all of the credit to inspiration from the Lord and would be reluctant to take any credit himself.

Dennis Atkin's wife sent the following information to Sister Sato to forward to me for inclusion in the book: (She mentioned to Tomiko Sato that her husband had passed away.)

ORAL HISTORY

Statement by President Clissold, October 1969 at the Clissold/Mauss reunion

Subject: Tatsui Sato's translation of the temple ceremony into the Japanese language

Typed . . . by Keith M. Munk from audio recording taken at the time. Audio recording is in the possession of Keith M. Munk.

I would like to say just a word or two about Brother Sato. There's a chapter in his life that I don't think many of you know very much about. In 1965, in the beginning of the year, Brother Hinckley, who was in charge of the Japanese mission, came to Hawaii and said there were a number of Saints that were desirous of coming to the temple. I was the president of the temple and he said, "What will we do with them when they come?" And I said, "Well, we will have temple sessions in Japanese." He said, "Is that possible?" And I said, "I don't see why it isn't." He said, "Well, has the temple session ever been translated?" And I said, "No." and he said, "Who can we get to translate them?" I said, "Well, I'm concerned there is only one man and that is Brother Tatsui Sato, in the mission in Japan." He said, "Well, I'm going there next month and I will inquire about it." And when he came back, he said, "The Brethren will call Brother Sato to come to Hawaii and translate the temple ceremony."

Brother Sato came to the temple and I gave him an office. And then I had a translation committee appointed, and we talked about the translation work. The thought was that we'd have the committee sit down in the temple and translate these ceremonies page by page. One day as I was giving thought to this, and some little prayer, it occurred to me that this would be a very difficult method to follow. That the thing to do was to place it all in Brother Sato's hands, let him translate the ceremonies from beginning to end and then have the translation committee sit down and go over his work. We did that. I told Brother Sato, "I am right here in my office, right at hand and near as the phone when I am not here, and any help I can give you, please call on me." He was there (in the temple) from early morning till late at night over a period of about three months. And finally the work was completed.

Then I called in the translation committee. And they had been eager, since they had been appointed several weeks before, and they had been rather eager to see the work. One Sunday morning we gathered in the temple and we took this translation that Brother Sato had made. And as we sat down after a word of prayer I said, "Now we'll go over this page by page and we'll interrupt Brother Sato or we will make comments and corrections as we go along." Brother Sato started to read, I motioned to the others not to interrupt him. I thought it would be well for him to read the whole ceremony from beginning to end, and then we could start correcting it if we had any corrections to make. We were there—I suppose it took us an hour and forty-five minutes or two hours—and Brother Sato read his translation of the Temple Ceremony. And when he was finished, there wasn't a dry eye around the table. And those, the Japanese, whom we called to assist us, they said, "We have never heard such beautiful Japanese in all our lives. We've been to the temple . . . , as we feel it now in our own native tongue, through the translation of Brother Sato." And then we had only two sessions after that, and I don't suppose there was more than ten or fifteen changes made in Brother Sato's translation.

And then we got a cast together and trained the cast. Brother Hinckley and Brother Paul Evans from KSL came down and brought all the equipment. We set it up in the temple and Brother Hinckley said this is going to take several days to tape all of these parts. But we had people selected, they had studied their parts and they read it, and we worked there all one Saturday morning. And when we finished at about 2:00 o'clock in the afternoon, Brother Hinckley said, "Well, I suppose that's all there is to it, except the correcting and the cutting." He knew nothing about Japanese, yet he seemed to know exactly where to cut the tape. Whenever we made an error in the recording, we didn't attempt to erase it, we just went on and made a repeat and kept the tape running. And so without knowledge of Japanese, he just kept cutting that tape and pasting and cutting and joining it, as I say, in the wee hours of Sunday morning. I wasn't satisfied that it was perfect, so I asked Brother Sato on Monday morning to sit down with two or three of the other Japanese and read, or listen to the tape. And they sat down and listened to the tape from beginning to end of the whole ceremony in the temple, and there wasn't one error in all of that recording of the ceremony.

> I don't believe there was a man on earth that could have done this work except Brother Sato who has spent eighteen years translating the Book of Mormon, *Jesus the Christ*, the Doctrine and Covenants, and the *Articles of Faith*. And I doubt there are many men in the Church that have the knowledge and understanding of the gospel that Brother Sato has. And I pay tribute to him and his devotion and for his faith and the great ability that he has acquired through his service in the work of the Lord.[1]

Brother Sato's Account of the Experience

Tatsui later wrote an account called "My Experience in Translating the Temple Ceremony" in which he relates, in his own words, how his prayers were answered and that they were even able to find the appropriate actors in a timely fashion:

> I am the first convert of the Church after World War II. The story of my conversion was written by Harrison T. Price, one of the first missionaries sent to Japan after the War. This story appeared in the *Improvement Era* several years ago.
>
> The first Mission President of the Japanese Mission, Elder Edward L. Clissold, appointed me as the official translator of the Mission in 1948. Since then I translated the Standard Works of the Church, the *Articles of Faith, Jesus the Christ,* and *The History of Joseph Smith by His Mother,* Lucy Mack Smith, etc. But, the highlight of my translation work was the translation of the Temple Ordinance into the Japanese language.
>
> Having received the assignment, I arrived in Hawaii near the end of January, 1965. Elder Edward L. Clissold, who was the Mission President, was the Temple President of the Hawaiian Temple, and he allowed me to engage in the work of translation in the office of the Temple President in the Temple. In this ideal environment and atmosphere, I could start my work of translation. However, according to the council of Professor Slack, one of the Temple Presidency and Professor of the Church College of Hawaii, I went through the Temple in order to listen to the

Ordinance spoken in English, and at the same time to catch the spirit of the Ordinance. By the blessing and help of the Holy Ghost, I completed the translation by the end of March.

The biggest part of the month of April was spent in Salt Lake City attending the Spring General Conference, and giving assistance at the office of the Genealogical Society. Returning to Laie at the end of April, I started to put the words of the Ordinance on the sound tape. However, the Japanese language had to be spoken by genuine Japanese lest the spirit of the language be lost. At the time when I started the rehearsal, there was only one Japanese missionary working in the Honolulu area who was Elder Uenoyama, a graduate from the University of Osaka, Japan. I obtained the permission of Elder Paulsen, then the Mission President in Hawaii, and Elder Uenoyama was sent to Laie. Still, at least, two genuine Japanese who could speak perfect Japanese were needed. I went through the Temple, and at the same time prayed for the help of the Lord to grant my petition. Answering my petition, Elder Okuyama, who was working in the area of the other islands of Hawaii, was sent to Laie to help in the work.

Then we lived together in the Temple Court, prayed, and went through the Temple every day, whenever it was possible for us and made a rehearsal of the Ordinance in Japanese. However, still we felt one character was lacking who could speak the genuine Japanese language. Again, we offered prayer, and in turn went to the Temple for the help of the Lord. Again our prayer was answered and Elder Niiyama came to Laie to get admission to the Church College of Hawaii. The Temple President assigned him as one of the narrators. Besides this, Japanese-American brothers and sisters were assigned as narrators of the Temple Ordinance, and once a week they came to Laie for rehearsal. They worked very hard to get the spirit of the language, and miraculously they could master the difficult pronunciation and intonation which fit their character in the Ordinance.

In the month of July, in order to put the words on the tape, or to record a narration of the tape, Elder Paul Evans, an audio expert, was sent to Laie, and the recording was started with Elder

Gordon B. Hinckley, Member of the Twelve, and President Clissold, presiding over the sacred work. The recording started at 7:00 a.m. and was completed at 10:30 p.m. that night. It was completed in one day, without missing even one word of the Ordinance, of which Elder Evans said was a historical record.[2]

A Completely Different Person

In an address at the Osaka Area Missionary Conference held at Nishinomiya on 6 March 1965, President Anderson cited a letter he had received:

> Elder Brown wrote and said Brother Sato is a completely different person. He is still steeped in translation. Elder Brown could feel his radiation as he saw Brother Sato at work translating. He goes through the temple every day and then spends the rest of his time translating the temple ordinances. He [Brother Sato] wrote back and said it was the most wonderful experience in his life.[3]

The importance of Sato's translation work was featured in an article in the *Church News*, dated 17 April 1965, entitled "Temple Work Planned in Japanese: Veteran Translator of Church Working on Ceremonies for Hawaii." The article includes pictures of Elder Boyd K. Packer, Tatsui Sato and Dr. C. Elliott Richards "Discussing marvel of the Salt Lake Tabernacle" and a picture of the Sato family accompanied by soldiers at the time of Tatsui's baptism in 1946. The article begins as follows: "Temple work will be inaugurated in the Japanese language this summer thanks to the work of Tatsui Sato, who, for the past two weeks has been enjoying his first visit to Salt Lake City. Mr. Sato," the article continues, "left his native Japan early this year to work on the translation of the temple ceremonies into Japanese at the Hawaiian Temple."[4]

Renewal of Friendships

The article noted that Brother Sato "took time out from his translating duties" to attend April conference and visit Church headquarters. "He was met at the Salt Lake Airport by Elders Boyd K. Packer, Assistant to the Council of the Twelve, and Dr. Elliott Richards . . . . It was a happy reunion for the three men, the renewal of a friendship that began just after World War II in the town of Narumi, Japan."[5]

Sato, himself, wrote a brief article for the *Seito no Michi* (Japanese *Ensign*) about his visit.

The following is a translation of the text:

> I stayed in San Francisco on the 2nd [of April] and visited the Golden Gate Bridge and the Japanese Garden, where cherry blossoms were in full view. On the 3rd, I arrived in Salt Lake City and went to Ogden where I stayed with the Mukais.
>
> On the 4th, I watched general conference on TV and left for Salt Lake before noon to attend the afternoon session. I met Lieutenant Boyd Packer, who is now an Apostle. He baptized my wife 20 years ago. President Packer prepared four admission tickets to the conference. Elder Richards, who also baptized me 20 years ago, is now a medical doctor—he took me into the Tabernacle. For 20 years I have dreamed of the Temple, the Tabernacle, the general conference—everything was in front of me and I was just overwhelmed.
>
> I attended 2 missionary reunions later that evening. I met so many missionaries. I was unable to count them. I shook hands and relived many blessings. That night, I stayed at the Richards' home, which is located in the hills of Salt Lake City.
>
> I attended conference all day on the 5th. When the evening meeting was over, the Prophet (Pres. McKay) was on the way back. I had a chance to shake hands with him and received some words of blessing. It was truly a warm handshake and the words came from his heart. After meeting the Prophet, a reporter from the *Deseret News* came and took pictures. On the 6th, I attended

Conference from the morning. The Prophet's message was very wonderful and I felt joy.

Brother Sato with the Richards
From left: Georgina Richards, Joel Richards (parents of C. Elliott), Tatsui Sato, C. Elliott Richards and his wife, Margaret Richards

Brother Richards also told me about the evening of April 5th, when President Boyd Packer invited Tatsui, Elliott Richards and his son Kent, to attend the priesthood session with him. Brother Sato's article continued:

> On the 7th, I visited This is the Place and went up to the mountains above Salt Lake City, but as the blowing wind was cold I covered myself with a blanket. Later that day, I visited the Genealogical Department. I was interviewed by Temple President Clissold and Directors Barton and Fudge, who are members of the Asia committee. I committed to help them with the genealogy of Asia. On the evening of the 8th, I received my endowment.[6]

Brother Sato stayed in Salt Lake City until April 22nd. While he was there, after conference sessions, he made several visits to the Genealogical Society and attended meetings and visited with those who were involved in Asian genealogy. He also attended a special reunion of former Latter-day Saint soldiers at Brother Ray Hanks' home.

Picture taken at the reunion
From left: Hanks, Richards, Bauman, Nixon, Arnold, Sato, Davis

Brother Sato wrote a letter to Brother Davis, dated 7 May 1965, in which he talked of coming to Utah via San Francisco and returning to Hawaii to return to his translating duties. His trip to Salt Lake City was a memorable one as he was able to meet many of his friends, shake hands with President David O. McKay and get a patriarchal blessing from Patriarch Eldred G. Smith. He called the trip to Zion "the highlight of my life" and expressed his gratitude for his many blessings and for the hospitality of the Davis family:

> I arrived at San Francisco airport in safety, 7:30 A.M. in the morning of the 22nd of April. The weather was fine and warm,

though it was cloudy in Salt Lake City. As Sister Terazawa of Chi's travel agency had written a letter to Brother Livingston, Bishop of Bay Ward, he telephoned to me in the afternoon and took me to his home in San Francisco. In the evening of the same day one of the brothers of our Church took me to Oakland Temple, and I could go through the temple, enjoying its magnificence and spirituality. The next morning at 9:00 A.M., I left San Francisco for Honolulu, arriving there about 12:10 P.M. I stayed in Honolulu for three days, attending Honolulu Stake conference and came back to Laie, my home in Hawaii, in the noon of the 26th of April. This ended my trip to Salt Lake City, which extended more than three weeks in inspiration and wonder. I shall never forget your love of brotherhood. Above all I shall never forget the thrilling experience we had when we visited the small hospital in your town.

Brother Davis, you and your wife Sister Davis welcomed me as an honorable guest and gave me all the possible hospitality during my stay there in Zion. When we met together at Brother Ray's home and enjoyed our wonderful reunion, I am sure the Spirit of the Lord poured abundantly upon all those who were present at the occasion and blessed them. Everyone was convinced that the Spirit of the Lord [will] always watch over and give blessing to those who seek after the Spirit and truth.

I was welcomed warmly and was given every possible blessing in Zion. I met and shook hands with President David O. McKay and received a patriarchal blessing of the Patriarch of the Church, Elder Eldred G. Smith. These are only a few of the wonderful blessings that I enjoyed in Zion, but these are rare blessings to Japanese Saints who live so far away from Zion.

My trip to Zion was really the highlight of my life. I am filled with the feeling of gratitude for the blessings given by the Lord. Thank you so much for all you have done to me, Brother Davis. Please give my best regards to Sister Davis. Thank you again. I am enjoying my work in Laie.

Your brother,
Tatsui Sato[7]

Andrus and Clawson on Tatsui's Accomplishment

Former mission president Andrus, exceptional in the Japanese language, was intimately involved as a committee member to review Brother Sato's translation:

> In preparation for the members to come to the Hawaiian Temple in 1965, the Church brought Brother Tatsui Sato to Hawaii and provided him a room in the Hawaiian Temple where he translated the temple ceremonies into Japanese. At the time President Edward L. Clissold was president of the Hawaiian Temple and I was a temple worker. President Clissold formed a committee to review Brother Sato's translations of the temple ceremonies. President Clissold was chairman with Tatsui Sato, Grace Suzuki, Hideo Kanetsuna, and me as members. I have many fond memories of our meetings with Brother Sato in the temple and with President Clissold and Brother Sato discussing the temple ceremonies in English and in Japanese. We all loved Brother Sato's translation because it's beautiful and impressive yet at the same time very easy to understand. Of course, Tatsui's involvement in family history and temple work eventually led him to move to Salt Lake City where, as his crowning work for the Church, he made a magnificent contribution to family history and temple work in Japan.[8]

Brother Clawson heard about Tatsui's translation of the temple ordinances into Japanese from several people. He mentioned that he spent many hours praying and studying in a small room in the temple. It was supposed to take three to six months but Brother Sato "did it in only 6 weeks." Everyone involved was very impressed by this master translator. Furthermore, he used the "most beautiful Japanese;" and when the translation was sent back to Salt Lake for evaluation, "only 3–4 words in the whole translation had to be revised." Several members of the translation committee commented that the "translation was so beautiful that tears came to their eyes."[9] The impact, of course, was huge, not only for Church members who were to make trips to the Hawaiian and Salt Lake temples, but also because of the opening of temples in Japan beginning with Tokyo in 1980 and then Fukuoka in 2001.

Japanese Saints in Hawaii

The tapes were made just in time for the Japanese Saints who came to Hawaii in the last part of July 1965. Elder Gordon B. Hinckley accompanied the group along with President and Sister Andersen and 163 members, including 29 children. Former Mission President Edward L. Clissold welcomed the group at the airport along with former Mission President Andrus and Elder Hinckley. The Japanese Saints stayed in college dormitories and in the homes of the Saints in Hawaii.

There are many touching stories of the interaction that occurred between families. The result was greatly strengthened testimonies and the accomplishment of considerable temple work. The Japanese members tried to include every session they could into their busy schedules, which included entertainment (including the recently opened Polynesian Cultural Center) and a special fireside.[10] Brother Sato's efforts and the "miracles" that occurred behind the scenes, though not generally known, were crucial in making this all happen. This temple trip was also valuable in preparing a new generation of leaders for service in Japan.

President Adney Komatsu replaced President Andersen in July 1965 as mission president. He wrote a letter of thanks to Tatsui, dated 26 April 1966, for his efforts on behalf of the Japanese Saints and for all he had done for the mission as a translator over the many years:

> Your willing response to the call of service, your faithful and diligent labors as the official translator of the Northern Far East Mission, entitles you the gratitude of all into whose lives you have been instrumental in bringing the light of truth, to the just

commendation of your fellow workers, and may I express my sincere appreciation for all you have done in this mission.

May the supreme joy that comes from the performance of a noble work well done be yours, and may your future life be enriched by the fruits of past experiences to further inspire you with a constant devotion to the gospel of Jesus Christ.

May the Lord's choicest blessings be with you and your family always![11]

Concluding a Career

Later on 13 October 1965, Brother Hanks responded to a letter from Brother Sato and mentioned visiting Tatsui at the Hawaiian Temple. He was happy that Brother Sato was coming to BYU (since the Hanks family lived in Orem) and offered help as a sponsor and dear friend:

Thanks for your nice letter of October 7th. It is nice to know that Yasuo has a good position in the national railways; give our kind wishes to him and his good wife. Thanks Brother Sato for your kindness to me Wednesday July 21, 1965, while in Hawaii. It was a real pleasure to be your guest. I enjoyed the day so much being with you and our visit together at the Hawaiian Temple grounds. I enjoyed also, so much, our stay Wednesday evening at your friend's home, Brother and Sister Takeuchi, and their Son, Tom, and his wife, Lillian. It was a real joy to enjoy the love and friendship of their children and George Takeuchi's children.

Brother Sato, Sister Hanks and I read your letter together and we are both very happy of your plans to come to BYU We both will be very happy and honored to be your sponsor. My good wife said you would be welcome to come and stay with us until you could get located. Kindly send the necessary sponsor papers. We shall be looking forward to having you with us here in the West.

Kindest of wishes,
Ray E. Hanks[12]

Sato also played an important role in helping to prepare for the visit of 314 Japanese Saints to the Salt Lake Temple, coinciding with October conference in 1970. He was set apart for the call on 13 May of that year by Elder Edward H. Sorenson, second counselor in the Salt Lake Temple presidency.[13] Soon after this historic trip of Saints to the Salt Lake Temple, the impact of new leadership and direction in Japan was felt. The first stake in Japan in Tokyo was organized in 1970, and a decade later a temple was dedicated in Tokyo in 1980. What Brother Sato felt was his greatest and most inspired contribution (the translation of the temple ceremony) has had a profound impact on members who have attended Japanese-language sessions at various temples over the years.

In 1948, President Clissold called Brother Sato to first translate the sacrament prayers and then to translate the Book of Mormon, Doctrine and Covenants and Pearl of Great Price. He had completed the work on 18 April 1956 after eight years of diligent labor. He was engaged to work as a translator until 1966, ending with the translation of the temple ceremony in the Hawaiian Temple. He reported in his brief history that he had translated the *The History of Joseph Smith by His Mother,* Lucy Mack Smith; unfortunately, when he returned to Japan the manuscript he had labored over could not be located. This turned out to be a disappointment.[14] His retirement and return to Japan were to be short-lived as he had a new opportunity.

Endnotes

1. Typed text from audio recording in possession of Keith M. Monk, comments by Edward L. Clissold at Clissold/Mauss Reunion, October 1969.
2. Tatsui Sato, "My Experiences in Translating the Temple Ceremony, 1965," Hawaii Temple history files, BYU—Hawaii Archives.
3. George M. McCune, *Testimony*, p. 128.
4. "Temple Work Planned in Japanese: Veteran Translator of Church Working on Ceremonies for Hawaii," *Church News,* 17 April 1965.
5. Ibid.
6. Article on Tatsui Sato's visit to Salt Lake City, *Seito no michi*, July 1965.

7. Correspondence, Tatsui Sato to Reed Davis, 7 May 1965.
8. Paul C. Andrus, "Memories of Tatsui Sato," revised copy, 25 August 2004, p. 5.
9. Video interview on "Tatsui Sato," Bountiful, Utah, 12 July 2001, interview by Brian Gubler.
10. Shinji Takagi and William MacIntrye, *Nihon Matsu-jitsu Seito-shi, 1850–1980-nen* [a history of the Latter-day Saints in Japan, 1850–1980], pp. 256–66.
11. Correspondence, Adney Y. Komatsu to Tatsui Sato, 26 July 1966.
12. Correspondence, Ray Hanks to Tatsui Sato, 13 October 1965.
13. "Tatsui Sato Plays Important Role as Translator," *Genealogical Society Observer*, August 1970, 6–5, pp. 1–2.
14. "Sato Tatsui Kyodai no ryakureki," [Brother Sato's concise history], 1987.

Chapter 8

BYU Professor & Marriage to Tomiko

TATSUI WAS ALMOST 88 YEARS OLD when, on 12 March 1987, he wrote a 17-page brief history (in Japanese) about his life. He described going to BYU after he completed translating the temple ceremony at the Hawaiian Temple. The following is a translation of his story:

> In 1966, I was hired to teach the Japanese language at BYU. I left for Laie, Hawaii to do the temple ceremony translation when the mission president was Elder Andersen. And when President Andersen was released from being mission president, I went back to Japan with a new mission president, Elder Komatsu. After I visited my first general conference in Salt Lake City, I went back to Hawaii. I met Brother Goya, the first missionary who went to Narumi. He asked me what I wanted to do since I finished the translation job. I told him, I really wanted to go to BYU and study there, but I didn't have money for the tuition. Brother Goya said that wasn't any problem at all. "You go there to teach. You should write a letter to them," he told me simply. At that time, Elder Wilkinson was the president of BYU. As Elder Goya told me to

do, I wrote a letter to President Wilkinson and said that because I did not have money for tuition, I would like to teach there while I attended BYU—would it be possible? I wrote the letter, because Elder Goya told me everything would work out fine.

After I returned to Japan, that same year on Christmas day, I received a letter that said BYU would hire me as a visiting professor. I taught there for two semesters in 1966. I was very happy for this opportunity.

Later, I got information about why I was hired to teach there. It was because Professor Paul Hyer went to teach in Taiwan, and another professor was called to become a mission president in Korea; they both left at the same time. A position was open that year. When I asked what I should teach, they told me to teach the Japanese language. I answered, "Yes." And they told me to teach the comparative religion too. I replied to them, "I can't do that." They said, "With your background, you can do it."

I quickly got materials ready for my classes. I did research about Shintoism and Buddhism. I had 21 students in my class; it was a big class. I found out that they were all returned missionaries from Japan. They were all good students, and they all helped me. Among those students, I still keep in touch with Professor Gubler at BYU—Hawaii and Brother Ogden, who visited me recently—he is a fine lawyer and is a mission president in Japan now. I forgot some of the student's names, but they gave me happy joyful days.

When I was ready to go to BYU, my mother was still alive. She was quite old at the time. She spent most of her days in bed. I told her, "I am going to America." She asked me when I would be back. I said, "In three years." It was just a random answer, but a miracle occurred in exactly three years after I left Japan—I was able to go back to Japan as a genealogy researcher for the Genealogical Department of the Church. And again, I returned a second time three years after that. That was the last time I saw my mother alive. She passed away at age 88. I am going to be 88 years old soon. . . .[1]

Among the papers that Tatsui treasured is an acceptance letter from Wesley P. Lloyd, Dean of International Students, dated 4 January 1965:

> Your application for admission to the Graduate School has been given careful consideration, and you have been admitted on a non-degree-seeking basis pending completion of your graduate application. We have received a letter of recommendation from Harrison T. Price. Letters from two additional references have not arrived. We must also have a copy of your grades for work done on a college level. We have received copies of notation of conferment of the degree, but we must have some indication of your grades to compute a grade-point average for your entrance into the Graduate School on a degree-seeking basis. Please arrange to have these sent to us.
>
> Please bring the enclosed registration permit with you when you come to register. If we can be of further assistance to you, we would appreciate hearing from you.[2]

Tatsui also received a personal letter from Earl C. Crockett, Academic Vice President, dated 16 September 1965, offering a half-time teaching position at BYU for the coming semester:

> I am replying to your good letter addressed to President Ernest L. Wilkinson, dated August 9. We have waited before replying until collecting information from several departments in the university. It now appears as though we could employ you one-half time to teach Japanese beginning the second semester of this year. The second semester begins the first of February 1966. This would allow you the balance of your time for studying . . . . We could probably assure you continued employment at least on a one-half time basis for the fall academic year, 1966–1967.
>
> Should you be interested in employment along the lines just indicated, I suggest that you write to Dean Bruce B. Clark, College of Humanities, Brigham Young University.[3]

Bruce B. Clark, Dean of the College of Humanities, wrote Brother Sato a letter, dated 29 October, to officially confirm the hiring:

> I am writing this letter to give official confirmation to what President Earl C. Crockett told you in a letter a month ago. We are pleased to tell you that all arrangements have been made for you to teach with us spring semester on a half-time basis. The spring semester begins on 1 February 1966 . . . .
>
> Your teaching assignment will be one section of Japanese language and one section of oriental culture and religion, if this is satisfactory.
>
> As President Crockett also explained in his letter to you a month ago, we can probably assure you continued employment at least on a half-time basis for the full academic year of 1966–67 if you so desire. Decision on this can wait until after you arrive here if you wish. Please regard this letter as an official notice by the University of your employment. I assume that you desire to accept since you have already expressed this to me. You should make plans to arrive in Utah at the latest by 1 February. Please keep in contact with me between now and then so that we can anticipate your arrival. Also, please feel free to write me on any matters that might not be clear to you.[4]

Since Brother Sato had applied for graduate study in religious education, Chauncey C. Riddle, chairman of the Department of Graduate Studies in Religious Instruction, wrote to him regarding what area he was interested in studying. He also asked for a picture to complete Tatsui's application. By that time, Tatsui had already made the move and was living in Orem:

> In order for your application to this department to be complete we need a clarification of your major area. In our department we have three areas: Bible and Modern Scripture, History of Religion and Religious Education. If you could let us know

which of these areas you wish to major in, your application will be processed without delay.

We also need a recent snapshot of you to accompany your application.[5]

Classes in Comparative Religion (Japan) and Japanese Language

The following are some of the subjects Brother Sato taught in his comparative religion class that were gleaned from his own voluminous notes. The first example is from a study guide that emphasized the noteworthy figures and sources of Japanese religious history:

1) Enki-Shiki, a collection in 50 volumes of the palace, the audience of the officials, the customs of the provinces, etc. It was published during the Enga era (927), hence its name.

2) Kobo-Daishi or Kukai (774–835) He entered the Buddhism temple while still quite young, and at 19, took the name of Kukai. In 804, he went to China, where for 2 years, he studied under the most famous masters. On his return, he engaged in a discussion organized by the emperor between the most learned bonzes and surpassed them all in eloquence and science. After that, he began to preach the Shingon doctrines. He invented the alphabet, called hiragana, and wrote the poem of 47 syllables after the manner of Japanese poems. In 921, Kukai received from the emperor Daigo the posthumous name of Kobo-Daishi, by which he is generally known.

3) Yamazaki, Ansai (1618–1682) He was born in Kyoto, and he was placed in the temple and destined to become a bonze. He studied Japanese antiquities, at same time devoting himself to Chinese sciences. He went to Edo (Tokyo), opened a school for young samurai. He established a new sect, the Suiga-Shinto, and left very many works in which he applies the doctrines of the Chinese philosophers of the Sou dynasty of Shintoism (960–1279).

4) Yoshida, Kenko, or Kaneyoshi and also called Urabe, Kenko (1283–1350) He cultivated literature. At the death of the emperor Go-Ura, his protector, he shaved his head and retired to the temple of the Shugaku-in (1324). He is the author of Tsurezure-gusa which is a classical work, composed in the 14th century. It is a collection of essays and anecdotes on all kind of subjects, and both for the matter it treats as for its style, it ranks high in Japanese literature. It contributed much to the spreading of Buddhist doctrines and the theories of Confucius and Mencius.

5) Ueda, Akinari (1732–1809) writer of Kyoto, left several works.

6) Inyou 5 Gyo Setsu. The teaching of Chinese philosophy in which everything in the world is divided into Yin and Yang.

7) Hayashi, Razan (1618–1680) He was born in Kaga. His father brought him to Kyoto at the age of 14; he studied literature at the temple of Kennin-ji. Tokugawa, leyasu (Shogun) bestowed on him scholar of doctor in 1606. He became a 1st secretary of the Bakufu. He published two books in favor of Shintoism. His historical philosophical and religious works amount to several hundred volumes.[6]

Besides the above class in comparative religion that focused on Shintoism and Buddhism in Japan, Tatsui also taught a third-year Japanese language and literature class. He used Hibbets and Itasaka's *Modern Japanese* as well as Yanaibara Tadao, *Nihon Kindai Keizu-shi Yoran* (an overview of modern Japanese economic history) as textbooks. He kept meticulous records of all his students including, their names, ages, majors and various test scores, as well as samples of student writings. For example, in his file, there are Brother Katsu Kajiyama's examinations and written work as well as Greg Gubler's writings. Katsu Kajiyama has taught Japanese for many years at BYU—Hawaii while Greg Gubler is a history professor and university archivist at the same university. The examinations included writing advanced kanji characters and translating sentences from Japanese into English.

The following are among the items to be translated in one of the exams; these items related to the text by Yanaibara are rephrased as follows:

> 1) Why American public opinion was united in opposing Russia.
>
> 2) Why the removal of Japanese military authority was essential before Japan could be democratized.
>
> 3) The policies taken in the Occupation to demilitarize Japan.
>
> 4) Why the foundation of the emperor system was lost with Japan's defeat in World War II.
>
> 5) The problems of denying the war in terms of self-definition and sanctions.
>
> 6) Why Occupation politics were modified to coincide with American political ideals.
>
> 7) After all, it was the intention of SCAP to promote Japan as a powerful member of the group of democratic countries in order to influence it to oppose communism.[7]

Tatsui discussed the great changes that had gone on in Japan during the American Occupation and taught the current language of politics and economics. Students were encouraged to participate, and Tatsui worked very hard to teach students to write characters correctly. And, with his long experience in translation, he taught them to translate passages and phrases in the spirit rather than literally. Translation was an art to him, and he taught students to avoid being too literal.

Among Tatsui's many keepsakes is a letter, dated 19 May 1966, from Roger Austin written to "Sato Sensei" (his teacher Sato). He was one of 23 students enrolled in the comparative religion class. From Sato's name lists and notes, one can determine the ages and majors of the students. The letter follows:

> I have been called back to Washington D. C. for a conference with the Department of State. If I am successful in this interview,

I will be sent by them to Vietnam this summer to work with the people there. Dr. Hyer will explain the situation to you.

I enjoyed your class very much and hope to be able to take another class from you next semester. I have handed in three papers instead of two and ask your permission to be excused from the final examination. I have studied the notes and feel that I know the information that we discussed in class.[8]

Tatsui and Greg Gubler. Tatsui kept several pictures of them together

Greg Gubler's name shows on Tatsui's name list in the beginning, and two of the exams are dated February 18th and March 4th in a third-year level Japanese conversation class. Gubler scored almost perfect scores in each of his tests. He willingly agreed to write the following memory of Tatsui:

The class I took from Brother Sato was one of the most memorable ones in college. The weather in February was unbelievably good that year, and he took us outside for *Aozora Gakko* [open-air class]. Everyone respected our *sensei* (teacher) as most were returned missionaries who had used the Book of Mormon and other scriptures in teaching. Brother Sato meticulously corrected our assignments and gave us immediate feedback. He suggested ways to improve our writing and taught us many useful expressions. The text (an economic history of modern Japan) was challenging and, in addition, we also had handouts and even wrote some poetry. As a result of the class and his careful guidance, I progressed greatly in Japanese composition and formed a lasting relationship with this master teacher. Later, when I replaced him at the Genealogical Society, I was fortunate to have him as a personal tutor for over three years. He was a man of great insight and ability. I will always be grateful for those opportunities.[9]

Graduate and Language Studies

In his file, there is the official grade report that showed what classes Brother Sato was enrolled in while he was teaching. These classes included, English as a Second Language, Latter-day Saint Church History, and Religion 242—a class in teaching the Book of Mormon. In his English class he wrote the following paper as a process theme:

How to Make a Japanese Delicacy

In Japan the gourmets not only appreciate the nourishing value of dishes, but also the color, the flavor and the tableware that harmonizes with the dishes.

The following Japanese delicacy is delicious and easy to prepare. First, wash soft leaves of beefsteak plant. Then, place one leaf on top of another and lay a stack of ten leaves at the bottom of a wide mouth jar. Sprinkle table salt on the layer. Repeat laying ten more leaves and sprinkling the salt. When the leaves reach the capacity of the jar, put an earthenware plate on the very top of the layer to give pressure. Let it set for 12 hours. After this process, take out the leaves and drip off excess saline water. Then put the leaves in another clean jar and add enough soy sauce just to cover the layers of the leaves.

> Next, cover the jar and keep it in a dark place. The pickle may be eaten after one month, but sometimes mold may be found on the surface of the juice. In this case, although the mold is harmless, the soy sauce should be renewed or else the mold will spoil the flavor. After three months the green leaves will be completely seasoned.
>
> Then take the leaves out of the jar, transfer them to another clean jar and keep it in a refrigerator. This pickle can be kept for years without spoiling its flavor. It is good for an appetizer, and especially goes well with hot cooked rice. The color, flavor and taste well represent the typical delicacies of Japan.[10]

Brother Sato kept almost everything. The following English paper comparing and contrasting two students is also interesting as it shows his great descriptive and story-telling abilities:

> All day snow was falling heavily and when night came freezing blasts from the mountain added more coldness. Teacher Tanaka was stooping over a coal stove of primitive type to which he had to supply several shovels of brown coal every twenty minutes. The dormitory inspector's room was dimly lit. The air of the room was thick with smoke and the phonemic odor of burning brown coal. Under the dim light Tanaka was pondering on his 16 years service as school teacher of the Miyagi Normal School of North East Japan. Footsteps on the corridor broke his meditation. He heard a knock at the door and saw a silhouette on the glazed door.
>
> "Come in," he said. With the rattle of the ill-fitted door a rubicund face with an enormous nose loomed against the dark corridor. The student said with the pause of attention, "I am Konno of the Room 25, Dorm, 1. I came to inform you about the Judo match, by order of vice-schoolmaster, Aihara." As he drew near to teacher Tanaka's chair, the floor board shrieked under the load of two hundred pounds. Konno was the captain of the Judo team of the Miyagi Normal School. "All right; but what are you going to

do with your chemistry lab work assigned for tomorrow?" Tanaka said to Konno. "Sir, I am sorry I can't attend the class, for our team has to have a warm-up meet from 9 A.M."

His answer was a challenge to Tanaka, who was just a common teacher working under vice-schoolmaster Aihara. Tanaka once visited Aihara's office and pointed out Konno's learning attitude, complaining that Konno was frequently found to be sleeping during his class, even snoring. To his surprise, Aihara said that unless Konno had not exhausted his energy so much that he was asleep during his class, our school could not have obtained victory in the Judo match. Tanaka felt the urge to warn Konno that he would flunk in chemistry, but before his urge took the shape of voice, Konno left the room saying, "Owari—I have done." His voice was so loud that anyone outside of the room could hear clearly. The rattle of the ill-fitted door was also loud when he closed it.

Tanaka again fell into his meditation, when he heard a knock at the door. "Come in," he answered, as one who was half asleep. When he distinctly came to senses, he noticed that a small-stature student was standing before him. The student spoke: "Sir, I am sorry I disturbed your meditation, but may I ask your favor to answer my question?" "Who are you?" "I am Sasaki of room 6 Dorm of #2." "Oh! You are Sasaki. What is your question?" "Sir, may I ask you concerning the adaptability of Pestalozzi's philosophy of education to our country?" "I am a teacher of chemistry. I don't think I have enough knowledge to help you on this matter."

"Sir, I know that you have rich knowledge not only of science but also of philosophy. Sir, as you know, our country is the country of the Shinto God, and our Imperial family is the direct descendant of this God. In October 1890, Emperor Meiji issued 'The Imperial prescript on Education' in which it reads: 'Our subjects ever united in loyalty and filial piety has from generation to generation illustrated the beauty thereof. This is the glory of the fundamental character of Our Empire, and herein also lays the source of Our Education.' I have studied the book Pestalozzi and his philosophy of education many times, but still I have a question in my mind: is Pestalozzi's philosophy adaptable to our country, the country of Shinto God?"

"Sasaki, your father is the Shinto priest of the Hachiman shrine in the neighboring village, isn't he?" "Yes, he is. He has been in that position over fifty years. I have been nurtured to succeed to his position, after his death." "I know what you mean. It is not the question of learning, but the question of the enlightenment of your mind. Study as you have been. You will be enlightened spiritually and your question will be answered by yourself." "Thank you sir, thank you very much." Sasaki went back to his room. The snow let up during the conversation and the moon was peering through the clouds.[11]

Featured at Special Fireside at BYU

While Brother Sato was at BYU, he was featured at a fireside conducted by the International Students Organization. An article entitled "Sato Addresses Fireside" appeared in the *Daily Universe* dated 11 March 1966; the article included a photo of him with a castle and a model Japanese junk from his personal collection of artifacts. The article, written by Steve Berry, follows:

> The International Students fireside Sunday will feature a talk by a visiting professor who translated the standard works of The Church of Jesus Christ of Latter-day Saints into the Japanese language. Professor Tatsui Sato is at the BYU teaching Japanese and studying LDS Church history. The fireside will be held at 8:45 p.m.; Prof. Sato will speak on the religious ferment in Asia.
>
> Professor Sato served 16 years as the official translator of the Japanese Mission, now the Northern Far East Mission. He retranslated the Book of Mormon into modern Japanese language and translated the Doctrine and Covenants, the Pearl of Great Price, Talmage's *Jesus the Christ,* and many other Church books. According to Prof. Sato, the translation of the standard works took

nine years to complete. He said that there were 50,000 copies of the Book of Mormon in Japanese in circulation for assistance to missionaries, members and investigators of the Church in Japan. Last year, Prof. Sato traveled to Laie, Hawaii, where he translated the Church temple ordinances into the Japanese language.

Prof. Sato was converted to the Church after he met an American serviceman in his home town of Narumi. The serviceman, Raymond E. Hanks, is now a resident of Provo. After his baptism, Prof. Sato was ordained an elder by the late Elder Matthew Cowley, who was a member of the Quorum of the Twelve. Prof. Sato was the only Japanese elder ordained by Elder Cowley. Before joining the Church, Prof. Sato earned a Bachelor of Science in chemistry from Tohoku Imperial University, where he remained as an assistant professor of chemistry. After finishing his studies at BYU, Prof. Sato plans to return to Japan and assist the missionary program of the Church and continue research and writing about the Church in Japanese.[12]

Marriage to Tomiko Hiranishi

Tomiko Hiranishi recalls in her own account of her life history, how she met her husband:

On April 1st, 1965, I met Tatsui during the general conference in Salt Lake. During that time, Tatsui gave a talk at the Dai Ichi Branch's (Japanese Branch in Salt Lake City) sacrament. That day, my first impression about him was that he must be a very earnest person. I can still recall how his speech was very refined and cultured, and his talk had a deep meaning to it.

In 1962, during [in] the *Improvement Era*, Tatsui's story about his conversion was printed. The title of it was "A Cup of Tea". I read it before I met Tatsui. The story impressed me so much that it seemed to be unreal when I was listening to his talk at Dai Ichi Branch. I was very surprised that he was actually there talking to us.

After our sacrament was over, we held a fireside at one of our members' homes in the evening. Mysteriously, I was assigned to give Tatsui a ride to the fireside. Many saints were gathered there. Tatsui gave a talk in English that time which was also a wonderful talk. After the fireside I gave him a ride to the home of Dr. Richards where he was staying that time. On the way, we chatted and I decided to help him with his shopping the next day. I remember that after the shopping, he treated me like [to] fried chicken.

I didn't realize that the Lord gave me the opportunity to meet him that time Tatsui met my daughter, Michiko, and they had a good conversation with each other. They became good friends. Michiko cut out the picture of Tatsui from the *Seito no Michi (Ensign)* and put it up on her bedroom wall. She was fond of him. Tatsui also liked Michiko. He told me that she had both the culture of Japan and America, and was a wonderful daughter. Hearing his words made me very happy.

After that, Tatsui and Michiko exchanged letters often. One day, Michiko suddenly said, "Mom, why don't you marry Brother Sato?" I was very much shocked and answered back to her, "Don't say such a silly thing," bashfully.

The following year, in July1966, I was reading my patriarchal blessing, which says, ". . . when you finish your life upon this earth, you will return to the Heavenly Father, and you will be able to receive the blessings of the Celestial Kingdom . . ." When I finished reading it, I felt that I would be able to marry in the temple for eternity.

The opportunity of marrying Tatsui occurred when one day I asked him to give me advice on my father's cemetery. Previously, Tatsui had told me about his former wife, Chiyo's, tombstone. I told Tatsui my father had passed away in 1960, and though I would like to purchase the tombstone, I hadn't paid for it yet. Therefore, I was going to visit the cemetery to make a payment. When I finished telling him about it, he offered to go to the cemetery and said that he would like to offer a prayer of blessing on the cemetery and the tombstone. I was so moved by Tatsui's prayer. My beloved father must also have rejoiced at this wonderful prayer. While I was listening, my heart was filled with happiness and was so impressed that I could not stop tears from streaming down. My heart was filled with peace and gratitude to Tatsui. When we returned to our car, Tatsui suddenly said, "I asked your beloved father, Shinjiro, whether I should marry you, and I got permission to do so. After meeting you, 14 months have passed away. Therefore, please do not say 'no' to me." I was very astounded and had no words to say, and kept quiet that moment.

When I returned home, I had a mysterious experience. As soon as I entered the house, I saw a bright light. In it, Tatsui was standing in white robes. I only saw him above the waist in the form of a cloud. Immediately, I heard a voice say, "He will become a good father to your children."

On July 29, 1966, we married in the Salt [Lake] Temple for eternity. Tatsui was always very kind to my children. He always supported them with their education and missions. I was always happy that Tatsui became my children's father. Tatsui was always kind to me. He talked to me with warm smile. He treated everybody with friendship, kindness and love. I am thankful to God that He gave me the blessing to meet Tatsui in this life and that I was sealed to him for all eternity.[13]

Tomiko Hiranishi was born on 8 January 1920 in Kemmerer, Wyoming to father, Shinjiro, and mother, Ayame Mito. She had four younger sisters and one younger brother. She lived in Wyoming until age 15. When America entered the Great Depression, the coal mine where her father worked was shut down. Her family went back to Japan, and she lived there for 13 years.[14]

She also wrote the following for a Church talk, the exact date of which is unknown:

When I was 15 years old, I left my birthplace—Kemmerer, Wyoming—and went to Japan. In Japan, I lived in Kure-City, Hiroshima Prefecture, where I attended school. I stayed at the home of my cousin-in-law's relative.

We were very comfortable in this beautiful home enclosed in a beautiful Japanese garden. Soon after, the master of the home, Mr. Takadono, wanted to teach me Nihon Seishin (when translated, it means "The Japanese Spirit"). He was a man of high character and was respected by the community. I'm sure he wanted to help me be happy in Japan. He said it would take at least 3 years for me to understand the Japanese Spirit. So for 3 years almost every night, after we ate supper, he talked about the Japanese Spirit. We had to sit on the *tatami* (straw) mat with our feet folded.

Mostly, I remembered my poor legs; they were so numb with pain. He said it was part of the teachings to sit erect and listen with our eyes focused singly on the speaker. Doesn't it remind you of the training we receive in sacrament meetings? Only we are lucky our legs are not folded in back while we sit on the floor.

There are only a few things that I remember out of the many hundreds of lectures Mr. Takadono gave us. In one of the talks we learned that the highest honor is to die for one's master. Such an honorable act was the highest in the headlines of the newspaper. I thought to myself, I could never take my life for anyone.

On another occasion, he lectured on the subject of *hara-kiri*, or suicide. When a promise is not kept or if you are not able to live up to the covenant you make with someone, you were to die, because it is a shame and dishonor to oneself and especially to your family.

I thought the Japanese way of thinking was very cruel and merciless, and I was glad to be born in the United States and not in Japan.

The point I'm trying to make is that when a Mormon missionary taught me the gospel of Jesus Christ, I was greatly impressed with the word "Mormon Spirit." The gospel teaches us that the Mormon Spirit is very similar to the Japanese Spirit. The gospel teaches us that we Mormons are peculiar people with a sacred covenant. If we do not keep and observe the covenant with Heavenly Father we will suffer spiritual death. Then we are unable to attain eternal life. Therefore, it is vital for us to keep our sacred covenant with our Heavenly Father.

Another thing that touched my heart was that Mormons build temples, as do the Japanese. I asked Brother Gubler about how many temples and shrines are in Japan, and he said there were over 80,000 Buddhist temples and over 100,000 Shinto shrines in Japan.

At the time of the dedication of the Mormon headquarters in Japan in 1949, my husband heard from Apostle Matthew Cowley in his dedicatory prayer that Japan will be dotted with temples. Japanese build temples and shrines to worship their ancestors and for the salvation of those who have passed beyond, and Mormons also build temples for the same purpose.

I'm grateful for the missionaries who came and taught me these sacred principles of salvation for the dead. I am really grateful to work for the Genealogical Department so we can help those people both living and dead to be saved.

I have a testimony that we are engaged in the important work of the gospel.[15]

Tomiko Reflects on Hiroshima

Tomiko endured the hardships of the war and was living in Kure, only a few miles from Hiroshima when the A-bomb was dropped in August 1945. It was an experience etched in her mind forever. The following is a text from one of her talks recalling the horrific event:

It was a clear summer morning, the 6th of August, 1945, at about 8:14 a.m. Japan time, when I heard the roar of a bomber. I was weeding grass in the rice paddy. I paused in my work and looked up into the sky. I recognized a single plane, a B-29, high overhead, trailing a long, white tail as it winged its way westward toward the city of Hiroshima.

If it were a formation of planes I would have been concerned and troubled. However, it was a single plane and even though I saw a black, oblong object drop from the plane, I did not give it much thought and resumed my work. I had no sooner bent forward and put my hand on a sheaf of grass when suddenly an intense glare flashed all around me. It was a million times stronger and brighter than the flash of a camera. The flash was even brighter than that of the noonday sun. Following the flash, an earth-rending explosion filled the air, accompanied by an eerie heat wave. I was hit by the heat wave and thrown on my back into the rice paddy. All of this occurred almost within the twinkling of an eye. I was numb with disbelief, shock and fear. I could not imagine that a single plane could have such a devastating effect and annihilate an entire city with a single bomb.

Even today, I find it difficult to adequately express the feelings that overcame me that fateful day. Surrounded by the eerie glare of heat, I thought for a moment that the bomb had been dropped into one of the huge oil tanks lined up in Kaitaichi City on the outskirts of Hiroshima City. When the roar of the blast was over, a foam-like substance started to shoot up into the sky. It was as though a giant champagne bottle had been popped open. As the foam-like substance ascended, a gigantic mushroom-shaped cloud formed in the sky. The surrounding area was soon enveloped in darkness. The mushroom cloud gradually changed its color—first to a light pink, then a darker pink and finally to a reddish pink. With a deathly pall setting in around me, the thought occurred to me that this was not a simple bombing incident.

I started to tremble with fear. I became terrified. I was thoroughly convinced that Japan's enemy had invented and inflicted upon us a deadly weapon by harnessing the energy from the sun and that the bursting of the bomb had produced a poisonous substance; furthermore, I believed that this huge blanket of clouds would soon drop over the population and smother us to death. The mushroom-like cloud started to move in my direction. I began to run for my life, away from the rice paddy toward the house. I cannot remember clearly what happened thereafter because when I reached my house my heart was pounding wildly.

I was breathless, exhausted and faint.

Standing in front of the house were my relatives and neighbors who had come to let us know that a deadly, new type of bomb had been showered upon us; that Emperor Hirohito had proclaimed to the nation that Japan had surrendered in order to prevent further loss of human life and property. The Emperor challenged the nation to accept defeat courageously and surrender valiantly.

The bomb took its toll. Hiroshima was left desolate and in ruins. Countless lives of innocent men, women and children were snuffed out. Many who survived were left maimed, wounded, and misshapen. Others were to feel the effects of radiation for years to come. Even unborn generations have been and will continue to be affected as radiation continues its relentless damage to offspring yet to come. No food, no clothing, no roof over their heads; loved ones gone or in agony and pain. The thought that humans can degrade themselves to such wanton destruction appalled me.

Though Hiroshima is today but a dark page in the annals of history, its scars continue to live on in the lives of many of us. Peace on earth and good will toward all men. Peace in our individual hearts and in our lives—surely, there is not a worthier goal for us to strive for as we live today in the aftermath of that fateful day on the 6th of August, 1945.[16]

Endnotes

1. Translation by author of Tatsui Sato's personal history.
2. Correspondence, P. Lesley Lloyd to Tatsui Sato, 4 January 1965.
3. Correspondence, Earl C. Crockett to Tatsui Sato, 16 September 1965.
4. Correspondence, Bruce B. Clark to Tatsui Sato, 29 October 1965.
5. Correspondence, Chauncey C. Riddle to Tatsui Sato.
6. Comparative Japanese religions, Winter Semester 1966, study guide in possession of Tomiko Sato.
7. Rephrased from class questions, Japanese 322 class, BYU, Winter Semester 1966, in possession of Tomiko Sato.
8. Correspondence, Roger Austin to Tatsui Sato, 19 May 1966.
9. Written statement, Professor Gubler on Tatsui Sato, May 2002, in possession of author.

10. Tatsui Sato, "How to Make a Japanese Delicacy," English as a Second Language, class paper, Winter 1966, copy in possession of author.
11. Tatsui Sato, Comparison and contrast theme, English as a Second Language, class paper, Winter 1966, copy in possession of author.
12. Steve Berry, "Sato Addresses Fireside," Daily Universe, 11 March 1966, p. 11.
13. Tomiko Sato, from her personal history, about 1985, copy in possession of author.
14. Ibid.
15. Tomiko Sato, Church talk, about 1979, copy in possession of author.
16. Tomiko Sato, memories of Hiroshima, undated, copy in possession of author.

Chapter 9

Pioneering Efforts in Genealogy

THE TRANSLATION OF THE TEMPLE CEREMONY in the Hawaiian Temple ended Tatsui Sato's long tenure as the translator for the Church. He had planned on graduate studies at BYU as he was extremely interested in comparative religion. However, his many abilities developed over years of service were sought as the Genealogical Society determined to learn more about Japan and sought to provide members with more tools for research. After earning a reputation as a master translator, Tatsui spent the next decade as a pioneer in Japanese genealogical research. While most people his age were retiring, he was making contributions of great consequence.

A Growing Interest in Genealogy

Soon after President Edward Clissold opened the mission in 1948, efforts were made to bring the programs of the Church to the Japanese Saints. Tatsui assisted in translating Church manuals and materials while he was translator. When President Paul Andrus began his long tenure as mission president in 1956, he assigned one of his missionaries, Joyce C. Worthen, to help write a manual for the Japanese Saints on genealogical research and records submission.

Tatsui and Tomiko Sato at the Mini Genealogy Workshop in Japan, 1972

Tatsui helped her considerably in this effort, which took two years before a handbook was finally completed.[1] In compiling the information, Sister Worthen had to seek the advice of Archibald Bennett, the general secretary of the Genealogical Society in Salt Lake City. He helped to resolve special problems unique to Japanese genealogy, such as lunar years, Buddhist posthumous names and the use of "and/or" names for adoptions. Tatsui was able to gain a firm foundation at this time on the fundamentals of Japanese genealogy. This was to prove valuable later as we shall see.[2]

At the time, the members in Japan were using translated versions of English materials and very little was available on Japanese research and sources. Because of the opening of new temples and missions, the Church realized the need to expand beyond the traditional preoccupation with English, Scandinavian and German genealogy. An Oriental committee was formed at the Genealogical Society to study the problems of East Asian countries. Japan, Korea and China were of particular interest because these countries used non-Roman alphabets and had unique dating conventions. The committee even solicited opinions from professors at BYU and returned missionaries from Japan.

Hiroko Nanjo was hired in 1964 to process Japanese names, and a submissions manual for Japan was published in September of that year. It showed the influence of Sister Worthen's earlier attempts to reconcile problems with lunar years, adoptions and the listing of various jurisdictions. There is no question that the planned temple excursion of Japanese Saints to Hawaii in 1965 had a large influence in these decisions.[3]

The Oriental Committee met during April conference on 7 April 1965. Frank Smith of the Research Department, translator Tatsui Sato, and several others were in attendance, including George Fudge, the new managing director of the Genealogical Society. The committee discussed the urgent need to prepare more names for the coming temple excursion. Tatsui's role in the translation of the temple ceremony was a major topic of discussion along with how he could continue to help the Church.

The following year, the Oriental Committee, now headed by Elwin W. Jensen, asked for a knowledgeable Japanese person to help with a preliminary survey. It was suggested that several months in Japan would be valuable for John Orton, who at the time was involved in the United States and was assigned to help out with Asian acquisitions. Orton, with no knowledge of the language, asked for assistance in carrying out his mandate to do a preliminary survey of Japanese records. After he returned from Hawaii, Tatsui was hired part-time to work on special projects. Among the foremost of these was a compilation of Japanese names. He continued this work while teaching classes at Brigham Young University in the winter and spring of 1966.

Elwin Jensen wrote a glowing memo on 6 September 1966 to Brother Fudge regarding Tatsui's accomplishments during the past few months. Jensen listed Sato's resumé and accomplishments and pointed out: "The importance of his Japanese knowledge to the Society cannot be overestimated." He discussed the progress of the

Japanese name catalog Tatsui was working on, which Brother Fudge had requested.

Tatsui had already provided the names and characters for over 12,000 Japanese names, including Romanization to help the Oriental Section in names processing. In addition, Tatsui had also acquired reference books and compiled considerable information on Japanese research methodologies and customs. Tatsui's assistance the previous November in 1965 during Van Neiswander's visit to Japan was also noted.

Jensen made the following recommendation regarding using Tatsui more to study the records of Japan:[4]

> Another field, where the Society has a great need, is in knowledge of record sources in Japan. Other than in the area of modern vital records, the Society has very few basic and specific facts concerning Japanese record sources . . . . Brother Sato could be useful in enlarging this fund of knowledge, if such project were engaged in. It would be necessary, of course, that such prime record researching be carried out in Japan, by direct contact, and by actual visits and search. A factual report could be prepared. Since Brother Sato has a good knowledge of Japanese history and knows the modern Japanese language, and also has a fair knowledge of the olden style language and writing, he could more readily determine the content and value of any given series of records. Brother Sato is also versed in Japanese protocol and in the ancient social graces of the Orient. He could more tactfully, and more readily, approach supervisors, directors, archivists, librarians and other Japanese officials than could any uninformed European.

Jensen noted that "we are practically in a virgin field" and that Brother Sato was the man to help the Society in this great undertaking. He also pointed out the following:

> Brother Sato has a B.S. degree (from Japan in chemistry) and would be welcome in universities and scholastic circles. Since

many of the ancient records and genealogies are housed in governmental universities and in historical libraries, a welcome contact with these places would be of great value.[5]

Brother Jensen made the following proposal, obviously excited by what Brother Sato had done for the Society over the past months:

> A scholarly and knowledgeable Japanese person is needed to assist with research . . . . The present Oriental Committee needs a well educated Oriental man to sit on committee meetings and projects. We do not, at present, know of any available person, who is as qualified as is Brother Sato, for such projects. A man with Brother Sato's knowledge and ability could be extremely valuable in assisting with a preliminary records survey in Japan. Such a project is vital to future planning. A minimum of six weeks to three months in Japan might be needed for such a preliminary survey. A comprehensive Japanese name catalog would be helpful to records work now, and invaluable to future computer indexing programs. It is recommended that when Brother Sato's contract with BYU has expired, he be considered for employment to assist with these vital programs.[6]

Frank Smith, head of the Research Department, wrote a "Progress Report of Tatsui Sato" later in the month (dated 21 September 1966). Despite Tatsui's part-time status and commitment to BYU, he had accomplished considerable work on the Japanese Name Catalog Project and in acquiring reference sources. Brother Smith recommended the "project be continued and completed" and saw considerable value in "future computer programs." He also commented about Brother Sato's contributions:

> During Brother Sato's employment with the Society, in addition to the name cataloging project, he has supplied much valuable information to the Research and Oriental departments.

He then mentions the marriage of Tatsui to Tomiko Hiranishi in the temple and that Tatsui was now "eligible for American citizenship as he has made application for a permanent visa and is now in the process." Brother Smith mentions his qualifications in detail from his degree at Tohoku Imperial University to his impressive list of translations. Brother Smith concludes:

> Brother Sato is presently holding a temporary position as professor at the Brigham Young University teaching Japanese language and comparative religion. His contract with Brigham Young University will expire with the close of fall semester, ending the latter part of January 1967. During Brother Sato's tenure with the Society, it was noticed that he took a great deal of enjoyment and personal interest in the name cataloging project. During the period of his employment he voluntarily worked two Saturdays without compensation and has volunteered to work his Christmas holidays, again free of charge, on this project. He appears very interested in enlarging his knowledge of genealogy and the correct procedures to follow: As a witness of this, he is enrolling in a basic genealogy class at the BYU this term (from Stevenson).

Brother Smith then also recommended the hiring of Brother Sato as soon as he was available on a full-time basis as the Japanese specialist for the Research Department of the Genealogical Society:

> Brother Sato would like to return to the Society on the 1st of February 1967, after his contract with BYU expires, and continue to work on the name catalog project. It is recommended that Brother Sato be employed and allowed to continue work on the name catalog project as well as to continue providing his assistance and knowledge of customs and genealogical sources of Japan.[7]

Frank Smith, in charge of research at the time, wrote the following memo to his boss, George H. Fudge, who at the time held the title of Manager, Research and Development Division. In it he discussed Brother Sato's move to full-time status on 1 February 1967 and job assignments:

> Brother Tatsui Sato, as you know, begins working today on an hourly basis 40 hours per week. I suggest his time be equally divided between compiling and establishing of the Japanese royal lines in the Romanized fashion and the compiling of Japanese name lists, both given and surname. These lists should have the Oriental character as well as the Romanized name, and should be flagged as to whether the name is male or female in each instance. Any variation of phonetic spelling should be indicated on the list. I realize that these lists will be quite a while in developing because of the phonetic spellings, but a principal Romanized spelling should be adopted for both a given and surname catalog.[8]

After his marriage to Tomiko Hiranishi on 28 July 1966, he was hired on a full-time basis to translate various records into English and to continue working on the names project. Tomiko Sato replaced Hiroko Nanjo on a part-time basis under Elwin Jensen in names processing. A year later she also was hired on a full-time basis. Interestingly, Tatsui asked his old friend Elder Gordon B. Hinckley for a letter of recommendation. As was his nature, he wrote a gracious letter of thanks, dated 13 February 1967:

> I am very glad to tell you that I was given a good job at the research section of the Genealogical Society and have been working since the 1st of February. At present my work is to make a name catalogue of Japanese people which is the continuation of the work that I did during the last summer vacation; also I am making the royalty pedigree which is the pedigree chart of the Imperial household of Japan. I am very happy to engage in this important work for the genealogical research of Japanese people.
>
> I am very grateful for this work and would like to express my heartfelt thanks for your kindness in writing a letter of good

> recommendation to President Burton of the Genealogical Society. My family also would like to join in expressing their happiness and gratitude for the blessing you have given to our family.[9]

Of course, Elder Hinckley, upon becoming a General Authority in 1960, was asked to supervise the missions in East Asia and became very well acquainted with Tatsui and his enormous contributions to the work. In order for Tatsui to work on a more permanent basis, however, he had to apply for permanent residence. A notification of this was sent by Claude P. Kidder of the Immigration of Naturalization Service, dated January 12, 1967: "I am pleased to inform you that your application for adjustment of status to that of lawful permanent resident of the United States has been approved."[10]

Since he was planning a trip to Japan soon, Brother Sato sought advice from Brother Harrison "Ted" Price—along with Kojin Goya, the first missionaries into Narumi and Nagoya—now a mission president in Tokyo, but formerly an official of the Immigration and Naturalization Service:

> I was very pleased to receive your letter of February 22, 1968 and learn that you will be making your first trip to Japan on or about May 2. Sister Price and I and your many friends here in the Church look forward to seeing you again. We had expected that your work would require a return trip to your homeland and are happy you did not wait too long. This will be a very pleasant visit for Yasuo, his wife and for your dear mother in Narumi.
>
> As you have been lawfully admitted to the United States for permanent residence, you may re-enter the United States with the alien registration card (Form I-151) without a new visa following a stay abroad of less than one year. You will, of course, need a valid passport or Japanese travel document. The passport which you now hold will become invalid upon your return to Japan. You may secure a new Japanese travel document from a Japanese consular office in the United States prior to your departure or you may apply for a new passport through the foreign

> ministry after your return to Japan. There should be very little delay in securing the new passport although the Gaimusho may request a more recent copy of your family register. You are still a citizen of Japan, of course, and will not require a Japanese visa or any other permission to return to Japan . . . .We hope that your busy schedule while in Japan will allow a little time to visit with us again.[11]

Surveying Records in Japan

In May 1968, Tatsui accompanied John Orton to Japan for a lengthy survey trip. They visited various *koseki* (household register) offices and had extensive deliberations about this vital Japanese source. They also visited Japanese Buddhist temples and were particularly interested in Buddhist death registers and cemetery records. At each repository, they took photos of various record types and made up a "Researcher's Record Evaluation" of each of the sources.

They also had a lengthy meeting with Akira Hayami of Keio University, Japan's foremost authority on the *shumon-cho* (examination of religion registers). Hayami had done extensive research on a large group of these records that had literally "surfaced" from a lake in Nagano Prefecture. This was a very productive trip in terms of surveying Japanese sources and repositories. Sato played a huge role in translating these materials and in helping produce a paper on the "Genealogical Sources of Japan."

An initial listing, dated from January 1967, was greatly updated, and various translated samples were added later in 1968. Many follow up letters were written to flesh out this information, including letters to several participants of the 1969 World Conference of Records. This became the basis of a more comprehensive paper published by the Genealogical Society in 1973.[12]

The trip was also mentioned by Professor Spencer Palmer in *The Church Encounters Asia*:

> During the Japan portion of the trip they were extremely successful in getting information from government offices and record keepers, as well as private and public depositories in the Tokyo and Kyoto-Nara areas of Japan.[13]

Of course, much of the success was due to preparation and Brother Sato's expertise in the various records. He had done an immense amount of research in order to understand Japanese genealogy and the various sources.

During this time, Sato spent much time in his major assignment in creating a Japanese surname catalog for the Research Department. Sato used Ryo Ota's monumental survey of Japanese surnames and lineages as a basis and included both Romanized and kana indexes for the various characters. Palmer records the following:

> The Japanese surname catalog has developed into a complex project. For nearly three years, Brother Sato has been compiling surnames from various sources. The catalog now boasts a total of some 80,000 surnames. He is now arranging them in a useable form, with volume one completed and a project total of ten to twelve volumes. The main purpose in the Genealogical Society's undertaking this project is to assist in clearing names for temple work when Japan is included in the computerized GIANT program. It is also anticipated that the surname catalog will serve as a guide for Japanese and Westerners alike in correcting pronunciation and spelling.

Besides the surname project, Palmer mentions Brother Sato's preoccupation with Japanese royalty. The Genealogical Society had assumed the responsibility to do the royalty research, and had submitted the lineage of the Imperial Family in order to prevent unnecessary duplication and to avoid research errors. Even then, Brother Sato had noted discrepancies in sources as to birth and death dates in the early Medieval Period. He certainly realized that more original research might be required.[14]

This required a huge effort and was accompanied by translations and research on the origins of surnames and an intensive list of Japanese research aids, repositories, and local history associations. An article on Brother Sato's role as a translator appeared in the August 1970 issue of the *Genealogical Society Observer*, recognizing his efforts.[15] The same article praises Tatsui's contributions to genealogy and family history, his involvement with the 1970 trip by Japanese Saints to the Salt Lake Temple and his quest for American citizenship:

> New U.S. Citizen: Tatsui Sato's years of service are a major contribution to genealogical work and to the progress of the Church among the Japanese.
>
> Brother Sato became an employee of the Genealogical Society after fulfilling his contract with BYU in 1966. Tatsui worked with Elwin Jensen, Oriental records analyst, and then was assigned to the Research Department to translate and assist with Oriental languages. His major assignment at present is translating a catalog of 75,000 Japanese surnames, written in Chinese, into Japanese and English for use in temple ordinance work. He also assists Brother John Orton, research specialist for Oriental and Eastern Asian nations, and accompanied Brother Orton on a trip to Japan in 1968.
>
> Another present work in which he is engaged is one which gives him great joy, that of working with other Japanese members in preparing for the visit and a series of special temple sessions scheduled in the Salt Lake Temple this fall for 315 members who will come from Japan at October conference time. He and other members of the Salt Lake Japanese branch of the Church were set apart to this preparation call on 13 May by Elder Edward H. Sorensen, second counselor in the Salt Lake Temple presidency.
>
> The Japanese branch of about 150 members meets in the 8th Ward chapel, Liberty Stake. Brother Sato is high priests group leader of the seven high priest members of the branch.
>
> On July 20, 1966, Brother Sato married Tomiko Hiranishi

> in the Salt Lake Temple. She also is a GS employee, working with Brother Jensen in the Oriental Records Section. She was born in Wyoming but is also a convert to the Church. . . .
>
> Brother Sato, who studied citizenship at the Horace Mann Jr. High School four months and then passed his test on 28 January, passed one more of many milestones when he gave the oath that made him a citizen of the United States on 11 May.[16]

The various projects Brother Sato was involved in were listed in a letter from John Orton to Frank Smith dated 31 July 1973. They included a guide for the old script, an article on the use of family crests in genealogical research, a study of the calendar system, studies of domain boundaries of the Tokugawa period, research and compilations on Japanese royalty and nobility and other projects already listed.[17]

The First World Conference on Records (1969)

The Genealogical Society, as part of its efforts to promote worldwide acquisitions and records preservation, planned a monumental World Conference on Records to be held in Salt Lake City from 5–8 August 1969 in conjunction with its 75th Diamond Jubilee. Over 7,000 participants from 46 nations attended sessions held in the Salt Palace venue. John Orton and Tatsui Sato were closely involved in the planning process and chose scholars closely involved in research on Japanese sources and research.

Dr. Norio Fujiki, a noted geneticist from the Aichi Colony for the Mentally and Physically Handicapped and later director of similar research at Fukui Medical School, delivered a paper entitled "The Koseki as a Source for Genetic Studies" based on village research by a group of doctors in Japan. This group, many of which are members of the Japanese Biological Association, has been very helpful over the years in assisting the Society in understanding and acquiring records in Japan.

Dr. Toshiyuki Yanase, of the faculty of medicine at Kyushu University, also presented similar research: "The Koseki as a Source for the Scholar of Japan." Masao Yoshida, head of the International Service Section of the National Diet Library in Tokyo, gave an overview of the operation and collections at Japan's Library of Congress: "The National Diet Library in Japan: Its Organization, Functions and Programs."

Two American scholars involved in Japanese records research also were involved. Ray A. Moore of Amherst University in Massachusetts presented "Family Records and Social History in Tokugawa Japan." Professor Noboru Hiraga of the University of Washington discussed "The Extent and Preservation of Original Historical Records in Japan."

These contacts and relationships proved very crucial in the years that followed, and provided an increased understanding of sources and even more contacts in Japan. Brother Sato, with his prestige and bi-lingual ability, was greatly responsible for bringing in these various experts and adding to the success of this breakthrough conference.[18]

Great Hopes for Acquisitions in Japan

At the time, there was considerable optimism about records filming prospects in Japan. Brothers Orton and Sato were enamored particularly with the *koseki* (Japanese household register) because of its coverage and particular preservation needs. This was especially true in light of news that older records were being destroyed. So John Orton, with translation and research assistance from Tatsui Sato, initiated a comprehensive survey of *koseki* record offices in February of 1971 to determine the policies of individual offices and the number of records involved.

Particular questions included:

- The number of volumes of *koseki* before 1900
- The number of *midashi-cho* (index) in the office
- The number of pages on the average for each volume

- Whether or not the office had submitted an application for permission to destroy the record
- What records were included in this decision
- Whether records were donated to archives or museums
- Questions on condition and preservation of records

The survey sample included records of offices in larger cities, towns and villages and proved very helpful for estimating the scope of a possible project.[19]

As acquisition of the *koseki* was still at the top of the priority list of the Records Selection Committee, John Orton made several proposals to elicit Church support for a huge project to film registers around Japan. In a letter dated 6 May 1971 from Elder Theodore Burton, who was then the General Authority manager of the Genealogical Society, to the First Presidency, permission was sought for filming an estimated 12–14 pre-1900 registers. This was to require 13 and one-third camera years and considerable budget. The estimate was based on a bid received from Microfilm Services, a Japanese contract microfilm company that had been approached about filming. Approval was given by the First Presidency to proceed if acquisitions could be negotiated.[20]

Once again, John Orton and Tatsui Sato went to Japan in 1971 for a survey trip and continued to visit archives, temples and *koseki* offices. They also contacted Professor Hayami and were able to peruse his large collection of *shumon-cho* (examination of religion registers). In addition, they visited cemeteries in Tokyo and Kyoto. The trip report also showed interest in and visits to several Shinto shrines to examine the genealogies of Shinto priests and tombstones near the shrines. This information was later compiled as part of the major sources paper. The trip resulted in further recommendations to the Records Selection Committee regarding acquisition: genealogies from the Mombusho Shiryokan, family genealogies found in archives and collections, and Buddhist sources to 1900.[21]

Attempts to get permission from the Ministry of Justice, Bureau of Civil Affairs, to film the early *koseki*, slated for disposal, continued as several letters were written with little response. Delbert Roach notified Theodore Burton of this on 21 September.[22] Tatsui Sato had translated a letter on behalf of the Society, and apparently there were efforts to get former mission president Harrison "Ted" Price to assist—Price was then district director of the Immigration and Nationalization Service in San Francisco. There is no record of the results of this strategy.

John Orton requested help in Japan for listing records in a projected nine-month project, preparing to film repositories under negotiation. One of the primary targets was the Mombusho Shiryokan, where an estimated 5.3 million exposures of mostly genealogies were awaiting budget approval and final negotiations. The following year, Akira Amano from Sendai was hired to represent the Genealogical Society of Utah in Japan. He set up operations in his home in Sendai and began to list and negotiate records for acquisition in various locations in Japan. In 1973 he was authorized to begin a pilot project to film Buddhist *kakocho* (death registry) in the Sendai area where he was able to negotiate the filming of the records of about a dozen temples.[23]

Tatsui was extremely busy studying and preparing materials on Japanese records and research at this time. The Research Department filed an annual report of the projects researchers were working on. His was most impressive. For example, in 1972 he was:

- Completing the extensive surname catalog of 62,000 names
- Working through the microfilm listings from Japan
- Researching and writing a large number of papers, including:
  - "Guide to Japanese Old Script" (for paleography classes)
  - "Japanese Genealogical Terms"
  - "Japanese Calendar System"
  - "Use of Mon (crests) in Genealogical Research"
  - "The Boundaries of the Tokugawa Period"

"The Koseki as a Genealogical Source"
"The Population Registers of the Tokugawa Period"
"Compiled Genealogies of the Kuge, Daimyo and Samurai"[24]

The following year (1973), Brother Sato was:

- Listing libraries and archives
- Training Kenji Suzuki (and the catalogers) in reading the old script
- Organizing and proofreading listings from Japan
- Doing more papers, including:
  New ones on local history groups
  "Chronology of Historical Events in Japan"
  "Migration, Immigration and Emigration" [25]

Tatsui translated considerable information on Japanese sources. For example, he thoroughly researched and wrote about *bukan* (books of heraldry), a record used by the samurai class to show "names, residences, domains, titles, fiefs, house crests, arms, genealogies, the kinds and amounts of presents offered to the shogun, and those received from the shogun, the names of principal retainers, etc."[26] Brother Sato continued with examples (including photos) and translations of several different types of *bukan*. This information was invaluable to management and later formed the basis for a paper on the major sources of Japan, though the paper did not contain as much detail.

In another paper entitled, "Helps for the Researcher," Tatsui wrote up a thorough list of Japanese terms—for example, "*Agemai*" (he included the Chinese characters). In 1722, Yoshimune, the eighth shogun (1684–1751), introduced a policy called the reform of the Kyoho era with the purpose of establishing feudal control. Every *daimyo* (ruling family) had to contribute one hundred *koku* (one *koku* equals 4.96 bushels) per 10,000 *koku* of rice or the equivalent in money. This contribution in rice was called "*Agemai*." Also, rice donated to feudal lords by farmers in order to relieve the financial difficulty of the *Han* (feudal domain) was called "*Agemai*."[27] Since the Genealogical Society was researching and acquiring land records and the records of samurai, this information was critical in understanding the makeup of these records.

John Orton was named the new manager of Asia and Pacific Acquisitions in 1974, as international acquisitions was expanded. Tatsui was still involved in translating and working on special projects. It is at this time that Kenji Suzuki was hired as Field Operations manager in charge of Japanese acquisitions. Kenji had received a master's degree in Linguistics at BYU and was initially hired in July 1973 to help out in the areas of cataloging and names processing. He was a valuable find because of his superb ability to work with people and manage the operation. Brother Amano came under his tutelage as the field representative in Japan.[28]

In retrospect, this was one of the most productive periods in terms of acquisitions. Brother Sato played a huge role in making this possible with his language and records expertise. Once again he was the pioneer and established the foundation for others who followed.

Continued Correspondence

Interestingly, Tatsui was being pressured to retire under the mandatory age limit, but continued to stave off his retirement. When he became 71 and received even more pressure from Personnel, he wrote a letter to Boyd K. Packer to help him; this letter was written probably in January of 1970:

> Brother Packer, may I tell you that I have been working for the Church for over 25 years since I was assigned as official translator in 1949; still I would like to work devoting my background and experience to the Church . . . May I ask you a favor again to seek for any possibility of employment so that I may continue to

> render service to the Church? If you would do so, I appreciate it very much.[29]

Apparently, the letter was successful, as there is no more mention of this problem. And he continued to work, though on an hourly basis, for the Genealogical Society.

Tatsui wrote a letter to congratulate Elder Boyd K. Packer when he was sustained to the Quorum of the Twelve Apostles on 6 April 1970. Elder Packer had been an Assistant to the Twelve since 1961 and was only 45 when he became an Apostle.

The following letter is dated 1 May 1970 and is addressed to Tatsui Sato:

> Dear Brother Sato and family:
>
> It was kind of you to send congratulations. I feel very humble in this new calling and responsibility. I appreciate your good wishes. We love and appreciate you good people and send our best and blessing to you.
>
> Sincerely,
> Boyd K. Packer[30]

Brother Davis mentioned in a letter dated 15 October 1973 that he had "talked to Brother Packer for a few minutes" at a stake conference. He was now living in the Los Angeles area and invited the Satos to visit.[31] The tone of the letter captured a great enduring friendship.

Another letter that should be included was written on 3 February 1975 from Tatsui to Elder Packer. Tatsui refers to Elder Packer's letter of 9 January and tells him: "I am very glad that you like my humble Christmas present which is the token of my appreciation for your brotherhood." He mentioned to Elder Packer that, "owing to your kindness," he continued to work for the Genealogical Society but on an hourly basis. Then he adds: "Since then, I have been working to the best of my ability, without vacation and without sick leave, being commended by my supervisor, Brother Frank Smith as the hardest worker in his [Research] department."

Tatsui then mentions the various activities he was involved in:

> Last year, I was sent to Japan by order of the Genealogical Society to open a way for microfilming major genealogical sources in Japan. Fortunately, I hit the best archives in Japan in Yamaguchi Prefecture, where more than 500,000 titles of precious old documents are deposited. The negotiations are concluded and at present a camera man of the society is taking the microfilm of the old documents at the archives.

Tatsui mentions beginning a class in Japanese paleography to help Genealogical Society staff learn to catalog and understand the records. The students included: Kenji Suzuki, who had just joined the Society in acquisitions, and catalogers Hiroko Mitarai, Kazuko Sasaki, Mitsuko Chinen, Yuri Noda and myself, Komae Mori.

Tatsui noted: "I believe their achievements will become the great assets of the society." He also mentioned that he had completed the "Japanese Name Catalogue," which "contained 62,000 Japanese names with their correct pronunciations in Roman letter and Japanese letter." He had hoped to publish it in Taiwan and believed it had great value for researchers and people involved in many fields dealing with Japan.[32] The catalog was put on microfiche; however, it was not published, though it certainly is a valuable but largely unknown source.

Though "retired," Tatsui continued to provide training for his successor, Greg Gubler, and to once again teach a weekly paleography class during 1976–78. He also was asked to help out in Translation Services as part of a calling from the Presiding Bishopric.

The following letter under the signatures of Victor L. Brown, H. Burke Peterson, and J. Richard Clark, dated 8 April 1977, is from the Office of the Presiding Bishop:

> Dear Brother Sato:
>
> With the approval of your stake president we are pleased to extend a call to serve as an Interpreter-Japanese to labor under the

> supervisor of Translation Services. This assignment will require your part-time Church service for an indefinite period of time. It will not be required that you be released from your present Church assignments.
>
> If you can accept this call, please advise us by letter at your earliest possible convenience. Ralph J. Richards, supervisor of Translation and Interpretation, will give you further information pertaining to this call. All of your assignments will be made under the direction of Brother Richards and those whom he may designate.
>
> In your labors we urge you to remember the lessons given by the Lord in this dispensation and recorded in Section Nine of the Doctrine and Covenants. As you are faithful you will be blessed with the gift of translation; the gift will come after you have expended your finest effort and to the degree you maintain an effective personal relationship with your Heavenly Father.
>
> We extend to you our appreciation for your willingness to serve and pray the Lord's blessing upon you.[33]

Of course, with a master translator/interpreter and a spiritual giant like Brother Sato, much of this advice seemed superfluous. He did help out for nearly two years until he and his wife, Tomiko, were called as temple missionaries in 1980 with the opening of the Tokyo Temple.

Working with Brother Sato

Greg Gubler felt fortunate to receive considerable training from Tatsui as his successor in the research department, now renamed Priesthood Genealogy. He had first met Tatsui in July 1963 at Chuo Shibu (Central Branch) in Tokyo. Like many other missionaries, he was very impressed by his quiet, scholarly bearing. He continued to see him at conferences in the Tokyo area. He was well aware of Tatsui's tremendous reputation and accomplishments. He was considered a mission icon. Later, as mentioned already, he had him as a Japanese teacher in the winter of 1966. Thus, joining Priesthood Genealogy and being able to work with Tatsui was a great joy to him.

With weekly training sessions for over two years (August 1976–February 1979), as well as a paleography class for over a year, Gubler learned to love and respect his *sensei* (teacher). Gubler fully credits his teacher for laying the foundation with respect to an understanding of Japanese sources and research. He also worked very closely with Tomiko on many projects. Despite Brother Sato's great reservoir of knowledge, he continued to live humbly in his small, pale-yellow house; and Brother Gubler would visit almost yearly. In his notes, besides volumes of information about records, Gubler also recorded insights Tatsui had into life:

> Tatsui believed strongly that Americans could learn from the Japanese in their appreciation for nature. He had gone through many difficult years trying to survive and felt fortunate to just have "running water." "On the other hand," he pointed out, "Americans use drinking water for everything and waste a pure and scarce resource." "American society," he stressed, "was very wasteful." He said: "Oriental cultures realize the importance of conservation." Tatsui felt that reliance on expensive drugs and vitamins in this country was not wise. He said, "People heal naturally, they don't need these various things." Once again, people were wasting their money.
>
> He did believe in *mokusa*, a Japanese art of healing through heat applied to certain spots and acupuncture. He was very skilled in this and tried it on a few close friends. He pointed out that Oriental medicine was proven by many years of trial and error. People, he felt, went to doctors too often. This was expensive. He advocated living the Word of Wisdom, in fact in using wisdom in all things, stressing the importance of balance in our lives. Likewise, he was disappointed in the morals and standards of American society. He pointed out the importance of righteousness and true gratitude to the Lord and others, and stressed that we should not take things for granted.

> He always felt strongly about the example of Ieyasu Tokugawa (who unified Japan under his banner). He felt he was an example of resolution, patience and bravery. The great Japanese virtue of *ganbarru* (pushing ahead despite the odds) greatly appealed to him. He also disliked using people and trying to get ahead by stepping on people. He used the example of the *gyoretsu* (retainers following their lord) as what many people do. We should not follow blindly; neither should we have false loyalty just to get ahead. Brother Sato felt strongly that people should follow virtue; he believed we all have a great debt to our ancestors, and he had a love for scholarship and discovering the truth.

Brother Gubler felt that he was sitting at the foot of a sage, a man of great wisdom and understanding—a humble man, yet a man of enduring greatness.[34]

Endnotes

1. Telephone interview with Paul Andrus by Greg Gubler, 4 August 2004.
2. Greg Gubler, "The Genealogical Society of Utah and Japan," Manuscript copy, 2001.
3. Ibid.
4. Ibid.
5. Memo regarding Tatsui Sato, Elwin W. Jensen to George Fudge, 6 September 1966, Microfilm copy of Asian Project Files, in possession of Greg Gubler.
6. Ibid., continuation of above memo.
7. Memo from Frank Smith to George Fudge, 21 September 1966, Microfilm copy of Asian Project Files, in possession of Greg Gubler.
8. Memo from Frank Smith to George Fudge, 1 February 1967, Microfilm copy of Asian Project Files, in possession of Greg Gubler.
9. Correspondence, Tatsui Sato to Gordon B. Hinckley, 13 February 1966.
10. Correspondence, Charles P. Kidder to Tatsui Sato, 12 January 1967.
11. Correspondence, Harrison "Ted" Price to Tatsui Sato, 28 February 1968.
12. Greg Gubler, "The Genealogical Society of Utah and Japan," Manuscript copy, 2001.
13. Spencer Palmer, *The Church Encounters Asia*, p. 84.
14. Ibid., pp. 85–86.
15. Article on Tatsui Sato in *Genealogical Society Observer*. May 1970, VI–5, p. 1.
16. Ibid.

17. Memo from John Orton to Frank Smith, 31 July 1973, Microfilm copy of Asian Project Files, in possession of Greg Gubler.
18. Greg Gubler, "The Genealogical Society of Utah and Japan," Manuscript copy, 2001.
19. Ibid., p. 27.
20. Memo from Theodore Burton to First Presidency, 6 May 1971, Microfilm copy of Asian Project Files, in possession of Greg Gubler.
21. Greg Gubler, "The Genealogical Society of Utah and Japan," Manuscript copy, 2001, p. 29.
22. Correspondence, Delbert Roach to Theodore Burton, 6 May 1973, Microfilm copy of Asian Project Files, in possession of Greg Gubler.
23. Greg Gubler, "The Genealogical Society of Utah and Japan," Manuscript copy, 2001, p. 31.
24. "Projects for completion by Brother Sato," Memo from John Orton to Frank Smith, 22 March 1972, Microfilm copy of Asian Project Files, in possession of Greg Gubler.
25. "Projects for completion by Brother Sato," Memo from John Orton to Frank Smith, 31 July 1973, Microfilm copy of Asian Project Files, in possession of Greg Gubler.
26. Tatsui Sato, Preliminary paper entitled "Major sources of genealogical information," manuscript copy, 1973.
27. Tatsui Sato, "Helps for the researcher," manuscript copy of definitions of Japanese terms, 1973.
28. Greg Gubler, "The Genealogical Society of Utah and Japan," Manuscript copy, 2001. p. 31.
29. Correspondence, Tatsui Sato to Boyd K. Packer, about January 1970.
30. Correspondence, Boyd K. Packer to Tatsui Sato, 1 May 1970.
31. Correspondence, Reed and Lula Davis to Tatsui and Tomiko Sato, 15 October 1973.
32. Correspondence, Tatsui Sato to Boyd K. Packer, 3 February 1975.
33. Correspondence, Office of the Presiding Bishop to Tatsui Sato, 8 April 1979.
34. Greg Gubler, "Notes from meetings with Brother Sato," 1976–78.

Chapter 10

Temple Mission to Japan

PRESIDENT KIMBALL, at an area conference on 8 August 1975, in Tokyo's Budokan, announced that a temple would be built in Tokyo on the site of the Azabu mission home.

This decision was greeted with great excitement as the dawn of a new day for the Church in Japan. Brother Sato was closely involved behind the scenes in the planning of the new temple, particularly in the decision to make a new translation of the newly revised English temple ceremony. Meetings were held in conjunction with the area conference. The following is taken from the minutes of a meeting held on August 8th, at the New Otani Hotel in Tokyo.

This meeting was a follow up to a meeting the previous day. Those present besides Tatsui Sato included Elder O. Leslie Stone (presiding), who was head of the Temple Department, Elder Adney K. Komatsu, Paul Andrus, Kan Watanabe, and D'Monte Coombs. The purpose of the meeting was to set up a schedule to revise the temple ceremony to fit the new film version, as the present Japanese version was nearly 30 minutes longer than the new film version.

Another objective of this second meeting was to make sure that the version that would be finally approved would be good enough to stand the test of time. The importance of input and having a mutually acceptable translation was emphasized. Elder Komatsu, Brother Andrus, Shuichi Yaginuma and Kan Watanabe (the latter two from the Translation Department in Tokyo) were asked to be on the committee to review the revision.

Tatsui Sato was asked if he would accept the assignment to make the revisions. Because Tatsui Sato was scheduled to retire in January 1976, Brother Coombs asked about transferring him from the Genealogical Department to Translation Services to complete this assignment. It was determined that if the translation went beyond the first of January, Tatsui's retirement could be delayed, if necessary. However, if he finished earlier, Translation Services could give him other work until his retirement date.

Tatsui Sato, Tokyo Temple

Brother Sato then asked how this would be administered. Brother Coombs, who was director of Translation Services, indicated that Roger Dock would provide Tatsui Sato his material, make available facilities and take care of his office needs. He would also supervise Tatsui's activities in Translation Services.

Tatsui expressed concern about any changes that may be suggested during the filming of the revised translation. He was assured that he would be there throughout the recording to provide technical assistance. Also, Shuichi Yaginuma would represent the Translation Department in Tokyo and would have the final say regarding any changes proposed, but it was pointed out he could not override Tatsui in final translation decisions. However, the desire of those assembled was for the two to work in harmony and with dispatch. If there were disagreements or questions of interpretation, it was suggested they be brought to Brother Coomb's attention and/or referred to Elder Stone and the Temple Committee.[1]

Still Busy in "Retirement"

After finishing this assignment, Brother Sato finally retired—actually, he was continuing to assist at the Genealogical Department in teaching paleography to staff members involved with Japan and teaching Brother Gubler about the intricacies of Japanese sources and genealogical research. He was also helping many patrons in submitting their family genealogies and writing characters on various forms. He continued to be much in demand as a translator and expert on traditional Japanese culture.

As usual, the Satos received a thoughtful Christmas greeting from Ray Hanks and his family in Orem just before Christmas in 1978. After inquiring about the Satos and wishing them a joyous Christmas season, Ray and Edith Hanks thanked the Satos for their "sweet friendship" and "love and devotion" to our "Heavenly Father's great Latter-day work."[2]

Elder Boyd K. Packer wrote Tatsui the following spring regarding assisting Dr. R. Lanier Britsch of Brigham Young University in his efforts to document the history of the Church in Japan. Personally addressed to Brother Sato, the letter follows:

> We have been attempting to collect the history of the Church in various places of the world by interviewing members who have participated in events of the past generation. In a meeting of the Historical Advisory Committee some two months ago, Brother Lanier Britsch was assigned to make an appointment with you for such an interview. We understand that you wanted to make sure that his interview was authorized. We hope that you will cooperate with him and recall with him all of the events that you can remember relating to the development of the Church activities in Japan, beginning with your baptism on July 7, 1946. I well remember the conference held the morning of your baptism, and then going out to the university to the swimming pool where I baptized Sister Sato and Elliott Richards baptized you. That was the opening of the work in Japan in this generation. I hope you will recall for Brother Britsch all of the events you have witnessed since that day, so it can become a part of the recorded history of the Church.
>
> We wish you and Sister Sato every blessing and value your friendship.
>
> Faithfully yours,
> Boyd K. Packer[3]

Mission Call to Tokyo Temple

Tatsui acknowledged his and Tomiko's mission call in a letter dated 19 August 1980 to President Dwayne N. Anderson, the new president of the Tokyo Temple.

The excitement of the call and returning to a temple in Japan is evident:

> May I express the sincere gratitude we felt when we found out that we were called to serve for the Church of Jesus Christ of Latter-day Saints to assist with the work in the Tokyo Temple. We accepted the call willingly feeling inspired that the Lord has a special will to use us as an instrument in His hand for the benefit of the living saints and their deceased ancestors. We are so glad to go to Tokyo and serve the Lord. We will work in the service of

God by keeping His commandments and following the counsel of the temple president.

Please give our best regards to Sister Andersen.[4]

With great thankfulness, Brother Sato wrote a letter to the First Presidency, mentioning Elder Cowley's prophecy and his own willingness to serve a temple mission:

Dear Brethren:

May I express the sincere gratitude I felt when I found out that I was called to serve as a missionary for The Church of Jesus Christ of Latter-day Saints, which is the true church restored by the prophet of God, Joseph Smith, Jr. I accept this call willingly feeling inspired that the Lord has a special will to use me as an instrument in His hand in performing sacred ordinances in the House of the Lord in Tokyo in behalf of the living saints and their deceased ancestors.

May I tell you that I am fortunately one of the witnesses that was present when Elder Matthew Cowley came to Tokyo to offer the dedicatory prayer for the mission home. In his prayer, he prophesied that the Japanese Saints would someday have a temple, even temples, in Japan.

I am so glad to go to Tokyo and serve the Lord in the temple, which is the realization of our fervent hopes. I will work in the service of God with all my heart, might, mind and strength—without looking for the worldly things—so that I may stand blameless before God at the last day.

Tatsui Sato[5]

The Satos immediately packed and left for Japan to be ready for the open house of the temple that was held on 13 September 1980. President Spencer W. Kimball formally opened the temple with the dedication on 27 October. This was the first temple in Asia and, as such, signaled that the Church had now become a "global Church."[6] Of course, for the first member after the war, this was an especially significant event, the fulfillment of a prophecy he had heard many years before.

Support from Friends

Two months later, the Satos received a message of support from Ralph Shino, a close friend and a member of the high council of the Liberty Stake in Salt Lake City:

> Enclosed, you will find a small token of our love and appreciation for the work you are engaged in. Please use the check for whatever you wish. All of us extend our love and greetings at this joyous holiday season and pray that you will be very successful this month in your proselyte work.
>
> Take full advantage of the occasion when the hearts and minds of most people are softened by the spirit of Christmas. They should be more receptive to your message than ever before. The Lord loves you and will continue to inspire and direct you to the honest in heart. Keep close to the Lord by doing what Enos did as recorded in the book of Enos, as well as the Lord's admonition to Oliver Cowdery in Section 8:2 and also in Section 9:8. You must feel that Spirit when you are teaching and likewise your investigators will feel that Spirit through you, as you look into their eyes and see that spark of light as you testify and challenge them for baptism.[7]

A Polynesian friend and member of the Liberty Stake high council wrote the Satos a letter of encouragement the following May:

> I'm grateful for the opportunity in which I have, to sit and write one of our Heavenly Father's humble servants. I would like to express my gratitude and the whole Liberty Stake for the great work in which you are doing. If we are happy, just think, how happy and proud our Heavenly Father is, with the great work, in which you are doing. He has no voices, no hands, but our hands, no feet, but our feet, here upon the earth, to spread forth His

gospel. He is putting all his trust upon you, to do his work, and we are all counting on it. He has many blessings bestowed for you, and it can all be yours, as you go forth in serving his loved ones who have not heard of the gospel. Remember that one spirit is more important than the whole world. You have been blessed, to come forth and called to be messengers of God, in these the last days, for everyone is the children of our Father in Heaven, but you have the key and the power to gather them to build forth the kingdom of God here upon the earth.

Remember, many have been called, but only few are chosen, and you have been called and chosen to deliver the truth. The doors are all opening for you, and the hearts of men are softened, to hear the truth, put on the whole armor of God, and go forth, our prayers are always with you. May God bless you, as you go forth in doing his work.[8]

The Passing of Ray Hanks

Brother Ray Hanks, who along with Mel Arnold initially met Tatsui, passed away just before the conclusion of Brother and Sister Sato's mission. Reed Davis and his wife, very close friends to Brother and Sister Hanks, wrote about this in a letter to the Satos in January of 1982:

> Time flies so fast and you have been at your job in the Tokyo Temple for over a year. Today is another day in our life to be remembered by you and me. Today I attended the funeral of our dear friend, Raymond E. Hanks. It was a thrill to attend his funeral, as I know that he is now with his God. Ray was truly a great missionary, and never failed to ask the "golden question."
>
> It was with great pride he has told me many times that meeting Tatsui Sato was his greatest testimony and that he really loved you and was so proud of you. We may miss Ray, but we can be happy to know that he will be there to meet us when we have fulfilled our time on this earth.
>
> I told Ray's wife, Edith, that I would inform you of Ray's

death, and she sends her love and best wishes to you and Sister Sato. . . . Enclosed is copy of the obituary and funeral program and our missionary contributions to the Satos.[9]

Tatsui credited Brother Hanks for opening his eyes and heart to the gospel in his response to Brother Davis:

> Thank you for your letter to inform me of the passing away of Brother Ray Hanks who was really the God-sent missionary to open my eyes and heart to the true Gospel restored by the true Prophet of God, Joseph Smith. I agree with your testimony that Brother Hanks is now in the Eternal Life, the Highest Glory where God the Father and Jesus Christ are. Even though he passed away which is the saddest news to me, it strengthens my testimony that the righteous man receives the highest glory, the Eternal Life. I enclosed a photograph which was taken when he visited Tokyo Temple and attended the missionary meeting held at Ginza, Tokyo. I am sure it will strengthen our dear memory of his sincere friendship and true love. May I express my sincere thanks for your generous donation to me.[10]

Ray's wife, Edith, welcomed the Satos home and wrote about his passing in December:

> Welcome back to Utah! I am sure you did a wonderful job at the temple while you were in Japan. I am so glad Ray got to go over to Japan for the temple dedication, and to visit with you.
>
> Have you heard that Ray passed away last January 12th? He went in such a hurry that it was a real shock to me. We went to church Sunday morning, and came home and he ate a good dinner. Then about 2:00 p.m. he took a stroke (or a cerebral hemorrhage) and I rushed him to the hospital. He went into a coma, and died Tuesday afternoon. It was a real shock, but I am glad he did not have to remain in a coma for weeks or months like some people do. I am sure he is receiving his blessings in heaven. It has

been lonely without him, but I try to count my blessings and keep cheerful.[11]

Sister Hanks wrote the following week to the Satos:

> I love you! Thanks so much for the picture you sent me of Ray, Amy, and you taken over in Japan. I will always treasure it. I have it on my mantel in the living room so I can see it and enjoy it every day. Just wish Tomiko was on it, too!
>
> I was so happy to receive your letter. I surely hope both of you are enjoying good health and happiness. You are most worthy to have our Lord pour out his choicest blessings upon you.[12]

From left: Ray Hanks, Amy Hanks, Tatsui, in Tokyo

Sister Hanks wrote the Satos during Christmas season 1985 and said:

> My husband, Ray, used to love you dearly also. Ray has been gone for four years, and I still miss him. I find it lonesome to live alone, but I am sure he is doing missionary work in the next world as that is what he loved to do. I was looking in one of my drawers the other day and found this article about Brother Sato. I

> thought you would like to have it. Brother Sato has done so much for the true Church.

She was also impressed with the Branch newsletter the Satos had sent her.[13]

Completion of Mission

Upon completion of his mission, Brother Sato received a letter of appreciation and a release from his sealing assignment from the Tokyo Temple Presidency:

> We wish to express our deep appreciation for the contribution you have made, as one of the first temple missionaries, in establishing a temple program in Japan. We have experienced some frustrations and hard work as the temple program developed. But out of it we have all reaped many blessings and rich, choice experiences. Thank you for your help in this endeavor.
>
> This letter is to inform you that you were officially released from yourTokyo Temple mission, including your assignment as a sealer, as of the 15th June 1982. We wish you much success and happiness as you return to America.
>
> Most sincerely,
> Tokyo Temple Presidency
> Dwayne N. Anderson, Temple President
> Yukiyoshi Y. Inouye, First Counselor
> Yasuhiro Matsushita, Second Counselor[14]

Brother Sato was asked to speak to the stake about his mission experiences on 23 October 1983; he gave a great testimony of missionary work and talked of his experiences:

> Dear Brothers and Sisters,
>
> I appreciate very much this special opportunity for us to bear our testimony before you this morning, which our stake president, Elder Schrasinger, arranged for us.

It was July 3rd, 1980, when I was called to serve as a missionary of the Church of Jesus Christ of Latter-day Saints to assist with the work in the Tokyo Temple. I was also recommended as one worthy to serve the Lord in working with sacred ordinances—also I was told that I am expected to devote my time and attention in serving the Lord, leaving behind all other personal affairs, and as I do these things the Lord will bless me in becoming an effective servant in the House of the Lord. Also I was told that the Lord will reward the goodness of my life, greater blessings and more happiness than I have yet experienced await me as I humbly and prayerfully serve the Lord in this labor of love among His children.

I bear my testimony before you that this is true and everything I was told has been realized. We arrived in Tokyo in the first week of September, 1980, when the open house of the Tokyo Temple was going on. The Tokyo Temple was built on the same site as the former Japan Mission Home, where I was working as the translator of the Japanese Mission from 1949 to 1965, almost 16 years. When we went there we found the mission home was taken down and the beautiful Tokyo Temple was standing magnificently. In 1949 Elder Matthew Cowley visited Japan to offer the dedicatory prayer for the newly built mission home of the Japan Mission. He offered the prayer standing at the same point where the present Temple is standing.

The prayer was a long one and in the prayer he blessed everything and every person having relation to the building of the mission home, and said "The mission home will be blessed and will stand safely until the due time will come." Also he said, "Japan will be dotted by temples." Everybody who heard the prophetic word was surprised and said in his heart that "Oh! More than two temples will be built in Japan."

Since then more than 30 years has passed and I saw the realization of the prophetic word that Elder Matthew Cowley said. When the time of the open house ended from December the training of the temple work started, and from January 1981 regular temple ordinances started.

In 1844, when April conference was held, Prophet Joseph Smith said, "There must, however, be a place built expressly for that purpose and for men to be baptized for their dead. It must be built in this central place for every man who wishes to save their father, mother, brothers, sisters and friends. We must go through all the ordinances for each one of them separately, the same as for himself, from baptism to ordination, washing and anointings, and receive all the keys and powers of the priesthood, the same as for himself."

According to these instructions, we temple missionaries worked and anointed the Japanese Saints who came to the temple to go through all necessary ordinances for them and for their dead relatives.

May I report what I could do from January 1981 to June 1982 (when I was released from temple work):

1) 274 endowments in behalf of deceased ancestors
2) 42 living couple sealings
3) Several hundred child to parent sealings in behalf of deceased ancestors
4) Several hundred couple sealings in behalf of deceased ancestors
5) Initiatory washing, anointing, and clothing for hundreds of persons
6) Assisted several hundred people at the veil
7) Trained several hundred new workers

When Elder Matthew Cowley traveled in Japan he noticed that every city, town, village, and even a remote country place has a Shinto Shrine surrounded by beautiful evergreens. And on the outskirts of a village there is always a tiny Shinto Shrine enshrining a divided spirit of the Goddess of Ise, who is the highest spiritual existence in Japan. Elder Cowley said, "Japanese people are a temple building people."

Also, when Elder Hugh B. Brown visited Japan he said, "Japan will become the ensign of righteousness in the Far East."

Now the Tokyo Temple is standing in Tokyo as the 1st temple in Japan, and Japanese Saints from Hokkaido to Kyushu, Okinawa, Korean Saints from South Korea, and Saints from other countries come to receive the temple ordinances.

As I said before in June, 1982, when I was asked to give a farewell address to the brothers and sisters who were working in the Tokyo Temple, "I worked with you almost two years in the same place, and at the moment of farewell I know that time flies like an arrow, according to the Japanese saying. Now time flew like an arrow or time passed by like a second, because I was happy to work with you."

Someone told me, "If you want to live a long day, stay in a jail, and you will live one day as if it would be ten years." When I was leaving Tokyo someone asked, "Why not stay here in Tokyo, because I know you'd be happy in Japan." I answered him, "No! Because, Salt Lake City is my home. It is Zion, the city of Saints who are in the service of God."

In Okinawa, mediums, i.e., spiritual mediums, are called *Yuta* (meaning the people in the service of their God). And when our missionaries answer the question "Where do you come from?" saying, "I come from Utah," people of Okinawa used [to] say, "O! Did you come from the country of the people in the service of God?"

Again I will say I love Salt Lake City because it is Zion, the country of Latter-day Saints. I bear testimony that Joseph Smith is the true prophet of God and he restored the true Church of Jesus Christ. I say this in the name of Jesus Christ, Amen!

May I add a story or rather a fantastic idea about the origin of the Japanese people, that is where the Japanese came from?

When I was in Laie, Hawaii, I was working to translate temple ordinances into the Japanese language in order to assist the Japanese Saints who came to the temple to receive the temple ordinances. One day I went through an endowment session in the Samoan language, and I was so much impressed because there were . . . similarities between the Japanese language and that of Samoans. First, the Samoan language vowel's ending—Japanese language has the same characteristic. Second, the Samoan language has many expressions using repetition, which the Japanese has too. For example, Niko Niko, meaning smiling. And I thought in my mind, probably we can find the origin of the Japanese [people] in Samoa or another island in the South Pacific area.

In ancient time, several thousand years ago, a people from Samoa or Tonga migrated from the South Pacific to Japan. There are many possibilities for this expedition. For example, the direction of ocean currents and monsoons helped them to navigate from east to west so they could reach one of the islands in the Indonesia area.

I could organize this idea into a story, but after all it was hypothetical.[15]

Returns as Sealer to Salt Lake Temple

The President of the Salt Lake Temple, Marion D. Hanks, received approval from President Gordon B. Hinckley, on 18 April 1983 to transfer Brother Sato to the Salt Lake Temple as a sealer:

Dear President Hanks:

Based on the request contained in your letter of April 12, 1983, approval is hereby given for Brother Tatsui Sato, who recently returned from service in the Tokyo Temple where he served as a sealer, to transfer to the Salt Lake Temple. Inasmuch as Brother Sato served previously as a sealer in the Salt Lake Temple, this letter will constitute authorization for him to begin to perform sealings in the Salt Lake Temple without the need to be given the sealing power again. At the same time, this transfer will have the effect of withdrawing Brother Sato's authorization to perform sealings in the Tokyo Temple.

In advising Brother Sato of this authorization, we suggest that you give a copy of this letter to him for his records.

Sincerely your brethren,
The First Presidency by
Gordon B. Hinckley[16]

Elder and Sister Davis on a Mission

Just after they returned, the Satos received a letter from Portland, Maine where Reed Davis and his wife, Lula, were serving. This time the situation was reversed, with the Satos assisting them:

> Here at last we are settled into our field of labor. . . . Brother Sato, you were so nice to give us your money and you know that we could do without, but the blessings that you are to receive I cannot take from you. You and your family have to be blessed of the Lord because of your goodness and love for the gospel, as you know you will always be first in our hearts.
>
> The thrill of going through the missionary training school at BYU was a treat. When we saw Michi and her family in the flip charts of the teaching lessons, it gave me a thrill. Now, she and her family's picture is being shown all over the world. Every time I show this picture, I have to stop and tell our people that they are close friends. Also, what a great family they are and . . . their mother and stepfather who . . . [led] them into the church. After our farewell meeting, everyone came and told us how interesting you were and how thrilled they were to hear your story. The little children were so interested to hear the Japanese language spoken and to have Sister Sato tell them what you had said. We will always treasure your words and pray that in our mission we can use your testimony to help others to gain that same testimony. Already, we have had the chance to tell people about you and the strength you have given to us and our desire to serve the Lord as missionaries here in New England.
>
> We wish to thank you again for speaking at our farewell and your other gift to us. We pray that you and yours shall always be blessed with choice blessings for your good. . . .[17]

This and many other letters are indicative of the great influence Brother and Sister Sato have had in the lives of their friends. It was a wonderful homecoming for Brother Sato to return to Japan and meet his many friends and to be close to his son and their family. He and

Tomiko were always grateful for this opportunity and to be part of the prophecy of a temple opening in Japan. Being called to help open the temple and to do temple work was an experience they always cherished.

Endnotes

1. Notes of meeting on revision of temple ceremony, Tatsui Sato's personal notes, 8 August 1975.
2. Correspondence, Ray and Edith Hanks to Tatsui and Tomiko Sato, 18 December 1978.
3. Correspondence, Boyd K. Packer to Tatsui Sato, 16 May 1979.
4. Correspondence, Tatsui and Tomiko Sato to Dwayne N. Andersen, 19 August 1980. Sent along with reply form acknowledging call as temple missionaries.
5. Correspondence, Tatsui Sato to First Presidency, August 1980.
6. "A Temple in Japan," *Church News*, 25 October 1980, p. 16.
7. Correspondence, Ralph Shinto to Tatsui and Tomiko Sato, 18 December 1980.
8. Correspondence, Sonasi Pouha to Tatsui and Tomiko Sato, 21 May 1981.
9. Corrrespondence, Reed Davis family to Tatsui and Tomiko Sato, 12 January 1982.
10. Correspondence, Tatsui Sato to Reed Davis, 5 March 1982.
11. Correspondence, Edith Hanks to the Satos, 13 December 1982.
12. Correspondence, Edith Hanks to the Satos, 17 December 1982.
13. Correspondence, Edith Hanks to the Satos, 17 December 1985.
14. Correspondence, Tokyo Temple Presidency to Tatsui Sato, 1 July 1982.
15. Tatsui Sato, Notes of testimony speech and mission report, 23 October 1983.
16. Correspondence, Gordon B. Hinckley to Marion D. Hanks, 18 April 1983, copy of original in possession of author.
17. Correspondence, Reed and Lula Davis to the Satos, 10 November 1982.

Chapter 11

Service in Dai Ichi Branch & Final Years

THE FIRST TIME THIS WRITER MET TATSUI was in May of 1973 at the Japanese Dai Ichi Branch. Members included Japanese immigrants, second generation Japanese and their descendants, a few returned missionaries from Japan, and students from Japan who were attending local colleges, including the University of Utah and LDS Business College. I still remember what my first impression was. Branch President Roy Tsuya and former Branch President Ralph Shino and other members welcomed me warmly.

Tatsui was a member that was respected and loved by everyone. President Ralph Shino took care of Tatsui while he lived in this life. Tatsui really respected him. I conducted a telephone interview with President Shino on 6–7 March 2004. He told me the following, including information about his own background:

In 1952, Ogden, Salt Lake and Provo were opened up as the Regional District Mission with Brother Shino called as the assistant to the mission president. He spent eight years helping with missionary work in this mission, which was primarily established to help foreigners, particularly Asians, Europeans and Mexicans. President Shino labored hard to help local Japanese and immigrants, especially those who had trouble with English. He said, "With the Lord's blessing, I even baptized some of them into the Church." As a result, a special branch, called the Dai Ichi (meaning Number One in Japanese) was officially organized in Salt Lake City in 1962. Shino became the first president of the branch.

President Shino first met Tatsui in 1966 when he first came to the branch. He was impressed that Brother Sato had "a lot of knowledge in many fields." In fact, "he impressed me greatly, as a great scholar." President Shino was released, but called once again to be the branch president in 1970. He immediately called Tatsui to be his first counselor. He recalled that Tatsui was "very happy at that time" as he was doing what he liked best, translating materials at the Genealogical Department of the Church. He was very thankful for the call, and they had a wonderful relationship.

President Shino then talked about the branch:

> At the Dai Ichi Branch, there were ten first generation Japanese, and also second generation of Japanese (Nisei), like me, Japanese students and returned missionaries from Japan—a total of 70 members. Brother Sato helped those Japanese who didn't understand English. Brother Sato's contribution to the branch was great with his great knowledge and spirituality.
>
> Steve Nelson was in our branch presidency. Everyone in his family had a true appreciation for everything about Japan and the Japanese people. Each time when we held our presidency meeting, Brother Nelson was always overjoyed by Brother Sato's wise, thoughtful and spiritual decisions. I often recall how Brother Sato used to talk about his experiences in translating the temple ceremony in the Hawaiian Temple. Brother Sato said that experience was very spiritual and the translation turned out great.
>
> After the branch was organized in 1962, I started having the newsletter to the members of the Dai Ichi Branch delivered in both English and Japanese—bilingual. The title was "To the Members of the Branch." Brother Sato contributed greatly as he patiently wrote to members almost every week, about Japanese

customs and traditions, culture, genealogy, and also tried to build up the members' spirituality with spiritual topics and discussions. All the members—whether immigrants, descendants, students, or returned missionaries from Japan—gained a great knowledge from his contributions; and it helped increase our faith and testimony. It's hard to explain how much Brother Sato contributed to us. In the latter years of Brother Sato's life, I was his home teacher. I visited him more than two times a week until he passed away. Every Sunday I went to visit him and blessed bread and water of the sacrament for him.

I am already 80 years old. My wife will be 80 soon. I can feel and see Brother Sato's meek and kind face. When I close my eyes, it seems I can even hear the soft voice of Brother Sato.[1]

Brother and Sister Shino

Visiting the Packer Home

President Packer wrote about Brother Sato visiting his home and telling the story of his conversion to his children:

On occasion he would come to our home. I remember I had surgery once, and he came to visit me. As I lay on the bed he demonstrated to me his expertise in acupuncture, showing me which pressure points would bring relief from pain and in which parts of the body. He was quiet and resourceful. He had a wonderful sense of humor.

We had a family gathering once and invited Brother Sato to come and talk to our children. We thought they should know and remember him, that he should be part of their lives as well. We had a wonderful evening. On that occasion he told our children of his first contact with the Church with Brother C. Elliott Richards and Brother Ray Hanks and one or two others. He was selling souvenirs at a little bazaar. He asked them, "What is different about you?" They did not know what he meant. But on several visits they seemed to be drawn to one another. He invited them to the teahouse and ordered tea. One of them said, "No thank you." . . . That is . . . the first he found out how they were different.

When we had him in our home, we sat on the lawn. All of our children were there. He told that experience and explained to our children they had simply said, "No thank you." . . . That was the beginning of his conversion to the Church.[2]

Brother Tatsui Sato's 88th Birthday

On 7 October 1987, as is the custom among Japanese, a special 88th birthday celebration was held for Brother Sato at the Dai Ichi Ward. Tatsui was dressed in the traditional 88th birthday ceremonial costume, a gold colored coat and hat, as shown in the picture. It was the writer's first time attending a traditional 88-year-old birthday party. I was very amazed to see the special costume on Brother Sato, who sat in front with his family members for that occasion. Over 200 people attended the event, which was held in the cultural hall. His son, Yasuo, and his wife came from Japan to celebrate. There were several former Latter-day Saint soldiers who attended—Reed Davis,

Mel Arnold, Elliott Richards, Boyd Packer, Bob Swenson, Thomas Bauman, and Norton Nixon.

Tatsui's 88th birthday party

Tatsui gave the following speech:

> Ladies and Gentleman, may I express my heartfelt appreciation for your sincere love and kindness to come and celebrate my 88th birthday.
>
> I was born in the last century; that is, I was born October 16th of 1899. Then the year of 1987 is the 88th year since I was born. In Japan, it is called "Beiju no iwai," that is "Celebration of one's 88th birthday."
>
> Now Japan is leading the world in long life, however the Japanese proverb says: "Man's span of life is but fifty years." "Man seldom lives to be seventy years." and "Time flies like an arrow!" Eighty-eight years have passed in a split-second! Why? Because I was happy except [for] some miserable times.

> In 1945 when everything was in commotion after the Great War, God the Father sent me three American servicemen to tell me the glad tiding of the true gospel. They were an advance party, and more than ten servicemen came after them. I accepted what they taught me, and I found true happiness to live in righteousness.
>
> I was baptized in 1946 at Sannomiya Kobe and was given the honor to be the first convert of the Japan Mission after the war. I can never thank you enough for your kind attention. *Arigato gozaimasu.* (Thank you!)[3]

An excerpt from a letter from the Baumans reflects on the great joy of the occasion:

> We want to tell you both how much we enjoyed attending your birthday party and dinner. It was so nice of you to invite us to this important occasion. It was a privilege and honor to be there. We enjoyed seeing Yasuo and talking with him. I knew him as a young boy about ten years old. I know you both must be proud of him as you are of all of your other children. Sister Bauman and I have valued our friendship with you over many years.
>
> We feel that to know both of you and feel your kind spirit and strong faith has been a privilege and a blessing for us.[4]

Sister Hanks, whose husband, Ray, had passed away, thanked the Satos for a special letter and photos of the special event: "We are thrilled and happy to have those pictures that were taken the night we came up to your church dinner to honor Brother Sato. We will cherish them all our lives."[5] The following year she wrote a special birthday greeting to Tatsui stating: "I hope Tatsui's health is very good at his age, and that both of you are living a very happy life."[6]

Tatsui continued to translate materials, even at this age. Upon the urging of George McCune, Brother Sato translated his book, *The Blessings of Temple Marriage*, which was published in Japanese in

1991. This was to be his last major project, as he had now entered his 90s.[7]

Tributes to Tomiko

Many people were impressed by Brother Sato's wife, Tomiko, and her efforts to make her husband comfortable in his later years. President Packer noted: "Tomiko was wonderful and took good care of him." John Clawson, who first met Brother Sato in 1949 in Tokyo, knew Tomiko before they were married and was very happy to see them together. He called her a "marvelous lady who really took care of Brother Sato in his later years."[8]

Sister Sato was especially known for her hospitality. Any visitor could expect a Japanese snack of some kind and a wonderful welcome whenever they came. She was always very generous with her time and spent many hours helping people with their genealogy and names submission. She was very skilled at Japanese crafts and knew the language and culture very well. After Tatsui's passing, she volunteered for a mission at the Hong Kong Temple and more recently went on a temple mission to the Washington D. C. Temple. She is a person of great enthusiasm and a wonderful friend to many.

She also was a great contributor to the social events and the various Relief Society activities of the Dai Ichi Shibu. She was always proud of Tatsui and felt he was a wonderful father and grandfather. Brother Sato always treated her children as his own, and she was very appreciative of his scholarship and great faith. She also was a person of great faith and generosity.

Last Visits to Brother Sato's Home

The last time the writer saw Tatsui was in early February of 1996. (He passed away on 15 June of that same year.) Just before my visit, I received a telephone call from Brother Wesley Jarvis who lives in Orem, Utah. His Father went to the Japan Mission in 1903 in the second missionary group to Japan. (In 1972, the author stayed at

Brother Jarvis' home and obtained free room and board while attending school.) Wesley's father strongly believed that the Japanese people are the descendants of the Nephites. He passed this theory down to his son, Wesley Jarvis. Brother Jarvis had called to inform me about the book that he was writing with Brother Keith C. Terry entitled, *The Remnant.*[9] Brother Jarvis really wanted me to meet Brother Terry, because the book is about the descendants of the Nephites—the Japanese.

Besides this, I had a strong feeling if I did not visit Brother Sato soon, I would not see him again. So I took a few days off from my school teaching in Oregon and flew to Salt Lake City. It was a cold, snowy day in Utah, as usual. I rented a car and drove to Brother Sato's humble home. I didn't tell them that I was coming to visit him. I opened the front door and entered his home. Brother Sato was sitting on the couch in the living room. He was staring at the hanging scroll on the wall.

The scroll is about 5 feet long and 2.5 feet wide. Without saying a greeting to me, he told me that he asked his son-in-law to translate Tokugawa Ieyasu's teaching on the conduct of life. He told me he had read it every day in his later years. Tokugawa Ieyasu was also born in Nagoya, so Brother Sato and he shared the same birthplace.

Ieyasu (1542–1616), the first Tokugawa Shogun, was an ingenious military tactician as well as a cunning politician. He is credited with completing the pacification of Japan begun by the powerful warlords Nobunaga and Hideyoshi, thus securing his family's hold on power for two-and-a-half centuries. Because of Ieyasu's patience and forbearance, he was a hero of Brother Sato, who in his later years translated Tokugawa's teachings on the conduct of life:

> A man's life is like a distant journey with a heavy pack. It should be made without haste. Remember that absolute satisfaction is denied to mortals, and therefore, feel no discontent. If your heart should be full of wishes and desires, recall your earlier days of suffering and poverty. Self-restraint and forbearance are

> the roots of peace and prosperity. Regard anger as your enemy. Obsession with victory without understanding and acceptance of defeat will bring to you calamity. Find fault with yourself rather than with others. To be wanting is better than to enjoy excess.[10]

History records that Ieyasu was a cruel persecutor of Christians. He also invited his eldest son to commit *harakiri* (ritual suicide) when it was learned that the 21-year-old had entered into relations with an enemy faction, the Katsuyori. It is not incongruous that a man like Brother Sato could learn from and even come to admire the Tokugawa Shogun; however, men like Brother Sato see the evolution of mankind from a higher perspective, where currents of ignorance and violence flow into powerful rivers of knowledge and peace.

Before it got dark outside, I needed to leave Tatsui's home, as I had an appointment with Brother Jarvis in Orem. Brother Sato told me to visit him again. I promised I would, and left his home. Brother Jarvis was waiting for me. He had prepared a beef stew dinner. I met Brother Keith Terry the next day and promised to take him to Japan to show him around so he could get ideas about Japan for his book. I wanted to take him to the ancient capitol of Nara and then to Kyoto, to show him the Japanese Shinto shrines and the Buddhist Temples.

While in Orem, I contacted Brother Masao Watabe who is a patriarch in a BYU stake. He had worked together with Brother Sato in the Translation Department in Tokyo. Brother Watabe had just lost his wife and was in a very deep depression. I asked him to join us for a Chinese dinner—he hesitated to come at first, but I changed his mind. I also invited him to go with us to visit Brother Sato the following day. First, he made an excuse not go, because he was overcome with grief from his beloved wife's death. However, he did go with Brother and Sister Jarvis and I to visit Brother Sato.

Sister Tomiko Sato prepared many traditional dishes for our lunch. One dish was a type of sukiyaki, and when I served it to everyone, they all enjoyed it. Especially, Brother Watabe who ate and ate—he said it was the first time he'd had an appetite since his wife passed away. He was so happy to see his longtime friend Tatsui. They clasped each other's hands and rejoiced. Brother Watabe told Brother Sato that he had been transformed into a god—he did not look like he was of this mortal life anymore.

Late in the afternoon, we excused ourselves to return to Orem. I decided I needed to take pictures of all the people who were gathered together at Brother Sato's home. If I missed this chance, this kind of glorious opportunity would never come again. I told everyone to wait for a while, and I went outside to look for a camera to buy. I found a store, bought an instant camera, went back to the Satos and took many pictures of us together. I think these pictures must be the last pictures of Brother Sato before he passed away.

Group picture taken in February 1996
From left: Tomiko Sato, Tatsui Sato, Masao Watabe, Wesley Jarvis, Komae Mori

Brother Sato asked me when I would visit him again. I told him I would come back to Salt Lake the next day to stay at one of my friend's home, so before I went there I would stop by and visit him. The day before my departure for Oregon, I stayed at my friend's home. Early in the morning of my going home to Oregon, I received a telephone call from Sister Sato. She had a message from Brother Sato for me, and because she didn't have my phone number had made many calls to locate me. She said, "Brother Sato has a message for you, so please stop at our home on the way to the airport." I quickly got ready and left my friend's home. I wondered what the message was.

Tatsui had the Book of Mormon and other scriptures on his lap. This writer received one of the last private lessons of the true principles of God from Brother Tatsui Sato. At the end, he said to me, "Komae Shimai (Sister Komae), you were born to be a Shinto priestess of Amami Island. Therefore you are very special and important to God. Serve God with all your heart."[11]

On the way to the Salt Lake airport, I could not stop the tears from streaming down my face. As far as I could see, the world was covered with snow, but Brother Sato had melted my heart one last time. This was truly an unforgettable experience.

Endnotes

1. Telephone interview, Shino, 6–7 March 2004.
2. Boyd K. Packer, Introduction, Masao Watabe, et al., *Ametsuchi wo miyo*, iv–v.
3. Notes by author, Tatsui Sato's 88th birthday celebration, 7 October 1987.
4. Correspondence, Tom and Donna Bauman to the Satos, 15 November 1987.
5. Correspondence, Edith Hanks to the Satos, 20 November 1987.
6. Correspondence, Edith and Amy Hanks to Tatsui Sato, 10 October 1988.
7. Telephone interview with Greg Gubler, 10 April 2004.
8. John Clawson, video interview on "Tatsui Sato," Bountiful, Utah, 13 July 2001.
9. Wesley Jarvis and Keith C. Terry, *The Remnant: A Novel* (American Fork, UT Covenant Communications, 1996.)
10. Tokugawa Ieyasu on the "Conduct of Life," translation by Tatsui Sato, copied by author, February 1996.
11. Tatsui Sato, words of parting to author, February 1996.

Chapter 12

Funeral

ON 16 JUNE, early in the morning, the writer received a phone call from two friends—Mitsuko Chinen and Kenji Suzuki, who live in Salt Lake City. They told me of Brother Sato's passing. My summer vacation had just begun that morning. I decided to drive from Eugene, Oregon to Salt Lake City; and early on June 18th at about 1:00 a.m. I left, arriving in Salt Lake City late that same afternoon.

My two sons, David and Christopher, and I stayed at Sister Gwen Pitts' home in Centerville. She showed me the obituary of Brother Sato that appeared in the *Deseret News* (Monday, 17 June 1996) and the *Salt Lake Tribune* (Tuesday, 18 June 1996). Accompanied by a photo were the following words:

> Tatsui Sato, husband, father, grandfather, Japanese LDS pioneer, scholar, scientist and leader ended his mortal journey on June 15, 1996. Born in Aichi Ken, Japan, on Oct. 16, 1899, to Magoichi and Tai Mizuta Sato, he became a consummate scholar, obtaining a degree in chemical science.

He became one of the first converts to The Church of Jesus Christ of Latter-day Saints in Japan after World War II. He immediately put his wonderful intellect and facility for language to work and, under the tutelage of the Spirit, became the official translator for the Church's Tokyo mission, translating the standard works, Talmage's *Articles of Faith* and *Jesus the Christ* and numerous other Church publications, thus building a communication bridge across which missionaries have reached thousands of new converts. Tatsui's wife, Chiyo Akizuki, shared his remarkable journey for 35 years until her death in October of 1958, leaving Tatsui and their son, Yasuo. Their daughter, Atsuko, preceded her mother in death, at age 3.

As a visiting professor at Brigham Young University teaching Japanese and comparative religions, he met and married Tomiko Hiranishi in July of 1966 in the Salt Lake LDS Temple. Together they became dedicated and talented genealogists providing untold hours of volunteer service to other Church members in their personal family history quest while holding fulltime jobs for the Genealogical Society.

He became a naturalized, committed citizen of the United States, a sealer in the Salt Lake LDS Temple, served in the branch presidency of the Dai Ichi Branch and, after retiring, he and Tomiko served as temple missionaries in the newly constructed Tokyo LDS Temple.

He continued learning almost unto his death. When age finally began to overtake him, Tomiko continued in her loving, patient and tender care for him, making him comfortable to the end.

He is survived by his wife, Tomiko; son, Yasuo and his wife, Minako Sato. In Tokyo, Japan; his sister, Fuyu of Shizuoka Ken, Japan; his adopted daughter, Michiko, her husband Douglas Matsumori and their children.

He is survived by an eternal legacy, leaving behind him spiritually guided, deeply thoughtful and rich literary Japanese traditions of the words of prophets, seers, revelators and of the Savior. . . ."[1]

Brother Tatsui Sato's Viewing

On 18 June at 6:00 p.m., Tatsui's viewing was held at the Wasatch Lawn Mortuary. The room was filled with flowers sent by family, friends, and associates. Many people were in attendance—among them there were former Latter-day Saint soldiers Mel Arnold, Reed Davis, Elliott Richards, Thomas Bauman and Bob Swenson. Tatsui's body lay at peace in the casket. He wore those scholarly round glasses, which he used to wear during his mortal life. His eyes were closed, his face had a peaceful smile, and a warm light was shining on him. All of the attendants' faces were also calm and peaceful. Brother Sato had a long, fruitful life and ended this mortal life without regret.

Brother Tatsui Sato's Funeral

The following day, 19 June at 11:00 a.m. at the Dai Ichi (Fairmont) Ward chapel, Brother Tatsui Sato's funeral service was held. The chapel was filled with friends and attendees, and it was lavishly decorated with many fragrant flowers. Brother Sato's casket was set directly in front of the altar, covered in red rose buds. The funeral service was conducted by the Dai Ichi Ward's bishop, Brian Nanba. He began the service with the following words:

> Brother Tatsui Sato, the first LDS member baptized in postwar Japan and . . . translator of the triple combination and numerous other LDS Church materials translated into the Japanese language, passed away peacefully at his home in Salt Lake City, Utah, on June 15, 1996 at exactly 96 2/3 years of age.

He then talked about Brother Sato's final days and his accomplishments.[2]

> Brother Sato was a member of the Dai Ichi (Japanese cultural) Ward since 1966 when he married his second wife, Tomiko

Sato. He had moved to the United States after 66 years of residency in Japan.

President Boyd K. Packer, Acting President of the Quorum of the Twelve, presided at the funeral and was the featured speaker. Also present were Elder Jacob de Jager, emeritus member of the First Quorum of the Seventy; Elder William R. Bradford, of the First Quorum of the Seventy; President C. Elliott Richards, who had served as president of the Jordan River Temple since 1993; and Sister Chieko N. Okazaki, first counselor in the Relief Society General Presidency.

President Packer had the privilege of baptizing Brother Sato's first wife, Chiyo Akizuki, in the swimming pool of the Kansai University campus in Sannomiya Kobe, Japan, on 7 July 1946. Chiyo's baptism was immediately following Brother Sato's baptism in the same pool by President Richards. Both, Presidents Packer and Richards, were serving at the time of the Satos' baptisms as Lieutenants in the United States military occupational forces in Japan.

President Packer read a letter of condolence from the First Presidency to Sister Sato which follows:

> Dear Sister Sato:
>
> We express our love and condolences to you at the death of your husband and our dear friend, Tatsui Sato. We shall appreciate your expressing our sympathy to other members of the family. Brother Sato was an honorable and just man who gave lovingly and unselfishly of his time to his family and fellow man. He made a lasting contribution through his untiring efforts in genealogical and family history work. We appreciate his meaningful assistance in the Church as a member of a branch presidency and as a missionary in the Tokyo Temple. We are especially appreciative of his dedicated labors in translating the standard works and other Church publications for the benefit of Japanese-speaking individuals.
>
> Brother Sato has now taken that essential step in his eternal progression and returned home to heaven. There he is experiencing

a happy reunion with loved ones who preceded him in death and will await being reunited with those he left behind. We pray that your knowledge of the gospel plan will bring you peace and comfort at this sensitive time and in the coming years. With love and kind regards.
Sincerely yours,
The First Presidency[3]

After reading this special letter of condolence, President Packer said:

> It's interesting how little we know. We lived with him, were close to him, and yet somehow never knew that this great man has walked among us and in one sense has been so little known. I have said on many occasions that if I were to name the ten most impressive people I have ever met outside the circle in which I stand certainly I would have to mention Tatsui Sato. I think he'd be about number two or three, this great and wonderful man.[4]

President Packer referred to three choice letters he had received from Brother Sato in 1947, 1948, and 1951 showing "something in transition." After reading the first part of the first letter written a year after Brother and Sister Sato's baptism of 7 July 1946, President Packer paused and said:

> I want to read this carefully, because this is poetry: "As a little flower and nameless weed can be welcomed by desert travelers, so every kind thing sinks to our heart and it lightens the darkness of our life like jewels." In reading on in the letter—about the Sunday School of the neighborhood children who "come to my home gladly. . . . The seeds that were planted by Brother Richards have come out and [are] growing up. I watch over them, giving nourishment, and dreaming of the time when they will thrive and bear good fruit."

President Packer continued, "Can you see a picture here of the man who is the Church—of the Church growing up around him?"

In reading the second letter, written about six months after the first, President Packer commented, "This is an insight that I think not 5% of the Latter-day Saints understand." Then he read the following words from Brother Sato's second letter:

> Truly Jesus is the foundation stone and love is the fundamental principle to rule over the Kingdom. I understand that the spirit world is not another world but it is merged into this world to be one, and to be real existence. I am seeing it, living in it, and [we] shall be living in it forever.[5]

In closing, President Packer said that when he thinks about this great man, Brother Sato, and the quiet place he has in the history of the Church, his "heart is full and glad . . . . Now, I appreciate what the bishop said to the children and grandchildren. You have a great heritage. This is a great chapter in the history of the Church. A nation really was built on this man, a temple was built."[6]

To Brother Sato's oldest son, Yasuo, President Packer said, "If you will be sensitive to the Spirit—this wonderful, venerable patriarch—Yasuo, he will be speaking to you and guiding you and correcting you . . . and the Lord will bless you and look after you and your family. You have a great heritage."[7]

After President Packer finished his talk, Brother Sato's farewell service concluded with the hymn, "How Great Thou Art."

"Kojo no Tsuki"

As Brother Tatsui Sato's casket was carried away by the strong arms of the priesthood holders, his favorite, most memorable song started to play—"Kojo no Tsuki" (The Moon Above the Ruined

Castle). It was composed by his former English professor, who was also the matchmaker for Brother Sato's first marriage.

Even now, this song is very well-known and sung by both the young and the old. When I heard this unexpected music, my breath caught up in my throat. I forgot everything else and was lost in my tears as many memories of Tatsui rushed back again. Brother Sato died a United States citizen, but at the same time lived by the Japanese traditions that were so important to him. But above all, Brother Sato lived by the teachings and word of God.

The words of his favorite song, "Kojo no Tsuki," seemed so fitting as we said our final farewells to a great man—one who truly touched so many people, both, through his translations and his long life of service and scholarship:

> Spring, reminiscing about the past, enjoying the view of cherry blossoms from the castle turret, passing the sake cup around and seeing the moonlight reflected in it.
> It must shine through the old pine tree branches.
> Where has the glory of past days gone?
> Autumn, with white dew shining on the samurai's station, as they prepare for battle and waves of crying wild geese pass through the sky.
> Weapons were lined up as if planted they must have shone so cold.
> Where has the glory of past days gone?
> Now, the midnight moon shines upon the ruined castle.
> The moonlight is the same now as in olden times, but for whom?
> Only vines trail across the crumbling stone walls.
> The lonesome sound of wind coming through the pine trees can be heard.
> The moon shines in the sky, the same as in olden times.
> The world flourishes and dwindles, while the moonlight illuminates the changing world.
> The midnight moonlight shines on the ruined castle.[8]

Burial and Parting

After the funeral service was over at the Fairmont Ward chapel, many of those attending followed the hearse and went to the grave of the Elysian Burial Garden. To the east of the graveyard, the precipitous Rocky Mountains were covered with snow and standing majestically. The sky was a perfect blue without any clouds. It was the middle of June in Salt Lake City.

The wine color of the coffin was covered with red rose buds and laid in the center of the freshly dug plot. Heaven and earth were in harmony. The early summer sunlight softly shone upon those in attendance.

Salt Lakt City Cemetery, February 1996

After the dedication of the grave, here and there, one by one, the gathered people left the cemetery. Finally alone, I quietly approached Brother Sato's coffin and thanked him with a silent prayer. As I said my final good-bye to him, I picked up three roses from his coffin and left. Though the funeral and burial were over, the example of his life would continue to have a profound influence upon my life.

A sage like Brother Sato, with scriptures on his knee and still studying, with author Komae Mori, several months before his death; probably the last photo taken of Tatsui, February 1996

When I think about Brother Sato, I am reminded of a character description given in *The Life and Teaching of Masters in the Far East* by Baird T. Spaulding, a book I read from Tatsui's collection. It seems very fitting when applied to Brother Sato, so I would like to contribute these words in his memory:

Brother Sato—
Ate simple foods, dressed simply and
    Lived in a humble house,
Never boasted nor was proud of himself,
    Humble, meek, gentle and thoughtful,
Cultivated his love and safeguarded it with armor,
    Loved and was loved by everyone for eternity,
Pure and innocent like a child,
    Loved and served the Lord.

Brother Sato will always be remembered for his noble, compassionate soul and sweet spirit. He became a legend in his own time.

Endnotes

1. Newspaper obituary, "Tatsui Sato," Deseret News, 17 June 1996.
2. Notes by author, funeral of Tatsui Sato, 19 June 1996.
3. Letter to Tomiko Sato from the Office of the First Presidency, 18 June 1996.
4. Address by Boyd K. Packer, author's notes, 19 June 1996.
5. Ibid.
6. Ibid.
7. Ibid.
8. English translation of "Kojo no Tsuki" by author.

Chapter 13

Visiting Latter-day Saint Former Soldiers

IN AN ATTEMPT TO LEARN MORE about Brother Sato and his servicemen friends who brought him the gospel, I determined to visit and contact as many as possible. This was a very rich and great learning experience for me. A brief account follows:

Ray Hanks (1914–1981)

In 1974, the writer visited Brother Ray Hanks' home, accompanied by Brother Sato and his wife, Tomiko. I still vividly recall seeing Brother Hanks that day. We had a barbecue in his beautifully decorated, amazingly organized backyard. Years ago, I had invited his family to come to my home for dinner. That was such a long time ago. He must have shared with me his experiences in Narumi, but I don't remember anything except feeling that Brother Hanks was a very kind, spiritual man.

In July, 2002, after meeting with former soldiers in Salt Lake City, I visited Sister Tomiko Sato to say good-bye as I was on my way back to Oregon. I noticed a blue folder on the living room floor. Sister Sato told me it belonged to Brother Hanks and if I wanted it, I could have it. I replied that I already had enough information about Brother Hanks—and the translation was done anyway—therefore, I doubted I would need it. But after that declaration, I decided to pick it up after all, and told Sister Sato I would take it just in case I needed some more information. When I came back home, I put the blue folder with the other stacks of paper on my living room floor and forgot about it.

Ray Hanks in front of the Satos' home (1970s)

One day the following month, early in August, I stopped translating as the shadows outside were lengthening and night was coming on. The memory of Brother Hanks flashed into my mind. It occurred to me that he would be so happy to see what I was doing with Brother Sato's life story. I stood up and began to walk around among the materials I'd been researching. I picked up the blue folder Sister Sato had let me take, and turned it over in my hands. On the back of the blue folder, there was something Brother Hanks had written, dated 6 June 1975: "To Komae, with kind appreciation for what she is doing for the Japanese people. Sincerely, Ray Hanks"

About thirty years ago, Brother Hanks had addressed the above message to me. As I finished reading it, I simply couldn't believe it. While he was still on this earth, he had wished for this publication! I realized that even though Brother Hanks was not here, he knew what I was doing for Brother Sato. Together with Tatsui Sato, he was watching over me and guiding me. Tears came to my eyes; I cried hard and could not stop for a long time.

Melvin Arnold (1920–)

In 1975, in the middle of a very hot summer, my son, David, was a year old. His father—the foreign student advisor at the University of Utah (he passed away in 1998)—and a couple he knew, went with me to visit the Mel Arnold family in Las Vegas. The five of us were going to stay at a hotel, but they insisted we stay at their home. Sister Arnold had all the beds prepared for us very quickly.

The Arnolds

I had wanted to visit them because I wanted to meet the soldiers who helped bring the gospel to Brother Sato—I guess it was just out of curiosity and gratitude. We stayed up late for two nights, and Brother Arnold told us about his experiences in Narumi. I don't remember much except going to a splendid steak house in Las Vegas. The decor of the restaurant was hard to forget. I also recall the delicious pancake breakfast Sister Arnold fixed for us the next morning.

Since then, I have had many chances to see the Arnolds. We have talked on the phone many times. The Arnolds still live in the same house where I visited them over thirty years ago.

C. Elliott Richards (1923–)

Brother Richards' wife and I served as members of the Young Women General Board of the Church during the 1970s. I first met Brother Richards when I was invited to their home along with the Satos for dinner. I don't remember the exact date, but I remember the kind hospitality on that occasion. After deciding to write Brother Sato's life story, I realized it was imperative that I talk to Brother Richards about the details of their meeting and the long friendship that ensued.

On 21 July 2002, at around four a.m., I left Oregon for Salt Lake City. I arrived at Sister Sato's home about three o'clock that afternoon. I told her why I had come to Salt Lake and asked her if she would help me accomplish my task. She called Brother Richards immediately and made an appointment for an interview over lunch the following day, Monday, at the Japanese Kyoto Restaurant.

Attending the lunch were Brother and Sister Richards, Sister Tomiko Sato, Sister Rose Pfaffle (my former missionary companion), Glenn Rowe (a director in the Church History department—we served in the Japan West Mission together), and Douglas Macdonald (Chief Economist of the Utah State Tax Commission—we also served a mission together). We all sat on the *tatami* (straw) mats and enjoyed some traditional Japanese food. Brother and Sister Richards answered all of my questions with a smile. However, I felt that the meeting at the restaurant wasn't enough time for me to get all of the information

I needed, so we arranged to talk at their home on Thursday morning, the 25th.

The Richards

The following entry is from my diary of that day at Brother Richard's home:

> July 25, 2002 before nine a.m., I left my former missionary companion's home in Bountiful to visit Brother Richards. I got lost, and I was a little late for my appointment. They welcomed me warmly into their home. I was there for two hours. My questions were mainly about Sister Chiyo Sato, because there was so little information about her—such as whether she looked like a typical, traditional Japanese lady. Brother Richards told me that she was the absolute opposite of me. He only knew two Japanese women—Sister Chiyo Sato and me. Sister Chiyo Sato always sat in the corner of the room, and never said anything through whole meetings, according to Brother Richards.

> My next question was whether Chiyo kept her house very neat or not, because I was very curious about her housekeeping. Brother Richards told me that "there was no way of knowing whether she kept her house neat or not, because there was only one charcoal heater in the middle of the room and no other furnishings at all!"[1]

In 1965, when Brother Sato finished his translation of the temple ceremony, he visited Salt Lake City during general conference. Brother Sato stayed at the Richards' home, and during that time, their son, Kent (now a surgeon), received a mission call to Mexico. Brother Richards suggested that Brother Sato stay at their home and use Kent's room, as he would be leaving soon.

Kyoto restaurant, from left: Douglas Macdonald, Komae Mori, the Richards, Rose Pfaffle, Tomiko Sato

Brother Richards recalled what Brother Sato had often said—that although Elliott was younger than him, he felt like Brother Richards was his spiritual father. Sister Richards also added to the memories of Brother Sato from those days:

> Brother Sato was always so calm and polite. He always bowed deeply and would kneel so respectfully. My 12 children always watched him curiously when he removed his shoes at the entrance before he came into the house.[2]

Sister Richards added at the end of my interview that Brother and Sister Sato, and their adopted children, Michiko and Koji, held their wedding receptions at the Richards' home. She also said that they paid many visits to Brother Sato.

Boyd K.Packer (1924–)

In the spring of 1975, I visited Elder Packer in his office and had a chance to interview him. I also taped that meeting. He told me the story of his involvement and relationship with Brother Sato. But, at the time, I was not as capable with English as I am now; and I was more interested in meeting a General Authority than in the interview. I was, therefore, happy to talk to him later in more depth.

President and Sister Packer

On 23 July 2002, I woke up early in the morning at my former missionary companion's home in Bountiful, Utah. In my heart I felt I should visit President Packer, but I thought that perhaps I was insignificant, and it would be impossible to visit him. Then, the next moment, I heard the still, small voice whisper: "*Do not fear—because he is an Apostle, and you are doing the work of God.*"

I waited for a while to call Sister Sato, as it was still early in the morning. At around eight o'clock, I called and told her who I thought we should visit. Sister Sato also felt that we should go see President Packer. I asked her to please make an appointment.

Shortly after our talk, Sister Sato called me back and told me President Packer was busy during the day, but he would be able to see me that night at seven o'clock. I called historian Glenn Rowe to be there with me. Tomiko Sato, Rose Pfaffle, Glenn Rowe, and Maya Nakahara accompanied me to President Packer's home that evening.

From left: Rose Pfaffle, Glenn Rowe, Komae Mori, President Packer, Sister Packer, Maya Nakahara, Tomiko Sato

President Packer had arranged chairs in his beautiful backyard, and he was there waiting for us. He and Sister Packer welcomed us. President Packer had laid out his picture albums from his soldier days in Japan.

When I sat next to him, my mind went blank, and my head felt empty. I was suddenly so afraid—though I am usually a courageous, optimistic, and easygoing person. I tried to explain to President Packer that I had come to visit because I wanted Brother Sato's book to be historically accurate and abundantly spiritual—instilling deep faith and building testimonies in its readers—and, also, to be a beautiful work (like Japanese literature). Graciously, President Packer let me use many of the precious pictures he had, as well as letters he had received from Brother Sato.

We had a wonderful visit, and President Packer was very cordial and cooperative.[3]

Thomas E. Bauman (1918–2001)

With Sister Sato, I went to visit Sister Bauman on Friday, 26 July 2002 at 10 a.m. Her home is located southeast of the University of Utah. She prepared all of Brother Bauman's picture albums and his biography and was waiting for us. She let me borrow all of the things I wanted. She also shared the most interesting stories about Brother Sato that her husband used to talk about; these are mentioned in Chapter 3. I was particularly happy to receive a copy of Brother Bauman's biography and pictures of the doctor with Brother Sato.

The Baumans and the Satos

Sister Bauman now lives alone in a beautifully organized, clean house. I asked her about Brother Reed Davis and where he lives, because I hadn't been able to get current information. Sister Bauman said that she had received a sympathy card from him a year ago when her husband had passed away. She located his card and gave me his St. George address.

Reed Davis (1916–)

After visiting with Sister Bauman on 26 July 2002, I visited Brother Rowe's office at the Family and Church History Department at the Church Office Building. I asked him if he would find the telephone number of Brother Davis on the Internet. When he called, Brother Davis answered the phone. Sister Tomiko Sato was with me, and we said that we would like to come for a visit. Brother Davis invited us to come to his home in St. George—300 miles south of Salt Lake City.

The Davises

The temperature was over 100 degrees that day. Sister Sato rode in the passenger seat as I drove my little Toyota to St. George. Brother and Sister Davis welcomed us warmly when we arrived. By the time the interview was over, it was eight p.m. As we were saying good-bye, Brother Davis said he could not let us go home without treating us to dinner. So he took us to a Chinese restaurant.

I was so happy that I was able to meet Brother Davis. And since I had not had any food that day, I ate and ate the delicious Chinese food. Our conversation never ended while we were eating, and the time went by swiftly. At eleven p.m., we decided to say good-bye to Brother and Sister Davis. They asked us to stay at their home, but we decided to return to Salt Lake that night.

We arrived in Salt Lake City on Saturday, the following morning, at four a.m. I was able to establish a close friendship with Brother Davis, and we have communicated many times since our visit. He has been extremely helpful in providing letters to and from Brother Sato as well as other material.[4]

In front of the Davis home, from the left: Komae Mori, Sister Davis, Brother Davis, Tomiko Sato. (Photo taken 26 July 2002)

Chaplain Warren Richard Nelson (1912–1964)

I truly regret that I was not able to meet Brother and Sister Nelson. I found a letter while I was sorting through Brother Sato's possessions, written by Sister Nelson 30 years ago. I immediately wrote a letter to her requesting any letters, diary entries or pictures from those days in Japan. The letter was returned as undeliverable. The following is the letter Sister Nelson wrote to Brother Sato, dated 25 June1970:

> I was so pleased to read the nice article about you in last Saturday's *Church News*. I feel like I have known you for many years. My husband was Chaplain W. Richard Nelson. Perhaps you remember him. He was present at the time you and your wife were baptized and you presented him with a beautiful book of Japanese art that we have really treasured. It also happened that we had a baby girl by the name of Chiyo at that time, and you and your lovely wife sent her some very precious little gifts.
>
> You have surely done a wonderful work for the Church with all of your translating services, and I am sure you can take a lot of credit for the tremendous missionary work being done in Japan at the present time. I don't know whether you know or not, but Chaplain Nelson died 14 years ago leaving me with 6 children, but we have really been blessed through the years. I have two married daughters with 7 grandchildren. My oldest son, Richard, came home from a mission in northern California. This leaves me a 17-year-old daughter and 14-year-old son still at home. I have been fortunate the last 11 years to have a very good position as secretary to the school superintendent.
>
> I hope some day I will be able to meet you and talk with you personally.
>
> I called in at the Genealogical Library one day, but they informed me that you were at the Bee Hive Bank and I didn't get up there. I rarely get to Salt Lake City, but maybe some day I can spend a couple of days there. I hope you are enjoying life in Utah and that you are being blessed for the wonderful work you are doing.
>
> I do appreciate your kindness to my husband while he was in Japan. He loved it there and often told about you wonderful people.[5]

As I didn't have any pictures or bits of information about Chaplain Nelson, I called Glenn Rowe of the Historical Department on 1 March 2002 for help. On 3 March, I received a fax from Brother Rowe containing Warren Richard Nelson's obituary from the *Deseret News*:

> **Funeral held for Chaplain**
>
> Manti—funeral services were held July 14 for Elder Warren Richard Nelson, a Utah National Guard Chaplain, the U.S. Army in World War II.
>
> Elder Nelson died July 10, in a Salt Lake hospital of leukemia. He had been instructor of seminary classes at the Institute of Religion at the University of Utah and before that had been director of the Institute of Religion at Flagstaff, Arizona, after having opened the Seminary system in Holbrook, Joseph City and Winslow, Arizona. He held an office of Seventies and had filled a mission to Brazil. Elder Nelson was born May 24, 1912 at Cedar City, Utah . . . .[6]

Chaplain Warren Richard Nelson's family, about 1953

Brother Rowe tried to find Chaplain Nelson's descendants, but was not able to locate any of them, until he looked in the obituary. After finding the obituary, Brother Rowe was able to locate Chaplain Nelson's family members and thus the phone number of his oldest daughter, Chiyo, and sent it to me.

I called Sister Chiyo and asked her to send me pictures of her father and, if she had any, some of his diary entries. She told me that when her father was stationed in Japan, a fire broke out in his barracks and destroyed his diary. But she promised to send some pictures of Chaplain Nelson, and she did.

I asked her why she was given the Japanese name, Chiyo, which is the same name as Brother Sato's first wife. Since she was born in 1944, before Chaplain Nelson met Sister Chiyo Sato, this seemed unusual. Chiyo explained to me that Chaplain Nelson had an administration job when the Japanese concentration camp was erected in Topaz, Utah. There he met a wonderful Japanese lady named Chiyo. When he went to Japan, he again had the chance to meet a Japanese lady whose name was Chiyo. Chaplain Nelson had named his first-born daughter Chiyo well before he met the Sato family. Brother Sato's first wife, Chiyo, was actually the third person he met who had the name Chiyo![7]

George Swett (1922–1997)

Brother Swett was quite a Good Samaritan during that time, dropping off bread and food for the Satos on his runs to and from Nagoya as his unit's quartermaster. I always wanted to contact Brother George Swett, but nobody had any idea where he lived. Last summer, Sister Sato told me that she couldn't get to sleep one night, so she decided to try and call the Swett family. The operator gave her many different "Swett" telephone numbers. One of the first numbers she dialed turned out to be Brother Swett's wife. Sister Sato apologized for having called so late, but Sister Swett was happy to speak with her.

Sister Sato asked her to call me, but for the next year I never heard from her.

The Swetts

On 29 May 2004, a Saturday morning, I received a phone call:

Hello. Is this Sister Mori? My name is Carlyle Potter, and I am calling about Sister Sato. She is on a mission right now. Do you know her? My friend and fellow ward member asked me to call you about the book you are writing about Brother Sato. She is Cathie Keller, and she is George Swett's daughter. Do you remember George Swett? Did you receive a photograph of George Swett?

They want to send you a photo for your book. Have you already published the book? The Kellers were reminded of your book and Brother Sato when they saw his photo with Elder Boyd K. Packer in the book *Saints at War*. They wondered if George Swett's wife ever sent you a photo for the book. They also wanted

> to get a copy of your book. That is why they asked me to call you.[8]

Brother Potter is a returned missionary from Hokkaido, Japan. Twenty-seven years ago he served his mission. He and his daughter and son-in-law said they would like to help with this project in any way they could. I asked them to send me pictures of George Swett during his military service in Japan. Brother Potter became a facilitator between the Swett family and me. I am so thankful for his help—thanks to him I was able to get pictures of Brother Swett.

Endnotes

1. Information from personal diary, entry for 25 July 2002.
2. Ibid.
3. Information from personal diary, entry for 23 July 2003.
4. Information from personal diary, entry for 25 July 2002.
5. Correspondence, Sister Nelson to Tatsui Sato, 25 June 1970.
6. Obituary for W. Richard Nelson, *Deseret News*, about 14 July 1966.
7. Telephone interview with Chiyo, June 2004.
8. Telephone conversation with Carlyle Potter, 29 May 2004.

Reflections

ALTHOUGH THE YEARS PASS by quickly, the image of Brother Sato is always in my mind. We, as his friends, can never forget him or his many contributions to the gospel work and building up the kingdom of God. Although I did not meet him until his early seventies, because of his long life, I was still able to benefit from his close friendship for over a quarter of a century. He was always a true friend and mentor to me. His advice and deep insights touched me on many occasions. In addition, he gave much service and genuine love to his fellowmen during what was a very productive and fruitful life. Even in his seventies and eighties, he was performing a great service to the Church. Everyone who knew him was impressed with his compassion toward others and his enduring faith. This volume is filled with many examples of this and also the genuine love and affection his many friends had for him. We can all take these examples into our hearts and allow them to influence our lives for the better.

I was very moved when I read a translation of *The Life and Teachings of the Masters in the Far East* by Baird T. Spaulding, a book from Brother Sato's personal collection. When I read about the description of a hermit, I could make a connection with Brother Sato in his twilight years. In fact, as the end of his mortal life drew nearer, Brother Sato fit the part even more. He sat on his couch or on a chair in a Japanese *yukata*, and speaking mainly Japanese, appeared like a sage sharing his great wisdom to those who were willing to listen and understand. He was very much caught up by the example of the famous Japanese Shogun, Ieyasu Tokugawa, and his Spartan lifestyle—a life of patience and reflection; a life of courage and integrity.

When I think about Brother Sato and his unique character and lifestyle, I am deeply moved. He ate simple foods, always thinking about nutrition and the health consequences of each food. His simple diet included rice, fish, bran muffins, and *mugi-cha* or Japanese wheat tea. He lived in a humble home, never aspiring for anything large or fancy. He never boasted, nor was he proud. He was frugal and careful about what he considered scarce resources. Moreover, he was humble, meek, gentle and always thoughtful. He cultivated his love for his fellowmen and guarded it with armor; he never said anything negative about anyone and was truly a man without guile. He had a sensitive and compassionate heart and loved people for who they were. People were instantly attracted to his personality, and he was loved by all. Pure and innocent like a child, Brother Sato served the Lord all of his life.

Brother Sato was also a saver. He kept his letters, cards and mementoes. He even kept the papers and exams of his students and a large assortment of photos and clippings. Because of this and the contributions of his many friends, the dream of collecting and presenting his life to his friends and admirers is coming to pass. This is not a project I volunteered for. The remarkable story of my own conversion and how I became involved in this undertaking are discussed separately in this book in a section entitled "About the Author." Because of Brother Sato and his great influence on my life, I will always be indebted to him. He was a true Christian in every sense of the word and, literally, has brought many people to Christ through his translations, good works, and great example, over the many years of his life.

Brother Sato always acknowledged his gratitude and the deep friendship he had for the Latter-day Saint servicemen who brought him the everlasting gospel. One cannot help but be impressed with the deep friendships that developed between the Satos and these men, who are wonderful examples of gospel charity and friendship. As I have read the letters, and talked with and visited many of them, I have been deeply touched. Since I translated many of the letters and experiences to share with the Japanese Saints in a Japanese version of this book, I have become more deeply involved than I ever dreamed possible. My great hope is that the wonderful example of Brother Sato may inspire the people of Japan to accept the gospel of Jesus Christ.

I particularly dedicate this work to the servicemen who valiantly took the gospel to Tatsui Sato. I am eternally grateful that I was able to understand—by visiting them (and their families) and learning about them through their letters—the deep and inspiring bond Brother Sato had with these wonderful men. The great love and compassion they had for the Satos and also, that Tatsui and his family had for them, is in itself, a remarkable story. And the great thing we know as members of the restored Church is that these bonds are eternal and will never be forgotten.

Bibliography

Correspondence

in the possession of the author or shared by the following families:

Arnold, Mel
Barrett, Ross
Bauman, Thomas E.
Clissold, Edward L.
Davis, Reed
Flygare, H. Grant
Hanks, Edith
Hanks, Ray
Hinckley, Gordon B.
Kocherhans, Lavor P.
Komatsu, Adney
Mauss, Vinal B.
Mellor, Max D.
Morley, Ralph
Nelson, [sister]
Nelson, W. Richard
Nixon, Norton
Packer, Boyd K.
Richards, C. Elliott
Sato, Chiyo
Sato, Tatsui
Sato, Yasuo
Swett, George

Interviews
by author and others:

Andrus, Paul (July 23 2004)
Arnold, Mel (August, 2001)
Clawson, John (video interview, 13 July 2002 by Brian Gubler)
Gubler, Greg (2002)
Hanks, Ray (1974)
Davis, Reed (25 July 2002)
Packer, Boyd K. (July 23 2002)
Price, Harrison "Ted" (15 August 2004 by Greg Gubler)
Richards, C. Elliott (22, 24 July 2002)
Sato, Tomiko (2000–2004)
Suzuki, Kenji (2001)
Swenson, Bob (2002)

Telephone Calls/Interviews

Andrus, Paul (4 August 2004)
Price, Harrison "Ted" (10 June 2004)
Potter, Carlyle (29 May 2004)

Personal Histories

Bauman, Thomas E.
Richards, C. Elliott

Newspapers/Newsletters

Church News (17 April 1965)
Salt Lake Tribune (1996)
Seito no Michi
Genealogical Observer (1970)
The Record

Manuscripts/Materials
on file at Family and Church History Department, LDS Church Archives, Salt Lake City, Utah

Japanese Mission History, 1945–52. Includes extracts from Tatsui Sato's diary, the opening of the branch in Narumi, early meetings and contacts, and Sato's move to Tokyo. LDS Church Archives, LR 4187 28.

Imai, Kazuo. Papers of Brother Kazuo Imai. Worked as typesetter/printer in Translation Services in Tokyo at same time as Tatsui Sato. LDS Church Archives, 14,913.

Sato, Tatsui. Interview with Atsuyo Wright. Includes address at Dai Ichi Branch, Salt Lake Liberty Stake, ca. 1980 in which Brother Sato discusses translation of scriptures and highlights of his life. LDS Church Archives, tape, AV 970.

Letter to Elder Harold B. Lee, ca. 1946. 4 pages. Discusses own Christian background and conversion to the Church. LDS Church Archives, MS 7248.

Translations and Collected Papers, 1910–1970. Experiences and translations of standard works, and many other projects including the *Essentials in Christianity*, *The Kingdom of God*, *The Principles of Conducting Music*, *A Rational Theology*, and *Jesus the Christ*. Papers include minutes of meetings of the early Narumi Branch, the Aoyama Branch in Tokyo, and the Tokyo 2nd Branch. LDS Church Archive, MS 2715.

Books and Articles

Andrus, Paul. "Northern Far East Mission Japan Memories of Tatsui Sato," Revised version, August 23, 2004. E-mail copy from author.

Britsch, R. Lanier. *From the East: The History of the Latter-day Saints in Asia, 1851–1996.* Salt Lake City, Utah: Deseret Book, 1998.

Greg Gubler. "The Genealogical Society of Utah and Japan," Reid Neilson and Van Giessel, eds. Centennial of the Japanese Mission, 2001 Proceedings. Provo, Utah, *BYU Studies*, 2004.

Hall, Andrew. "A History of the Church in Western Japan, Chapter 2: The Reestablishment of the Japanese Mission, 1945–1953. Internet manuscript, Andrew Hall@hotmail.com, downloaded, July 21, 2004.

"Ro-karu pe-ji [local page]," *Seito no michi [Japanese Liahona]*, pp. 40–41 (October 1996), special inset dedicated to Tatsui Sato, 6 pages.

MacIntyre, William and Shinji Takagi. *Matsu Jitsu Seito-shi, 1850–1980 [A history of the Latter-day Saints in Japan, 1850–1980].* Kobe, Japan: Beehive Shuppan-sha, 1996.

McCune, George M. *A Tribute to Brother Tatsui Sato: Scholar, Professor, Father, Researcher, Interpreter, Translator, Church Leader, Temple Sealer, Genealogist, Temple Missionary, Saint.* Brief limited copy brochure published about 1991.

The Blessings of Temple Marriage in The Church of Jesus Christ of Latter-day Saints. Japanese edition translated by Tatsui Sato as *Matsui Jitsu Seito Iesu Kirisuto Kyokai no Seito shinden kekkon no megumi*, Tokyo, 1991.

Nihon Dendou Hyaku-nen Jikkou Iinkai, eds. *Seiki wo koete: Matsu Jitsu Seito Iesu Kiristuto Kyoukai dendou hyakunen no ayumi [Beyond the Century: A Centennial History of The Church of Jesus Christ of Latter-day Saints in Japan],* Tokyo: Meibunsha, 2002.

Packer, Boyd K. *Memorable Stories and Parables.* Salt Lake City, UT: Bookcraft, 1997.

Palmer, Spencer J. *The Church Encounters Asia.* Salt Lake City, UT: Deseret Book, 1970.

Price, Harrison T. Price. "A Cup of Tea: A True Story of the Church in Postwar Japan," *The Improvement Era.* October 1962, pp. 160–61, 184, 186.

Smith, Henry A. *Matthew Cowley: Man of Faith.* Salt Lake City, UT: Bookcraft, 1954.

Sato, Tatsui. "Sato Tatsui Kyodai no ryakureki" [Brother Tatsui Sato's brief history]. Manuscript copy in possession of author, dated 12 March 1987.

"Watakushi no kaishu [my conversion]," *Seito no michi,* December 1958, pp. 13–15.

Takagi, Shinji, and William MacIntyre, *Nihon Matsujitsu Seito-shi, 1850–1980-nen [History of the Latter-day Saints in Japan, 1850–1980]* Kobe, Japan: Beehive Shuppan-sha, 1996.

Takagi, Shinji. "The Eagle and the Scattered Flock: Church Beginnings in Occupied Japan, 1945–48. Manuscript copy, August 2001.

Tate, Lucille. *Boyd K. Packer: A Watchman on the Tower.* Salt Lake City, UT: Bookcraft, 1995.

Watabe, Masao, Kazuo Imai and Koichi Ishizaka, eds. *Ametsuchi wo miyo: Sato Tatsui Okina no omoide [Looking at Heaven and Earth (nature): Memories of Our Venerable Tatsui Sato]* Tokyo: Yunikkusu, 2004. Includes brief reminiscences from among the following: Boyd K. Packer, Masao Watabe, Kazuo Imai, Paul Andrus.

About the Author
(In her own words)

I WAS BORN IN 1945 on the little island of Amami, which is between Kyushu Island and Okinawa. My parents moved to Okinawa when I was eight years old.

When my older brother was a college student, he joined the Church. He took me to a Halloween party at the church and introduced me to the missionaries and some members in 1961, when I was a middle school student. He never invited me to attend church, however.

The following year, I entered the Naha high school, which is very close to the Latter-day Saint meeting place. They were renting an old Japanese inn. When I found out that missionaries were teaching a free English conversation class, I was very curious and anxious to attend. When I took one short English lesson, two very kind-looking sister missionaries came to me and asked if it would make me happy to learn about the teachings of Jesus Christ. At first, I hesitated to answer, because ever since I was born, it was expected that I was to be a Shinto priestess. But I could not say no because they seemed to be so special. I felt like I had never met anyone who made my spirit so happy and overjoyed. I made an appointment for a cottage meeting to take a lesson from them.

I didn't want to be alone with the sisters, so I asked about four of my girl friends to go with me. I told them to listen carefully to the missionaries, because I was not supposed to learn any other religion than Shintoism. Sister Apo, who was from Hawaii, and Sister Course from Utah taught us the lessons. We had never heard about Jesus Christ and didn't have any knowledge of Christianity at all. We couldn't understand what the missionaries were saying.

After we met a few times, the sisters talked about the Word of Wisdom. All my friends promised them that they would not drink tea, but I said, "It's impossible for me not to drink tea." That day, when I went back home, my mother brought me a cup of tea. She put it on the table, and I tried to pick it up to drink. I couldn't lift up the teacup—I tried again and again, but I couldn't move it from the table. Then the missionaries' lesson of the Word of Wisdom came back to me.

Then I knew they must be teaching the truth from God. I decided to pay more attention to their teaching from that moment on. I was not afraid to tell my parents that I was taking lessons about Jesus Christ. They were very shocked upon hearing this news. I tried my best to obey all of their teachings and tried to be a very good daughter to them; but after the incident with the cup of tea, I made up my mind to be strong and stand for my beliefs no matter what. All of my friends were baptized, because they could get permission from their parents. I was the exception. Missionaries diligently visited my parents to get permission for me to be baptized. Finally, my parents gave up and said, "You can be baptized, but when you finish high school, you need to quit."

In July, 1962, when I was 17 years old, I was baptized in the ocean by Elder Egerretzen in Okinawa. There was a typhoon the day before, and the Nami no Ue beach sea was rough. It was Saturday morning. I went into an angry ocean of high waves. I can still recall the day of my baptism like it was yesterday. I couldn't stop smiling; my whole spiritual body was very happy.

In the middle of August, I was supposed to attend the district conference in Naha, Okinawa. I left home and started to cross Highway # 1 (now #55) to catch a bus. After that, I don't remember anything except seeing my body lying on the highway. Then I saw myself in an ambulance with my father watching me. I kept hearing the voice of the elder who baptized me saying, "Mori Shimai, Mori Shimai." I couldn't answer him, but I heard him call me every time I was about to go into a deep sleep. After many hours passed, I finally had the energy to reply, "Yes!"—and I was awake. My face was so heavily bandaged I couldn't see, but I sensed my mom nearby. I asked her what the date was. My mother explained to me that I'd had a car accident in the morning, and I was in the Red Cross hospital. I'd been unconscious since morning, and my face was wrapped in a bandage.

In the evening, shortly after waking, I knew my father came to visit me. He was called by a physician to step out of the room into the hallway. I could overhear them. The doctor said he had tried his best, but there was nothing they could do, and I was going to die that night. The doctor advised that relatives should come to say good-bye. My father replied that he would give up all his wealth to save me, even if I was to be physically or mentally handicapped—he begged the doctor to save my life. Overhearing this, I was calm, because I was happy to have been baptized. I did regret that I had to die so young, before I could do anything good for my parents.

Shortly after that, several Church members, the mission president, and a few missionaries came to visit me. They heard about my accident in the news and on the radio. My district president was Kensei Nagamine. I think I heard his voice asking my dad whether they could please pray for me. I heard my dad's voice say that the doctor had already given up on my life, and the Shinto god couldn't save me either—but if their American God could help, he would give me to the Church. Then I don't remember anything until the next morning when the doctor awakened me from a deep sleep. The doctor couldn't believe I lived through the night—miraculously, I was alive. The doctor questioned me, "What is your name? How old are you? What school do you attend?" He asked me three times. I had survived, and I promised God, at the age of 17, that I would devote my life to Him.

After I finished college in Okinawa, I went to the Church College of Hawaii. My bishop was Dwayne Anderson, the former mission president of Japan. He remembered me, and told me he'd blessed me while I was in the hospital. In the summer of 1969, Bishop Anderson told me that I owed a lot to God; and, therefore, I should go on a mission. I was not happy about it, because serving for two years was too long for me.

One day, after eating dinner at the cafeteria, I was strolling to my dormitory. It was summer vacation time, and it was very quiet on campus—like a ghost town. I went to the little pond that was located in front of the religion classroom. I fed bread to the fish in the pond. I noticed the door of the classroom was open. I went inside. The room was dark, but someone's handwriting on the blackboard caught my eyes: "I will go and do the things which the Lord hath commanded, for I know that the Lord giveth no commandments unto the children of men, save he shall prepare a way for them that they may accomplish the thing which he commandeth them" (1 Nephi 3: 7). Reading this scripture, I knew this was a message from God.

Tears streamed down my cheeks. My fear of going on a mission left, and I knew that the Lord would take care of me and help me accomplish my mission. I went to see the bishop and told him I would go on a mission. I wanted to go to the mission in Brazil, to see another land and teach the gospel to Japanese immigrant descendants. Then I found out that I was called to go to the mission in Japan, where I was from.

In August, 1969, I received my mission call to Japan and entered the Language Training Mission (LTM) at the Church College of Hawaii, presently BYU—Hawaii. At one of our evening worship meetings, President Donald Ross Black who taught speech there and was a counselor to President Kenneth J. Orton at the Hawaiian LTM, gave a talk about his missionary experiences. He quoted Alma:

> Yea, I know that I am nothing; as to my strength I am weak; therefore I will not boast of myself, but I will boast of my God, for in his strength I can do all things; yea, behold, many mighty miracles we have wrought in this land, for which we will praise his name forever. [Alma 26:12]

Since that time, this scripture has remained in my heart and has become the direction for my life.

When I went to the Japan West Mission, I served under President Kan Watanabe. He was very spiritual, and I was trained by him to be a good missionary. When I started missionary work in Japan, I faced a big problem. The Japanese people (young and old, male and female) whom I contacted to teach the gospel of Jesus Christ asked me the same question: "Why do we need to learn about the teachings of the American God?" I didn't have an answer for them. I also questioned myself about it.

I decided to fast and pray to God, "Why am I here? How do the teachings of the American God benefit the Japanese?" If I wouldn't have gotten the answers to these questions, I could not have continued to be a missionary and would have gone back to my Shintoism. Before I left on my mission, I had never thought about these questions. I simply attended the Church, because the prayers of the priesthood holders saved me. I was faced with the reality of having to find out what connection Jesus Christ had to the Japanese people.

Although I had graduated from a Christian college in Okinawa, and studied the Bible during those years—taking Old and New Testament classes were a requirement—I had never been able to make a meaningful connection between Christ and his importance to the Japanese people. After reading and studying the Bible with this dilemma in mind, I began to fast and pray to the Lord as I read the scriptures. One morning, I read Exodus, Numbers, and Leviticus. I felt like I was reading with my spiritual eyes. It had never happened to me before. All of the scriptures came to my mind, as if alive. Here and there, I found old Japanese Shinto teachings and Japanese customs in the scriptures. I couldn't believe that old Japanese Shinto teachings and Japanese customs were based on the Old Testament.

The following scripture from Exodus helped me to realize that Japanese Shintoism is based on the teachings of Moses:

> And the LORD spake unto Moses, saying,
>
> On the first day of the first month shalt thou set up the tabernacle of the tent of the congregation.
>
> And thou shalt put therein the ark of the testimony, and cover the ark with the vail.
>
> And thou shalt bring in the table, and set in order the things that are to be set in order upon it; and thou shalt bring in the candlestick, and light the lamps thereof.
>
> And thou shalt set the altar of gold for the incense before the ark of the testimony, and put the hanging of the door to the tabernacle.
>
> And thou shalt set the altar of the burnt offering before the door of the tabernacle of the tent of the congregation.
>
> And thou shalt set the laver between the tent of the congregation and the altar, and shalt put water therein.
>
> And thou shalt set up the court round about, and hang up the hanging at the court gate.
>
> And thou shalt take the anointing oil, and anoint the tabernacle, and all that *is* therein, and shalt hallow it, and all the vessels thereof: and it shall be holy.
>
> And thou shalt anoint the altar of the burnt offering, and all his vessels, and sanctify the altar: and it shall be an altar most holy.
>
> And thou shalt anoint the laver and his foot, and sanctify it.
>
> And thou shalt bring Aaron and his sons unto the door of the tabernacle of the congregation, and wash them with water.
>
> And thou shalt put upon Aaron the holy garments, and

> anoint him, and sanctify him; that he may minister unto me in the priest's office.
>
> And thou shalt bring his sons, and clothe them with coats:
>
> And thou shalt anoint them, as thou didst anoint their father, that they may minister unto me in the priest's office: for their anointing shall surely be an everlasting priesthood throughout their generations. [Exodus 40:1–15]

This scripture is just like describing a Shinto shrine. (Shinto means "way of God" and is the Japanese national religion.) At the entrance of each Shinto shrine, there is a laver. Before entering the shrine, we wash our hands and purify ourselves. In the shrine, there is an altar. There are candlesticks, incense, and offerings on the altar. And there is a veil behind the altar, in front of a box. I realized that we Japanese were just keeping and practicing the teachings from the Old Testament times. The Lord heard my prayer and answered my questions. Yes, Jesus Christ is not only God to the Western Hemisphere, indeed He is God to the Japanese and to the whole world.

In 1970, we had Expo '70 in Osaka. The Church built an impressive Mormon pavilion as one of the exhibits. Many Japanese went through the pavilion and purchased copies of the Book of Mormon. One of them was a brother from Amami Island, my homeland. Brother Maki said he bought the Book of Mormon because it wasn't expensive. He went home and read it, and he couldn't stop reading it throughout the night. He knew immediately that the Book of Mormon was true. He could relate to the teachings of his ancestors in the Book of Mormon. In Amami Island, there was no Latter-day Saint Church at that time. Brother Maki contacted our mission president, Kan Watanabe. On that day, we had the district conference in Fukuoka Branch (where Japan's second temple is now located).

Brother Maki came to attend the conference and asked to be baptized that same day. Shortly after his conversion, the mission president sent elders to open the branch in Amami Island. Shortly after the elders went there, I asked the mission president to send me there, too. Sister Pfaffle and I made the journey together. My father, who was not a member, came along with us to help our missionary work. One day, my father suggested that we go to the next village. It was the day after a typhoon. We couldn't get there by boat, because the bay was not calm—there were still strong, high waves at the beach. My father suggested we climb the mountains and go to the village. It was hot, humid August weather. My father carried the copies of the Book of Mormon on his back. We climbed the steep, green-covered mountains as we listened to my father's explanation about those areas. Anciently, villagers trapped wild pigs, and there were many poisonous snakes that lived there.

When we arrived in the village, we announced to the villagers that they should come to the meeting place and hear the teachings of Jesus Christ. Many came to hear from us. The people of Amami are so pure and innocent in their hearts.

My missionary companion left for the mission home in Fukuoka to return to America. She had finished her two-year mission already. I stayed on Amami Island helping the elders. I mainly wrote articles for the newspaper and asked an editor to publish them in the daily newspaper. I wrote articles on the relationship between the teachings of Jesus Christ and the customs and traditions of Shintoism.

I also did research in my village and wrote papers about their history, which were published by the head librarian in Naze, the capital of Amami Island. I learned so many interesting things while I visited and interviewed many of the elderly people in my village. The most interesting story that was handed down from generation to generation is very similar to the story of the appearance of a white god in the Pacific. One of the oldest members told me the following story:

> The white God lived on East Mountain. Each time when the villagers prayed to Him, He came to visit the villagers. He dressed in a white robe and had white skin and rode on a white horse, and came down to the village with a loud sound like cymbals which echoed even to the neighboring villages. All the

> villagers knelt down on the ground to worship Him. It was very impolite to look at His face. The white God taught them how to build canoes and houses. Among some of the village houses, there are sacred streets. When God came down to the village, it is said that He walked on these streets. Only the holy people who were mediators to God could walk on these narrow alleyways. If commoners walked these lanes or climbed the holy mountains, it was believed they would become sick for defiling holy places.

Around the *Ashage* (villagers' meeting place), some of these streets, only a few feet at most in width, still remain today. An elderly man mentioned that when he was a little boy, he still remembers how he occasionally heard the loud, clapping noise of the cymbals echoing through the valleys and hills—but God did not come down to the villages anymore. The time was about 1920. The old gentleman concluded the reason God had stopped coming to visit the village was because there had become too many disbelievers, including my uncle, who was said to be one of the main offenders!

When I played the tapes of this interview later for my dad, he told me I should have asked him about the legend of the white God. My father knew the stories just as well, and indeed the origin of our family lineage is tied up in this mythic past.

I had been in Japan for over two years. Sister Pfaffle, who was my companion in the Language Training Mission in Hawaii and also my companion for most of my mission, had returned home. I went back to the mission home and told President Kan Watanabe it was time for me to finish my mission. I was blessed to have a wonderful mission president and outstanding missionary companions. Because Sister Rose Pfaffle and I were companions for almost two years, she greatly influenced my spirituality, and we are lifelong friends.

At the end of my mission, I received a letter from President Kenneth Orton of the LTM in Hawaii. In his letter he mentioned that Elder Gordon B. Hinckley wanted to know about the Japanese and their religion, customs and traditions. He thought I would be a perfect person for the task. So I went back to Hawaii and lived with sister missionaries while working on my new project.

One day, I was going to write a chapter on the origin of the Japanese people. I read many books on that subject, but I couldn't agree with any of their ideas. One night, I dreamed of a peaceful and beautiful city. I knew it must be Salt Lake City. I really wanted to go to Salt Lake City to finish this chapter.

When we held a missionary conference in Miyajima, which is close to Hiroshima, all of the missionaries of Japan West were gathered there. I was asked to give a workshop for them. The topic was the similarities between Christianity and Shintoism. In my workshop, I quoted many scriptures. When I finished, one of the elders asked a question: "What is the origin of the Japanese?" I replied, "I don't know." President Kan Watanabe announced that he'd received a couple pages of someone's research paper from President Benson in Salt Lake City. I remembered only one thing from the paper—that one of the brothers thought that the Japanese people are Nephites.

I had never been to Utah, but I knew that the beautiful, peaceful place I'd dreamed of must be Salt Lake City. I decided to go there in search of the brother who said the Japanese might be Nephites. I didn't know where he lived, nor did I know his name. I kept asking people that I met, "Do you know who says the Japanese people are Nephites?"

I was not successful in Salt Lake City, so I went to Provo to look for this elusive brother. That day was the third day since I had begun to fast. I was determined to find that brother! On the BYU campus, I decided to contact a religion professor. At the first door I knocked, a humble, unassuming man opened it and told me that he was busy. I told him I was busy, too. Later when I learned more about him, I found out he was a very famous scholar—Brother Hugh Nibley. I went into his office and found many papers on the floor and everywhere. I picked up one paper from the floor which had an ancient language on it. "I have a similar writing to this," I told him. The writing came from under the ground in an ancient Japanese shrine's backyard.

I asked him whether he said that the Japanese people are the Nephites. He immediately told me, "Eighteen years ago, I heard it from Brother Jarvis." He didn't remember his first name, so he began to call the various Jarvis families listed in the phone book. After he tried several phone calls, he finally reached Brother Jarvis' son. He gave us his father's phone number. Brother Nibley drove me to Orem, Utah, where Brother Wesley Jarvis lived. Meeting Brother Jarvis was a most unforgettable spiritual experience. I faced a tall, handsome, meek, kind, and very familiar-looking brother. Brother Nibley dropped me off and left.

Brother Jarvis, his wife, daughter and her fiancé were on their way to a restaurant for dinner. They invited me to join them, and I happily did. I didn't understand much English in those days, but everything he explained about the Nephites made me happy, and I believed that he was speaking the truth. My spirit was overjoyed at meeting Brother Jarvis. I told him I'd been fasting for three days and enjoyed eating the delicious food in the restaurant.

My visit to Salt Lake was very successful. I went back to Hawaii and finished the chapter on the origin of the Japanese. It was the end of July. I was planning to go back to Japan, but I accepted an invitation from Brother Jarvis to stay at his home and attend BYU. I was too late for my registration, so I asked President Theodore Tuttle to call the BYU foreign student office and ask them to consider giving me special permission. Because of his help, I was able to attend BYU that fall semester, in 1972. Almost every night, Brother Jarvis gave me lessons on the Book of Mormon. The Lord blessed me abundantly.

The following year, when the spring term was over, I decided to go back to Japan. I stopped in Salt Lake City and attended a meeting on Sunday. There I met Brother Tatsui Sato. He told me that instead of going back to Japan, I should go to the University of Utah. One day, he took me in a little old Toyota to the administration officer who was a former Latter-day Saint soldier, Norton Nixon. Brother Sato had just obtained a driver's license, at the age of 74. He drove very carefully from the Church Office Building to the University of Utah. (I was very scared, thinking I was probably his first passenger!) Because of the help and encouragement of these two great brothers, I stayed in the United States until the present time.

In the middle of August 2000, Sister Tomiko Sato came to visit me in Oregon. She brought a few things of Brother Sato's to help me remember him, as we had been close over the interim years. She also mentioned that if I wanted his collection of books, I could have them. She confided that she knew he would like me to have his books. So just before school started at the end of August that year, I drove to Salt Lake City and gathered Brother Sato's 150 most precious books and loaded them into my car. Sister Sato told me I could also have all of his boxed material if I wished, so I brought it all back home.

When I opened the boxes, I found the history of Tatsui Sato's life contained in innumerable letters and articles. I wondered how I could possibly be worthy to compile all of his precious materials. He was the most humble, spiritual and compassionate person I had known. He was a man of many distinctions—a scientist, professor, genealogist, temple missionary, temple sealer, and a pioneer of The Church of Jesus Christ of Latter-day Saints in Japan. I never dreamed that I would even think about putting his lifelong materials together. Yet I began to have a strong impression that I should put this material in order, to tell the story of Tatsui's life and the history of the Church in Japan.

I only knew of Brother Sato's later life—therefore, before I started this project, I felt that I needed to visit the place where he was born. (I mentioned visiting Narumi in Chapter 1.) After I came back to the United States, many months passed before I worked on the project. One night, a memory from my youth came back to me—when I was 17 years old and was baptized in Okinawa. I just remembered the promise I had made to God, and I decided to work hard on Brother Sato's project.

In the middle of June, the school year ended, and summer vacation began. I took all of the material from the boxes, and according to date, I separated and organized it all over my house—in the dining room, living room, bedrooms, and across countertops—spread out over 2,400 square feet. I left just enough room for a path for me to walk around it. Each day, I worked around the clock, from 6:30 a.m. until 2:30 a.m. the next morning. I translated and typed in Japanese at the same time. I cut off my life from the outside world, and patiently, day after day, while fasting and praying to the Lord, began to work on this big job. I didn't know I could do a translation; but I found I could translate without much difficulty, because I had help from God and Brother Sato.

One night, I translated Brother Sato's journal, and went to sleep with a question in my mind—"Is there any other word for the translation of 'soldiers?'" In my sleep I heard "shinchugun" three times, and I realized I should use that word. Translating the 40 handwritten pages of Brother Sato's journal and the letters from the Latter-day Saint soldiers made me cry because they were so spiritual.

Then one night when I was about to translate a poem from President Packer's funeral speech, the words came to me in my ear as if from a breeze—spiritually, without me actually translating. After I finished typing the poem, I wondered about one of the words that came to me—were there really "wildflowers" in English? And sure enough there were.

After 2 a.m. one morning, I was translating Brother Sato's talk given at a sacrament meeting about his temple missionary experience, and I was almost able to do it without even reading his own words. Every day, spiritual things like this happened as I worked on this project. In two and a half months, I finished putting all of the materials together. I have a testimony that God gave me the talent of translation to accomplish this task—I can humbly say this is my testimony.

To conclude, I would like to thank my parents, Fukujiro and Yoshie. Like Nephi, I was lucky in "having been born of goodly parents."

My mother, still alive at 88 years of age, lost her third son last summer, my younger brother, Hiro. Though she is old, her spirit remains strong. When she asked me if I would make money from this book, I told her no and that the purpose of this project is to strengthen the testimony of others and preserve this important history. Therefore, I sold property I had in Idaho and also poured in all of my time and energy to research and finance this work. My mom told me that since she is old, money is nothing for her, and she wants to help me publish this book in Japanese and English. Originally, she wasn't happy about me joining the Church, but she trusted me, and I've never been a burden to her.

To hear my mother's approval of this task was so gratifying to me; and although she is not a member of the Church, her support has been invaluable. Thanks to my mom, I realize what true wealth is; and I know now that she has accepted my role in the Church.